The
Divine Voice

The
Divine Voice

Christian Proclamation and the Theology of Sound

Stephen H. Webb

BrazosPress
Grand Rapids, Michigan

© 2004 by Stephen H. Webb

Published by Brazos Press
a division of Baker Book House Company
P.O. Box 6287, Grand Rapids, MI 49516-6287
www.brazospress.com

Printed in the United States of America

Library of Congress Cataloging-in-Publication Data
Webb, Stephen H., 1961-
    The divine voice : Christian proclamation and the theology of sound / Stephen
H. Webb.
        p.   cm.
    Includes bibliographical references and index.
    ISBN 1-58743-078-9 (pbk.)
    1. Preaching—History. 2. Rhetoric—History. 3. Sound—Religious aspects—
Christianity. 4. Word of God (Theology) 5. Theology—Methodology. 6. Reforma-
tion. I. Title.
BV4207.W39 2004
251—dc22   2004000337

For A. B. C. and D. too, of course
And R. R. R.

"The Lord God has given me
the tongue of those who are taught
that I may know how to sustain
the weary with a word.
Morning by morning he wakens—
wakens my ear to listen
as those who are taught."

Isaiah 50:4

Contents

Acknowledgments

Two centers gave me the time and energy to write this book.

I am grateful to Mauri Ditzler, dean of Wabash College, for appointing me a senior fellow of the Wabash Center of Inquiry in the Liberal Arts in the fall of 2002. The support of that community, in the splendid Trippet Hall, made for a congenial way to begin this project. One question the Wabash Center posed during my appointment concerned the appropriate size of a liberal arts college, and I had time to explore my hunch that the answer has to do with the relationship between space and sound. Liberal arts colleges offer students the intimacy of hearing their professors, as well as each other, in close quarters. It is a lack of proximity of sonic space, in part, that makes both large universities and "distance learning" so problematic for effective teaching and learning. A colleague once told me that Wabash College should never grow so large that all the students cannot fit into the chapel, and that sounds just about right.

Thinking about the architecture of sound also led me to inquire into why so many liberal arts colleges have Protestant roots. Wherever the Christian church has put preaching at the center of its worship services, education in the liberal arts has flourished. This was certainly true for the reemergence of the liberal arts in the universities of the High Middle Ages, a revival that was directly dependent on renewed interest in Augustine and a renewed emphasis on preaching in the Franciscan and Dominican orders. It was also true, of course, for the Protestant Reformation, which, in its alliance with the humanists and their revival of classical learning, put public speaking at the center of Western culture and sealed the connection between preparation for the task of ministry and the dissemination of the liberal arts. The fact that this union of preaching and pedagogy is largely forgotten in higher education today does not make it any less important. I will not address the plight of higher education directly in these pages, but these issues were in the back of my mind as I turned my attention, near the end of my semester at the Wabash Center, to the soundfulness of God and the vocal shape of the church.

My change of focus was made productive by the Center for Theological Inquiry at Princeton, and I am grateful to Wallace Alston for selecting me to be a member there for the spring of 2003. The camaraderie among the members, led by Robert Jenson's probing mind, as well as the splendid support of the staff, proved an inspiring context for writing the bulk of this book. My only regret is that conversations at CTI kept making the book longer rather than shorter! I could not have asked for a better group of scholars to show me how much I needed to keep thinking, even when I thought I was done: Tom Guarino (whose pastoral presence was as graceful as his careful questioning), Kevin Hughes, Stacy Johnson, Neil MacDonald (who has made his own creative way into the topic of God's voice), Patrick Miller, Peter McEnhill, John Muddiman (who seemed to know everything about the New Testament), Ed Noort (and the ever wonderful Emsi!), Peter Ochs (whose questions were always intense, honest, and generous), Gerbern Oegema, Ron Piper, Gene Rogers (whose comments were models of theological thoughtfulness), Paul Rorem, and Gerhard Sauter. Jenson read the whole manuscript when it was much too long and persuaded me to rethink Martin Luther at several key points. I know he will still disagree with me, but I hope the revisions I made will at least strike him as plausible, if not reasonable.

While at Princeton, I had the opportunity to meet with and learn from a remarkable group of theologians—James Kay, Charles Bartow, and Michael Brothers in homiletics and Bruce McCormack in systematic theology—who inspired me with their interest and suggestions. I could not have been at a better seminary for support in thinking about the performative aspects of preaching.

The idea for this book began when Walter Jost and Wendy Olmsted solicited an essay for their volume *A Companion to Rhetoric and Rhetorical Criticism* (Oxford: Blackwell, forthcoming), and I am very grateful for their support and encouragement over the years. At a crucial point at the beginning of this project I was inspired by Serene Jones, who in one conversation covered much of the ground of this book with me and whose own theological voice is surely one of the soundest. At Wabash College, Bill Placher, as always, offered the most careful advice, exercising a true gift in service of the Word. Bill also invited me to present an overview of this project for the 2003 Lafollette lecture, an honor for which I am grateful. Jon Baer, a wonderful new colleague, helped me think about American religious history, and David Blix answered some of my more obscure queries. I am grateful for conversations with several former Wabash students who have now found their own theological voices: Derek Nelson, Alex Wimberley, Matt Rose, Scott Seay, Jeff Marlett, and Zach Hoover. Derek and Alex read the long version of this book, thereby overpaying any debt they might have owed me for the hours I spent grading their papers. Margaret Adam, one of my favorite theologians, was the first person to read the penultimate draft, staying up all night to do so on a visit to Princeton. She was also my hardest reader (perhaps, I like to think, due to the late hour of her reading), at least so far. I am sorry I had to edit my discussion of the work of her husband, A. K. M. Adam. In a long blogger conversation, AKMA was instrumental in helping me to clarify my position on the status of biblical authority. Shirley H. Showalter, president of Goshen College, shared with me some of her own research into the religious nature of sound, and I am grateful for her words of wisdom and her generous spirit. Correspondence with Marjorie O'Rourke Boyle and Stanley Hauerwas was very helpful, as were conversations with David Tracy. Aron Aji continues to awe me with his gentle spirit of deep listening and wise knowing. I also need to thank the ever patient Isabel Wollaston, who has given me much by providing me room to write what I want for the journal she deftly edits, *Reviews in Religion and Theology,* as well as Don Ottenhoff, a superb editor at *Christian Century* who has graciously supported my writing over the years.

I could not ask for a better editor than Rodney Clapp or a better publisher than Brazos Press. Rodney has a sharp ear for good prose that is quickened by his keen sense of both divine and authorial voice. He demonstrates how an editor can be faithful to God and his writers at the same time, drawing both closer together.

Just when I thought it was safe to read over the copyedited pages from my publisher, my manuscript was subjected to a delightful and spirited discussion at Loyola College in Maryland. I am grateful to Stephen Fowl for the invitation and his friendship, as well as the generous and helpful comments of Trent Pomplum, Maiju Lehmijoki-Gardner, Claire Mathews-McGinnis, Brian Sholl, John Betz, David Hall, and Rusty Reno. David brought up more connections between my topic and the church fathers than I could ever properly master. Rusty speaks in a tone of voice that sounds like it came from a better theological time that is now long past. For years people have asked me if I knew him and were surprised that I did not, and now I know why. He listens as one who has been taught, and his words give me hope.

Most of all, this book is a tribute to my wife's passion for teaching voice for the actor. Diane Timmerman began studying Kristin Linklater's approach to voice four years ago, and she completed the requirements to become a designated Linklater teacher just as I was finishing this book. Since I had to live through this arduous process, I decided to make the most of it. The more I listened to her, the more I realized I needed to apply what she was learning to Christian theology. In whatever she says, she is always a graceful teacher, and I have heard more of God's will in her voice than in any book of theology. She is "the voice of my beloved" (Song of Solomon 2:8). Needless to say, our conversations were always interrupted by our children, Charis, Barek, and Asher, and I would not have it any other way.

one

Witnessing to a Noisy World

The First Word

Sound is invisible and thus it can penetrate walls and barge unannounced through closed doors. It is this invisibility that makes sound so convenient for thinking about our relationship to God. Sounds have a seemingly spiritual capacity to seep into our souls in intimate and uncontrollable ways. The effect can be disturbing—an innocent screech on a chalkboard can make us cringe—or uplifting—the booming bass at a party can make us want to dance. Nothing is as reassuring as the voice of a loved one, but the opposite is also true: victims of violent assault can spend years getting an unwanted voice out of their head. Loud sounds can be so overwhelming that military planners have begun researching ways to use them to deafen and disorient enemy troops, which puts the story of Joshua bringing down the walls of Jericho with the blast of trumpets and a great shout into a whole new context.

To escape our noisy world, we go to movies, where every image is perfectly synchronized with a sound. Or we use the latest technology to construct a sound cocoon of utterly private rhythms that put us out of sync with everyone else. Ironically, the very technological advances that allow us to turn our lives into isolated sound systems have transformed public spaces into acoustical battlefields, because we keep cranking up the decibels as our hearing grows dimmer. Besides, even when it is not blared or boosted, sound has the tendency of drifting beyond our control and forcing its way into other people's attention.

Something is going on with sound that is worth paying attention to. Or at least something is going on with the study of sound, which has become an increasingly important topic for many scholarly fields, including communication, rhetoric, film, theater, and what has come to be called performance studies.[1] It is a topic that theologians usually neglect. This is a book about what it might mean to take sound seriously as the most characteristic medium of biblical revelation and Christian mission.

Christians believe that all sound has its origin in God because God spoke the world into being. Christians also believe that the destiny of sound has a particular form because Christians have heard in Jesus Christ's call to discipleship the voice of God. Of course, God can make any kind of sound God wants. The psalms, for example, imagine God speaking through nature, although more typically they call upon nature to sing the praises of God. God can speak in many different ways, even though for Christians the divine voice is always identifiable as the Word. The point is that everything God "says" does not take the form of vocal speech. Even when God speaks vocally, the divine voice can be hard to describe. God spoke to Job out of the whirlwind, and the psalm states that when "he utters his voice, the earth melts" (Ps. 46:6). To make matters more complicated, God can speak without making any sound at all—by communicating through acts of history, for example, or by revealing the divine plan directly to the human mind. Nevertheless, the Bible, as I will argue in chapter 2, puts a premium on sound as God's most typical choice of a medium for communication, and vocal speech is the form the sound of God most frequently takes. Christians believe that the voice that created the world is the same voice that sustains and

---

1. For an example of the growing literature on the history of sound, see Constance Classen, *Worlds of Sense: Exploring the Senses in History and across Culture* (New York: Routledge, 1993). Studies of sound and Christianity are rare, but there are exceptions. See T. J. Gorringe, *The Education of Desire: Towards a Theology of the Senses* (Harrisburg, Penn.: Trinity Press International, 2001), 13–16, 65–69. The topic of negative theology also frequently raises the issue of sound. See, for example, Oliver Davies and Denys Turner, eds., *Silence and the Word: Negative Theology and Incarnation* (Cambridge: Cambridge University Press, 2002). The topic of sound is becoming prominent in the history of religions. Guy L. Beck, in *Sonic Theology: Hinduism and Sacred Sound* (Columbia: University of South Carolina Press, 1993), argues that no religion makes sound more central than Hinduism. In certain strands of Hinduism, mantras, as the effective cause of sacrificial rituals, are more powerful than the gods themselves. Also see Lawrence E. Sullivan, "Sound and Senses: Toward a Hermeneutics of Performance," *History of Religions* 26 (August 1986): 1–33. Finally, for the most sophisticated (and decidedly doxological) defense of orality from Jacques Derrida's accusation that it masks a "metaphysics of presence," see Catherine Pickstock, *After Writing: On the Liturgical Consummation of Philosophy* (Oxford: Blackwell, 1998).

saves it, so that the history of sound, as it is orchestrated by God, has a vocal richness that harmonizes every dissonant note. This raises the question of the relationship between instrumental and vocal music, which I will explore in chapter 9 by reflecting on the end of all sound in heaven.

We can add our voices to the divine harmony because we were created in God's image. Theologically construed, speaking is not a trait projected upon God by analogy to human experience. We do not speak first and then think about God as speaking too. On the contrary, we can speak only because God created us to be hearers of God's Word. We are created in God's image, but that image is more like an echo than a mirror. God spoke us into being so that we too might have the joy of sharing in the spoken Word.

We are God's echo, but this does not mean that all earthly sound is our echo. Everything that is answers to the sound of God, not us. Nevertheless, we were created not only to listen to God but also to speak on God's behalf. Adam's naming of the animals represents the way we are called to mediate the authority of God's voice to the rest of the world (Gen. 2:9). Being stewards of God's creation requires us to attend to the sounds of nature as well as to prune those sounds with the human voice. What things mean is inseparable from the words we give them, whether those are words of chemistry or poetry. Of course, God hears everything, while we do not, and many of the sounds of nature that we can hear exceed our comprehension. The fact remains, however, that the meanings of things find their expression in our voices, just as it is in Jesus' voice that we come to know ourselves. This is not to imply that the creatures of the world do not have voices of their own. There is much wisdom to the medieval legend that on Christmas Day God grants animals the ability to speak as a reward for keeping the baby Jesus warm on the day of his birth. To be given a voice is to be set free. Even the groans of creation will one day be transformed into a chorus accompanying the transcendent solo of the Word (Rom. 8:22).

The creation story in Genesis provides further reasons why we should be humble about our sonic prowess. When God first spoke, there were no human ears to hear God's creative pronouncements. And even after God called humanity into a relationship of sound, giving humans the capacity to respond to God's voice, we quickly forfeited the benefits that stemmed from this privilege. That Adam could give names to all the animals suggests that his power of speech was not completely dissimilar to that of God's creative Word. When Adam and Eve disobeyed God, however, they lost not only their natural voices—which would have been naturally authoritative—but also the innocence of their hearing, which is indicated by the way they interpreted God strolling in the garden during the evening breeze as the menacing sound of impending judgment (Gen. 3:8). The fall begins with a case of "bad" hearing—Eve listens to the serpent—with the result that ever since people have let their ears lead them astray. Listening henceforth becomes an arduous task, whether it is listening to God, to each other, or to our own consciences.

Our hardness of hearing is compounded today by a cacophonous soundscape. The psalms invite us to hear the whole earth making a joyful noise to God (Ps. 66:1), but we are much more likely today to hear the sounds of urban congestion instead. If nature still speaks to us in God's voice, noise pollution makes it awfully hard to discern. In Eden all sounds would have spoken, gently and sweetly, of God's grace, but after the fall, God had to raise the divine voice to get our attention. God shouts not to scare but to save us, though our distorted senses can make God sound fearsome and menacing. In order to help us hear God more clearly, the Word that existed before the creation of the world became human. Sound would never be the same.

Prophet's Task

Prior to the incarnation, and in anticipation of it, the Hebrew prophets were chosen to proclaim God's Word. When God raised up prophets to speak on God's behalf—as recorded in the Old Testament—public speaking became the centerpiece of the divine drama. God spoke as well through mighty historical events, like the exodus from Egypt, but the prophets had to explain what God intended such events to mean. From a biblical perspective, then, the prophets set the stage for all subsequent reflections on the significance of the human voice. Since human speech encroaches upon the divine prerogative, it is fraught with significance and danger. While all speech should be worthy of God's hearing, speech on behalf of God carries an enormous responsibility. This is why the prophets were often reluctant to open their mouths to God's will. The stories of the prophets illustrate how public speaking can be both empowering and terrifying—an activity made necessary by divine revelation but for that very reason an activity that is never easy.

The New Testament extrapolates the extraordinary vocal demands on the prophets to cover all believers, requiring them to testify to their faith in God. Being a follower of Christ cannot be separated from the task of learning how to speak about Christ. "I believed, and so I spoke," declared the apostle Paul (2 Cor. 4:13). In what could be a gloss on this passage, Karl Barth writes, "Cognizance becomes knowledge when man becomes a responsible witness to its content."[2] Just as we frequently do not know what we think about something until we open our mouth to talk about it, Christians do not know what they really believe until they publicly witness to their faith. In other words, faith is not something we possess and then hope we can express if and when the time comes to speak out. Faith is embodied when the confidence required to be a witness is experienced as a gift from God.

In fact, Christianity intensifies the pressure put on public speaking to a nearly unbearable degree. Being a witness is not only an occasion but also a test of faith. The fear of taking the risk of testifying before others is not of a different order from the fear of taking the risk of turning to Jesus in the first place. Jesus calls us to witness in his name; we have a vocation to speak the faith. Standing up to speak in front of others about our faith is what it means to stand up for Jesus. In his *Exhortation to Martyrdom* Origen declares, "I would go so far as to say that it is better to honor God with lips when one's heart is far from God than to honor God with the heart and not to make confession with the mouth unto salvation."[3] Even in our day, public confession can be an anxious event. The phenomenon of stage fright, as I will show in chapter 4, is integrally connected to Christian theology. To many people it will come as a surprise to discover that the Bible demonstrates an intimate knowledge of a wide range of speaking disabilities, and that a biblical analysis of the sometimes suffocating weight public speaking carries makes stage fright an especially key element of a theology of sound.

The fact that we can and do speak out on God's behalf testifies to the power of God's Word to make our words true. Nevertheless, when we find ourselves speechless, we are not abandoned by God. Of course even in Eden our speaking skills would have been finite, compared to God's perfect Word, but we move from finitude to fault when we use our voices to deceive, manipulate, or betray. We can also move from finitude to despair when we misinterpret our slowness of tongue as God's rejection of us. This process typically begins with the social isolation that can accompany any speech impediment. Because we feel keenly the social expectation to speak up and listen carefully, we can end up exaggerating how others judge our communicative failures. When we

---

2. Karl Barth, *Church Dogmatics* 1/1, trans. G. W. Bromiley (Edinburgh: T & T Clark, 1936–1977), 188. Barth makes Paul's statement his own when he writes, "I believe, therefore do I speak" (ibid., 108). (Most subsequent quotes from the *Church Dogmatics* will be cited parenthetically in the text.)

3. Origen, "Exhortation to Martyrdom," in *Alexandrian Christianity*, ed. John Ernest Leonard Oulton and Henry Chadwick, Library of Christian Classics 2 (Philadelphia: Westminster, 1954), 396.

internalize those judgments by blaming not only ourselves but also our Creator, we end up in despair.

The good news of the gospel is that Jesus Christ has redeemed our agony, so that no matter how isolated we feel, we know God is with us. If God is the source of our confidence when we testify to the truth, then God is also present when our tongue is tied by doubt. The Holy Spirit speaks to us even when, in our anguish, we cannot find the strength to speak for ourselves. The harsh truth is that when we judge ourselves, we are really judging Jesus Christ, because we are saying that he has not done what the Bible says he did. That harsh truth, however, does not redound upon us, because Jesus Christ has already taken all judgment upon himself. No matter how much we reject him, he has already suffered in our place, restoring our hearing and setting our tongue free.

Learning to Speak: A Personal Aside

On speechlessness, I speak from experience. Losing my voice while giving the eulogy at my best friend's funeral was the closest experience I have had to what damnation must be like. My heart was racing, my breath was short, and my mouth was dry. My head seemed empty, except for an impending sense that it might explode. I felt a crushing weight of judgment, perhaps a result of feeling unworthy to survive Erik and unable to say the right words to bury him. I could not free my voice from my body's anxiety, and I did not trust myself to allow my mourning its guttural noises. I had to act as if I were halfway normal by pretending I could talk, though I could manufacture sound only in a mechanical way. I could pass for me, but I knew that what I heard when I spoke was coming from someplace else. Thus began years of battling with what is appropriately called stage fright. In the aftermath of that eulogy, I felt as if I had survived a car accident and was now afraid of driving. Demons seemed to descend upon me with the very thought of public speaking, threatening to possess me if I opened my mouth. I had lost faith in myself and feared losing faith in God if I could not regain my public composure.

This led me to reflect on the role of voice in my life and in my faith. I was raised to believe that there is no higher calling than preaching the Word, and though I was still a boy when I gave my first sermon in junior church, I eventually found that I am more at home in the classroom than behind the pulpit. My teaching, however, is always a form of preaching; my pedagogical confidence depends on my theological convictions. When I began losing my voice, I needed to find a theology that could speak to my speechlessness—one that would restore my confidence in the Word of God that I had grown up listening to and that I had so wanted to proclaim.

I wanted to speak with confidence precisely because listening to a voice full of authority was what religion meant to me when I was growing up. This was especially true of Sunday mornings. When I was very young, I sat through the worship service with my parents, no doubt squirming the entire time, but soon I began a journey through various Sunday school classes that was meant to prepare me to reenter the sanctuary with all the stillness of an adult. When we were almost old enough to attend the service, we had our own junior church that we treated as a rehearsal for the real thing. What we needed to practice most was the self-discipline required to listen to someone talk for forty minutes. Our church did not believe in children's sermons. There was only one sermon in the church, no matter what the biblical text was, and it always circled around the same set of themes about sin and salvation. The point of Sunday school was to teach us enough about the Bible so that we could answer Jesus' question, "Who do you say that I am?" (Matt. 16: 15). Portraits of Jesus standing at a door adorned our Sunday school classrooms, and the message was clear. We had to give a public answer to the question of who Jesus is as evidence of our salvation.[4]

When I finally was old enough to sit in church and hear the sermon, I still did not always understand what the preacher was saying, but that only made the act of listening to him all the more religious in my young mind. Keeping still took an incredible amount of energy, and I was sure that what the sermon meant was not unrelated to my attempts to stop squirming.[5] In my conservative church, we were not supposed to listen with our body; that was for Pentecostals and charismatics. The Word of God was supposed to set us free from our physical desires, which meant that self-discipline was a sure sign we had rightly heard what we were told.

What faith means to me has changed over the years, but there are also some basic continuities with my youth. I still think that attending to a sermon on Sunday is one of the fundamental practices that sustain my religious identity, even though nowadays I try to listen with my whole body, rather than with my head scrunched down on my stiff neck.

4. One of the best sermons I have read on the power of the public confession of faith is by Fred B. Craddock, "Stand Up and Be Quiet," in his book *The Cherry Log Sermons* (Louisville: Westminster John Knox, 2001).

5. The patient attention required to transform boredom into something like peace is a virtue found in many religious practices. See Michael L. Raposa, *Boredom and the Religious Imagination* (Charlottesville: University of Virginia Press, 1999), chap. 5.

Being a father teaches me how much the voice is a matter of the whole body, not just the neck up. When we had our first baby, I waited anxiously for her first word. It was a longer process than I anticipated! She flung out her arms like a televangelist preacher in order to try to purse her lips. When she cried, it came from every pore of her being, and it pierced me down to my toes. My wife and I cooed and babbled to her, surrounding her with an "envelope of sound."[6] I soon came to the conclusion that the idea of the very first word was a myth of origins—a good myth, but a myth nonetheless. Her baby sounds took shape gradually, and I could not say exactly when they became words. Still, patiently waiting for those sounds to converge into a voice was a large part of what it meant to be a parent. She needed us to listen, and we wanted her to talk. She became her own person when she could convert her cries into words. She was a person before she spoke, of course, but her voice seemed to reveal the person we already knew her to be.

Sometimes voices reveal what we would rather hide. When I found myself speechless in public performance situations, I was afraid that my anxiety bared the tumultuous state of my soul. Discovering how common this problem is was some comfort, but it was also troubling to find out how little is written about stage fright from a theological perspective. I needed to understand how God is revealed through speech acts, and I needed to experience grace in my own speaking.

Back to Barth and Beyond

The most logical place to search for a theology of public speaking is the Protestant Reformation, with its emphasis on proclaiming the Word of God. The Reformers put public speaking at the center of their understanding of faith. Chapters 5 and 6 make the case that their ideas about speech, orality, and performance are as vital today as they were in the sixteenth century.

Nonetheless, to speak of a theology of the Word of God today is, in the ears of many theologians, merely to echo the polemical rhetoric of the Protestant Reformation, especially the incessant bellowing of Martin Luther. The Reformation sounded a note of deep baritone in the history of theology that has given way to lighter and more varied religious

6. The phrase is from Didier Anzieu, who has argued that infants begin to develop self-awareness through discerning the sources of sounds. Surrounding a baby with soothing sounds, what Anzieu also calls a sound bath, is used in France as a way of treating infants with developmental problems. See Didier Anzieu, *The Skin Ego*, trans. Chris Turner (New Haven: Yale University Press, 1989), pp. 157–73.

harmonies. In the academy, historians have turned against the hype of early-twentieth-century German scholars that portrayed the Reformation as the beginning of all things modern. Now the pendulum has swung the other way, so that the Reformation is frequently relegated to a mere footnote in studies of the late medieval period.[7] The Reformation may have brought an era of church history to an end, but many historians now argue that it did not provide for any new beginnings.

In the twentieth century, Karl Barth revived the Protestant Reformation's theology of the Word by speaking in a voice that was as original as any heard in the history of theology.[8] I use his theology throughout this book, but I will focus on it in chapter 7, in the context of thinking about the Trinity and the doctrine of creation. Following Barth too closely has its dangers, because his voice is inimitable. His texts have a unique sound. It was as if he wanted to prove the continuing legitimacy of the Reformation by shouting loud enough to pierce the droning monologue of modernity that had been ringing far too long in the ears of liberal Christians. Even he could not sustain the breathless exclamations of his early work, which was written in response to the crisis of World War I. When he wrote the first edition of his famous commentary on Romans, as he observed many years later, "it required only a little imagination for me to hear the sound of the guns booming away in the north."[9] All of his work responded to the need for a new theological sound by preparing the groundwork that makes Christian proclamation both possible and confident. He masterfully reaffirmed the freedom of the Word from all worldly constraints in order to rejuvenate preaching at a time when Christians had become much too inundated by secular noise.

7. Much of the change in Reformation historiography has been motivated by an attempt to rethink the relationship between Protestantism and Catholicism in the sixteenth and subsequent centuries. John W. O'Malley develops an excellent analysis of the anxiety that has led to countless debates over how to name Catholic developments in relationship to the Protestant Reformation in *Trent and All That: Renaming Catholicism in the Early Modern Era* (Cambridge: Harvard University Press, 2000).

8. Different lists could be drawn up of those who participated in the twentieth-century revival of the theology of the Word. Harold Stahmer traces the origin of the theology of the Word to the period immediately after World War I and includes figures such as Eugene Rosenstock-Huessy, Franz Rosenzweig, Martin Buber, and Ferdinand Ebner. See *"Speak That I May See Thee!" The Religious Significance of Language* (New York: Macmillan, 1968).

9. From Karl Barth's preface to the English edition of *The Epistle to the Romans*, trans. Edwyn C. Hoskyns (London: Oxford University Press, 1968), v. Barth's commentary on Romans is full of auditory images that resonate with the battlefields of World War I. When he later reflected on the impact made by this book, he used predominantly auditory rhetoric, such as bell ringing and the roaring of lions. For a full analysis, see Stephen H. Webb, *Re-figuring Theology: The Rhetoric of Karl Barth* (Albany: State University of New York Press, 1991).

Barth's impact on America, perhaps due to the controversies stirred up by his explosive style, was mediated by theologians like Dietrich Bonhoeffer and Emil Brunner. A movement formed that became known as neo-orthodox theology—a term Barth did not like—which was held together as much by style as by substance. It is no coincidence that the neo-orthodox version of the theology of the Word became popular in America at a time—the post–World War II era—when preachers were often among the most educated persons in town and thus were still highly respected in their communities. Neo-orthodox theology was not only a theology that could be preached from the pulpit, it was also a theology that dealt with the complex issues inherent in the art of preaching. Neo-orthodox theology flourished only for as long as preaching was considered a unique and authoritative form of speech.

The second generation of the Word of God theologians, who followed in the footsteps of Barth from a comfortable distance, had the burden of confronting the legitimation crisis that afflicted the special status of preaching. Their theological research was motivated by an attempt to provide believers with resources to speak with confidence about Christian claims in a world that was growing deaf to the sounds of religion. This generation of Word of God theologians was especially interested in the technological revolutions that had degraded the status of the human voice to a technical instrument void of revelatory power. A good example of this group is Gerhard Ebeling, a student of Rudolf Bultmann, who tried to bridge the gap that separated Bultmann from Barth.

Ebeling set out to provide a more systematic foundation for Bultmann's argument that Christ is to be found not in the past tense of history but in the present moment of proclamation.[10] Writing his most significant work in the 1960s, he thought the problem of his time was a widespread "boredom with language."[11] Although Ebeling does not isolate it as a

10. Bultmann's *Christus praesens*, the Christ who is present in the proclamation of the gospel, might seem to be a natural resource for my own attempt to develop a theology of the Word, but it does not explain how the voice of Jesus Christ we hear in the sermon today is the same voice God used to create the world and to call the people Israel into an everlasting covenant. For the best recent work on Bultmann, see James F. Kay, *Christus Praesens: A Reconsideration of Rudolf Bultmann's Christology* (Grand Rapids: Eerdmans, 1994).

11. Ebeling's brief volume, *God and Word*, trans. James W. Leitch (Philadelphia: Fortress, 1967), is an example of the Word of God theology at its highest pitch, right before it fell into disrepair by the end of the 1960s. It also shows how central apologetics is to his theological task. These lectures were given at a conference at the Pacific School of Religion in Berkeley, California, in 1966, and it shows Ebeling to be very sensitive to the American context of the death of God theology then so popular and the search for a means of revitalizing the church. He wants to understand how Christianity has been reduced to dull sermons and pious platitudes, so that preachers can once again speak the Word with

cause of the crisis in communication, it should not be ignored that the generation that came of age during World War II was subjected to more propaganda than any other generation in history. People had heard all too many words, which made it hard for preachers to speak a saving Word. For Ebeling, each generation must hear the Word anew, because the Word can affect us only if it is spoken to our unique time and place. Yet what happens when people no longer want to listen to what institutions like the church have to say? The task of the theologian, Ebeling argued, is to restore people's confidence in language by demonstrating a basic human need for truthful communication.[12] For Ebeling, Jesus was unique precisely because of his confidence in proclaiming the good news.[13] The preacher must breathe new life into the old words of the Bible in order to convey the spirit of Jesus' communicative confidence to a contemporary audience.

After Ebeling, the theology of the Word faded from the theological scene. Proclamation became the special preserve of homiletics, and systematic theologians turned to more pressing concerns of social justice and political engagement. Arguably, Ebeling himself was somewhat responsible for the end of the neo-orthodox era, with its pronouncements about the centrality of proclamation for faith. His Bultmannian version of the theology of the Word was ruined by its own ambitions. He tried to provide proclamation with twin foundations, both of which proved unstable: a metaphysical basis in grandiose claims about the nature of language and a historical basis in the renewed quest for the historical Jesus. If there is to be a third generation of theologians of the Word, such a theology today needs to be rethought in the more modest context

confidence and vigor. As with most apologetics, he offers a mix of sociological observations and metaphysical foundations. For the former, he adopts Heidegger's account of modernity's devaluation of the meaning of words. For the latter, he investigates the resources within the nature of communication that might enable a retrieval of the gospel. "It is precisely the consideration of the nature of words that leads to an understanding of what God means" (p. 6). In other words, we cannot say "Lord, Lord" today before we undertake the task of figuring out what it means to say anything at all. Also see Gerhard Ebeling, *Word and Faith*, trans. James W. Leitch (Philadelphia: Fortress, 1963), 296–7, and *Theology and Proclamation*, trans. John Riches (London: Collins, 1966), 89.

12. See Gerhard Ebeling, *Introduction to a Theological Theory of Language*, trans. R. A. Wilson (Philadelphia: Fortress, 1973).

13. It is no exaggeration to say that faith for Ebeling is the confidence and courage to speak the right word at the right time. This is why he was so interested in the "inner certainty" that he thought defined the core of Jesus. For Ebeling, the preacher participates in the confidence Jesus experienced in his self-understanding as the one chosen by God to proclaim the gospel. This is why Ebeling wanted to renew the quest for the historical Jesus. He was joined in that quest in Germany by Günther Bornkamm and Ernst Fuchs and in America by James M. Robinson.

of recent scholarly developments in rhetoric, orality, and performance studies. It will still have broad ambitions, but those ambitions will be a function of its attempt to speak systematically about the whole range of Christian beliefs, rather than trying to ground faith in metaphysics or historiography.

The Declining Status of the Sermon

If Ebeling was the last significant Word of God theologian, it was not entirely the fault of his metaphysical and historical ambitions. Social trends since the 1960s have given the sermon such a low status that a theology of the Word appears to have little to say. Indeed, when comedians like Lenny Bruce, Richard Pryor, and George Carlin began defying the censors by using profane language in their televised appearances, the whole notion of sacred speech began to collapse.[14] If there are no limits to speech—everything can be said because words are just words—then nothing we say can convey the sacred or the profane. Without demonic speech, in other words, it is unlikely that we will be able to hear something of the divine in speech either. The coarsening of public speech has made the theology of the Word sound awfully naive and abstract. Words have become so divisive and polemical that it is hard to imagine a Word of such singular power that it could be heard above the clamor of competing interest groups.

The contemporary context for proclamation can be best understood if we compare it to the period in American history that was most favorable to neo-orthodox theology. The sound of Protestant worship in the generation following World War II was made cohesive by the authority of the preacher's voice. Preachers, just like public school teachers, could expect their audience to listen to them because of the status society granted their profession. They were predominantly male, and they lived in a time that equated authority with the volume and pitch of the male voice. With the entry of more women into all the professions, including the ministry, that equation no longer holds. Women expanded the tonal range and expressive quality of preaching, but the fluidity of gender roles has left little consensus on what characterizes the authority of sound. Indeed, churches have become one of the primary sites in our society where gender roles are contested according to the qualities of sound.

Perhaps the prestige of the postwar sermon was more of an exception than a rule in American history. As Martin Marty once wrote, we are

14. See Stephen H. Webb, "What Did Lenny Bruce Really Die For?" *Reviews in Religion and Theology*, forthcoming.

a nation of behavers, not believers.[15] We let our actions speak louder than our words. This was especially true after the 1960s, when many churches decided they had to take action rather than merely repeat the same old story. The national trait of pragmatism—whatever works is true—which Americans seem to inherit at birth, renders all religious speech problematic, but it is especially hard on Christian proclamation. Christians are commanded to speak boldly in the name of Jesus Christ, whatever the consequences. It is inevitable that in a pragmatic culture, preaching becomes equated with irrelevant and sanctimonious platitudes. The easiest way for unbelievers to shun proclamation is to tell Christians that they do not practice what they preach.

The charge of hypocrisy is thus used to censor Christianity's most central practice, which is preaching. It is a charge that fundamentally misunderstands the nature of Christian speech. Christians know that they can never live up to the words they speak, but they also know that God has spoken a true and perfect Word. Christians learn to speak the Word by hearing it, so a grateful listening is the habitual disposition that makes preaching possible. Karl Barth goes so far as to define preaching as "the speech which obediently listens." The preacher, in a way, is the church's chief listener. Barth expands this point by suggesting that the church should be understood as "the listening Church."[16] Free speech in our age means that people have the right to express themselves, no matter what they have to say, and that without such expression there is no freedom. Christianity teaches just the opposite—that freedom begins in the ear before it reaches the mouth.

The church has suffered more than most institutions from the loss of a commitment to listening as a lifelong discipline. People change churches until they find one that says what they want to hear. Indeed, as denominational loyalty began declining in the 1960s, preachers had to assume that their congregants did not know much about any particular tradition within the Christian faith. Without this shared theological grammar and vocabulary, preachers had to go out of their way to change their speaking habits. The unchurched had to be cajoled and affirmed, so that preaching increasingly became convivial and inspirational rather than exclamatory and exegetical. No doubt the influence of television forced all public speaking into a more conversational mode. Private words of counsel came to sound more authentic than pronouncements from the pulpit, which contributed to the transformation of the ministry into a helping profession, making psychology and not the art of public speaking paramount for ministerial

15. Martin E. Marty, *A Nation of Behavers* (Chicago: University of Chicago Press, 1976).

16. Barth, *Church Dogmatics* 1/2, trans. G. T. Thomson and Harold Knight, 803, 813.

education. Perhaps most important, churches updated their music in order to surround their congregants with an envelope of warm and familiar sounds.[17] The soothing rhythms of praise music now set the tone for worship services more than the sermon does. As a result, the spoken word seems to accompany the music, rather than the other way around.

How can the Word be preached with authority today if we have lost the ability to listen to it? Sermons keep getting shorter and shorter as our attention span continues to shrink in reaction to the onslaught of the ever multiplying media. The church is not alone with this problem. We pay less and less attention to political speeches, listening with cynical reservation if we listen at all. Ministers frequently respond to this dire situation by supplementing their sermons with visual aids, which only reinforces the idea that the spoken word does not matter. The pulpits are not empty, but the words spoken in them have become increasingly irrelevant to what many Christians believe and do.

The decline of public speaking does not mean that we have become a quiet nation. On the contrary, the spoken word abounds in talk-show America, where people get opportunities to say whatever they want, no matter how outrageous or banal. The consequences are anything but encouraging for the church. The spoken word has become so democratized that it has been inflated and devalued. It does not help that televisions are left on in homes and businesses, so that disembodied voices drone on in the background of everything we do, while e-mail is rapidly replacing the telephone, which long ago diminished face-to-face conversation.[18]

Indeed, the efficiency of technology has made us impatient for the content of communication: forget the niceties, just get to the point. Computers speed up communication to the point where the spoken word feels clumsy and inept as it works its way through our vocal apparatus of lungs, larynx, and tongue. The *New York Times* recently reported on the invention of a digital time machine that will shorten audio recordings by up to 12 percent through a process of micro-editing.[19] Digital

17. A Methodist church in West Hollywood, California, has filled its empty pews by incorporating Broadway songs into worship, on the principle that what makes music sacred is its emotional impact, not its cognitive content ("Broadway Tunes Make a Joyful Noise," *New York Times*, February 16, 2003, sec. 1, 31). The article notes that they even sing "the occasional hymn."

18. See Todd Gitlin, *Media Unlimited: How the Torrent of Images and Sounds Overwhelms Our Lives* (New York: Henry Holt, 2002). Also important is Richard Winter, *Still Bored in a Culture of Entertainment: Rediscovering Passion and Wonder* (Downers Grove, Ill.: InterVarsity Press, 2002), and John L. Locke, *The De-voicing of Society: Why We Don't Talk to Each Other Anymore* (New York: Simon & Schuster, 1999).

19. *New York Times* (October 2, 2003), E1 and E6. Also see James Gleick, *Faster: The Acceleration of Just about Everything* (New York: Vintage, 2000).

compression can eliminate thirty milliseconds of a vowel without altering the pitch of the voice. This technology trades on the fact that people
speak at a typical rate of 140 to 180 words a minute, while people can
comprehend speech at rates much faster than that. The tongue turns
out to have evolved at a slower rate than the ear. Real-time speaking,
speaking 1.0, might someday go the way of WordPerfect. This thought
is not as fantastic as one might think. Scientists are currently working
on brain-computer interface systems that, through the implantation of
electrodes, will enable the paralyzed to speak by translating thoughts
directly into words, bypassing the body's muscles. If it could work for
the paralyzed, why couldn't it work for all of us? Why rely on the tongue
when the tongue is so slow? Now more than ever, it is imperative for
those concerned about the future of the church to rethink the theology
of the Word by putting it in the context of the study of sound.

Christian Acoustemology

The proper relationship of the sound of worship to the voice of the sermon is what I want to call the acoustemology of the church. Epistemology
is philosophical reflection on how we know what we know. Acoustemology is theological reflection on how Christians know what they know in
worship. Different church traditions have different acoustemologies. My
Roman Catholic friends talk about the sound of the Mass, which has the
same intonations and rhythms regardless of the language used. Since the
Mass surrounds them with a wall of familiar sound, they can attend Mass
anywhere in the world without needing to know the local language. Perhaps
my friends are idealizing the Mass, given all the changes in Roman Catholic
worship in recent years, but the contrast with the din of Protestant noise
is significant. While Protestant worship should orchestrate the sounds of
prayer and praise in order to heighten the pitch of the sermon, more often
than not the sermon sounds like a dull interlude in the midst of emotionally
charged singing. Too many preachers use the same tone of voice to make
the announcements as they use to announce the gospel message.

The acoustemological distinction between summoning and inviting
might be helpful here. Jesus did not invite his disciples to follow him;
he summoned them. Inviting and summoning are two different speech
acts, and they are useful categories for understanding the shift in preaching from the middle of the twentieth century to the beginning of the
twenty-first. This was, in part, a shift from a transcendental to a more
immanent understanding of the Word, although a proper homiletics will
always try to hold those two categories together. As worship became
more corporate, preachers strove to become the collective voice of their

congregation, rather than the voice of God. Preachers embraced their status as "one without authority."[20] A passage from an incisive essay by Thomas G. Long is worth pondering:

> The older sermon, even if preached by a popular and accomplished preacher, will often seem to contemporary ears to be overly long, heavy, and ornate, full of excessive rhetorical flourishes and moral exhortations. Today's sermon, by contrast, is often less theologically and conceptually weighty, more dialogical and conversational in tone, less linear in structure, and more open-ended. The contemporary sermon will typically display far greater reliance upon image, narrative, and evocative phrase, and it will be focused upon ordinary, everyday events and how it is that they are the environment for the experience of the gospel, rather than upon heroic subjects and well-defined dramatic themes. In short, today's sermons tend to be more "impressionist," inviting the listener to get in on the act and to join with the preacher in the creation of meaning.[21]

Sermons have become softer as communication theorists abandoned the idea of a passive audience. Another way of putting this is to note that the tone of preachers changed from the asseverative (making assertions) to the associative (conjuring images).

Changes in the acoustemology of Christian worship can have profound implications for Christian doctrine. Unfortunately, theologians are trained to be close readers, not attentive listeners, which might help explain why few theologians pay any attention to the oral nature of the Christian witness. Karl Barth defined theology in terms of a dogmatics that stands between exegesis and proclamation (he might have said that theologians should learn their exegesis from proclamation), but under the pressure of increasing specialization in the academy, biblical scholars tend to ignore theologians as much as theologians, trying to prove that they belong in the secular academy, ignore homileticians. The irony is that both biblical scholars and homileticians have recently embraced the fundamentally oral nature of the biblical witness in ways that theologians have still to learn.[22]

20. This is the title of a groundbreaking book on preaching by Fred B. Craddock, *As One without Authority* (Nashville: Abingdon, 1979). The very first page of this book, first published in 1971, talks about the new sound of "the noise outside in the street" that drowns out the relevance of the sermon. Craddock's answer to this problem is an inductive method that begins with the religious experiences the preacher shares with the congregation. The task of the preacher is to activate the meaning the congregation brings with them to church through a process of intent listening. Many of the shifts in preaching that I will analyze in this book can be traced back to Craddock's influence.

21. Thomas G. Long, "And How Shall They Hear? The Listener in Contemporary Preaching," in *Listening to the Word: Studies in Honor of Fred B. Craddock*, ed. Gail R. O'Day and Thomas G. Long (Nashville: Abingdon, 1993), 170.

The turn toward orality in thinking about Scripture does not mean that biblical scholars have nothing to learn from theologians. The fact that most biblical scholars are still in the throes of historical criticism suggests that they can go only so far in attending to the essentially oral nature of Scripture. A comment by Richard A. Horsley, one of the most prominent New Testament scholars to turn to orality, is representative of this point: "To appreciate Mark's story as oral performance, modern readers would have to 'identify' themselves with the historical audience in context, probably a step few are willing to take."[23] For Horsley, the historian needs to understand the orality of the Bible in order to peel off the layers of tradition that have encrusted the biblical text. He is thus more interested in the orality *behind* the Bible—what the gospel would have sounded like to its original hearers—than the orality *in front of* it—what it sounds like today. Horsley ignores the fact that how we listen to the Bible today determines what we make of its original meaning.

Exegesis is usually considered a precondition for homiletics, but from the perspective of a theology of sound, homiletics is just as much a precondition for exegesis. Although we need to pay attention to the historical dimension of sound—that is, the way that the social conditions for speaking and hearing have changed throughout history—we also need to acknowledge the short life span of sound waves, which throughout most of history have dissipated without a trace. Consequently, our best efforts to reconstruct how words were used in the past are necessarily shaped by how we pronounce them out loud today. In chapter 8 I will elaborate on the thesis that reading is actually a form of hearing, with the aim of arguing that the most appropriate context for understanding the Bible is listening to the sermon. We can begin to understand the difficulty of the shift from thinking of the Bible as something we see to associating the Bible with what and how we hear when we begin attending to the way visual cues saturate our habits of thought and action.

At the Crossroad of Eye and Ear

The perspective of the history of sound—which is itself a component of the sociology of the senses—generates many surprising insights into

22. For a good overview of this discovery process, see Brian K. Peterson, *Eloquence and the Proclamation of the Gospel in Corinth* (Atlanta: Scholars Press, 1998), chap. 1. Also see the very important book by Whitney Shiner, *Proclaiming the Gospel: First-Century Performance of Mark* (Harrisburg, Pa.: Trinity Press, 2003).

23. Richard A. Horsley, *Hearing the Whole Story: The Politics of Plot in Mark's Gospel* (Louisville: Westminster John Knox, 2001), 77.

Christian faith. A theology of sound will be both a theo-acoustics of the Word of God and a practical theology of public speaking. It will traverse a broad range of topics, from the sound of God in the trinitarian conversation that created the world to the turbulence that keeps us from hearing God today. This way of putting my topic, however, is a little misleading, because I believe that sound has no history outside of the voice of Jesus Christ. I thus will not assume a theory of sound and then apply that theory to Christian faith. Perception does not precede theological reflection. That is, perception is not a rudimentary form of cognition that theology raises to the order of conceptual thought, as if we need to polish our senses in order to make them transparent to the divine. Instead, my governing insight is that theology itself is a form of perception, so that how we hear and how we speak cannot be separated from how we think about God.

Theologians have long noted how our images of God are metaphorical and thus drawn from our sense perceptions. We think about God with our body, so that when we talk about visions of God, for example, we are at the same time talking about the habitual patterns of perception we deploy through our body. Unfortunately, as that example demonstrates, theologians typically privilege sight as the primary source for our metaphors about God, rather than drawing from the whole range of our sensory perception. In fact, the very language of "models of God" relies on the visual activity of picturing and representing, in which we see one thing as something else. "Model of God" theologians like Sallie McFague inspect images of God in order to ascertain their power and alter their configurations.[24] Biblical images of God that do not fit their conceptual models are expendable. As a result, religious language is treated as an abstract and soundless object. Theologians who adopt the models of God approach are not positioning themselves as hearers of the Word. Hearing leads to a process of internalization and enactment or performance (you signal the fact that you have successfully understood what someone has said by doing something) that is quite different from the speculative activity of reenvisioning or the detached activity of remodeling.

The battle between the eye and the ear has been waged throughout Western history, with different agendas and varying results. I do not mean to restage that battle here, if only because I believe that the redemption of the world will entail the restoration of all of our senses. In fact, in chapter 9 I will argue that Christian eschatology entails the proposition that heavenly grace will saturate our whole body, making synesthesia—the mingling and

24. For further analysis of Sallie McFague, see Stephen H. Webb, *Good Eating* (Grand Rapids: Brazos, 2001), 234–40, and Webb, "Should We Love All of Nature? A Critique of Sallie McFague's *Super Natural Christians*," *Encounter* 59 (summer 1998): 409–19.

mixing of the senses in a unity that transcends their differences—a reality. Nevertheless, I want to do more than recommend sound as a neglected topic worth retrieving for theologians. I want to argue that knowing God is not just a matter of seeing the world in a particular light. Nor can the way in which we think about God visually simply be supplemented by adding the dimension of sound to sight, so that we learn to listen to the sounds of the world as God's orchestration. Instead, we need to explore the extent to which all aspects of Christian faith are soundful. In chapter 7 I will go so far as to argue that sound is the most fundamental category by which we can conceive of God. The world reverberates with the divine harmonies that are the source of the physical laws that govern matter and the spiritual energy that sustains life.

One of the favorite terms theologians use is *shape*. Theologians talk about the shape of Christian doctrine. Or they talk about how faith shapes our beliefs and practices. This simple word betrays a deeper set of convictions about how theologians should go about their work. Christianity can be turned into an object of reflection, a spatial grid across which various beliefs can be positioned and connected in order to make a pattern that is a delight to the mind's eye. But Christianity also has a particular sound, an oral quality, not just in the fact that its tradition was originally passed down by word of mouth but also in every Christian's love for certain words, whether heard, chanted, or sung, and the church's receptiveness to the idea that the divine can be heard in speech. In fact, our love for certain words is made possible by the reality that God made and loves us through the Word, a Word that had all the specificity of an embodied voice. Without that belief, all words sound alike.

The disciples did not seem to care what Jesus looked like, since no physical descriptions of him or likenesses were passed down to later generations. But they cared about his voice. This is especially true in the Gospel of John, which reports that the temple police said, "Never has anyone spoken like this!" (7:46).[25] The disciples witnessed more with their ears than with their eyes. If they had had a tape recorder, they surely would have recorded Jesus' voice, since it attracted multitudes. It was a voice that accomplished what was said without further action, as when Jesus ordered Lazarus to rise from the dead—a scene that echoes the Genesis account of God creating the world by calling it into being.

25. John is often read as emphasizing the illuminating vision of God—it is often observed that the Eastern Church is Johannine and visionary while the Synoptic, Pauline Church of the West is auditory—but there is a case to be made that John's Gospel restricts the power of vision (see, for example, 1:18; 6:63; 8:51) in favor of voice. For a good discussion of this issue, see Werner H. Kelber, "The Authority of the Word in St. John's Gospel: Charismatic Speech, Narrative Text, Logocentric Metaphysics," *Oral Tradition* 2 (January 1987): 108–31.

That we cannot hear the voices of most of the saints who have pre-ceded us, though we can read the books some of them have left behind, is an accident of technology that gives us a biased sense of the qualities that bind us together.[26] Surely it is the prayers of the faithful, both the vocal and the inarticulate longings of their hearts, that unite all Christians more than the jottings of the literate few. To God those prayers must sound like a constant humming emitted from the very properties of matter, a melody that accompanies the universe as it resonates with God's Word. By listening, God makes all of our sounds—from guttural moans of despair to tearful shouts of joy—matter.

There is, in sum, a soundscape to Christian theology, and it is often overshadowed by talk about the landscape of sacred places. This is ironic, because Christians did not revere special places until the fourth century and the time of Constantine, when Constantine's mother, Helena, trav-eled to Jerusalem and discovered what she took to be the sites connected to the life of Jesus.[27] Christians did not have a temple, a place marking the center of the earth and its consecration by the divine. Instead, their Temple was the person of Jesus Christ, who ascended to heaven and left women and men to speak in his place. Such speaking can be a precarious activity, as battles over the related roles of the oral and the written in church history attest. Even when we read the Bible, however, we listen for the sound of a voice among the marks on the page.

The life of the pilgrim is not just a spatial journey, as if we could ever really progress from a point of sin toward some spot on the spiritual map closer to the glory of God. It is also, and perhaps better, described as an audition in which we take the Bible's words as our own, except in this audition we are trying out for a play in which we have already been cast. The church is more like community theater than a professional production, and I will return to that analogy in chapter 8, where I will discuss the performative aspects of the Christian faith. In the church everyone has a role, and the pressure is off, but we still have to practice our lines. We meet on Sundays for vocal exercises, in a space created by a sound theology, where we learn how to turn all noise into something joyful. That is what I hope to say.

26. Scholars do try to reconstruct the sounds of the past. For an attempt to imagine what Shakespeare's plays must have sounded like in the space of the Globe Theatre in 1599, see Bruce R. Smith, *The Acoustic World of Early Modern England: Attending to the O-Factor* (Chicago: University of Chicago Press, 1999).

27. Constantine ordered the construction of a basilica on the site, previously occupied by Hadrian's temple of Venus, that was thought to be Jesus' tomb, but some scholars think Bishop Cyril of Jerusalem was the author of the legend that Helena found the tomb, since she seems to have arrived in Jerusalem after construction of the new church had already begun.

two

Theo-acoustics

Voices in the Night

Hearing sounds at night while lying in my dark bedroom was, for me, the epitome of childhood helplessness and vulnerability. If only I could see what was going on, everything would be all right. Not knowing where sounds came from made them unnerving. After all, sounds are always sounds *of* something. We don't hear sounds themselves; we hear things making sounds. We hear the voice of someone talking or the creak of a door opening, rather than a voice or a creak in the abstract. Not knowing who was talking or what was making the door open could be scary. For me as a child, night sounds conjured a world that was full of the foreboding of adulthood. They upset me not because I could not imagine where they came from but because I could imagine all too many possible sources for them. Could that be strangers talking or a monster behind the door? I had not yet learned to restrict my hypotheses to the range of the most plausible causes. Perhaps only in such experiences can we understand the mystery and power of sound to the ancients, who lived without the benefit of electric illumination.[1]

---

1. The loss of the oracular voice—the way our auditory imagination conceives of the divine—has been discussed by poets, historians, and scientists but neglected, for the most part, by theologians. For a popular account of the role of "hearing voices" in the origin of culture and religion from the perspective of a reductive evolutionary neuropsychology, see Julian Jaynes, *The Origin of Consciousness in the Breakdown of the Bicameral Mind* (Boston: Houghton Mifflin, 1976).

In the dark, demons speak, but that means that the gods can speak as well. When it turned out that behind the creaking of my bedroom door stood my father wishing me a good night, I knew that sounds could save as well as condemn.

Someone very close to me has related an experience of God's voice that I find irrefutable, though he has hesitated to make his testimony public for fear of skeptical reactions. He was a child of about eight, very devout and intent on being a minister when he grew up. One night, while he slept, he felt a presence enter his room. He was in a hypnogogic state that was neither slumber nor wakefulness. That is, he was too alert to be dreaming but too somnolent to be lost in reverie. The presence was unlike anything he had experienced before or since. It was a feeling of perfect inner peace and security, but it was also a feeling of something external that objectively surrounded him. The presence so completely saturated the room that the spiritual and physical seemed fused together. True, my friend did not think of the experience in exactly these terms when he was a boy, but it is still vivid in his memory, and even at the time he understood it to be a unique event for which any words would fail.

As the presence descended (for that is how he felt the Spirit enter the room), he felt a physical hand on his shoulder and heard the words, "Do not be afraid." He knew immediately that it was the voice of Jesus. From the distance of many years, he understands that the voice, which was deep and rich and masculine, was an accommodation to his young mind. Jesus Christ surely has a voice capable of an inimitable range of pitches and intonations. Speaking in the voice of a man was a way of assuring this boy, who did not have the happiest relationship with his father, of the love he desperately needed. But my friend also remembers that he immediately recognized the voice as belonging to Jesus, as if Jesus had but one voice, the one people heard when he spoke during his time on earth. In any case, Jesus addressed him by name and then gave him the Great Commission, as it is found in the Gospel of Matthew. At that point Jesus asked him to repeat this summons, and as he did so, the hand, voice, and presence receded into the night, leaving behind a silence that was forever changed.

Of course, there are many ways such an experience could be interrogated. One of the fundamental projects of modern psychology is to investigate how children develop a growing ability to distinguish between reality and fantasy through play and the imagination. Nevertheless, I do not know why the testimony of such purportedly empirical experiences should automatically and always be discounted. The boy in question was not physically ill, and although he may not have been as happy as he could have been, he was not in a disoriented or agitated state of mind.[2] He was not the victim of a traumatic assault, and he was old enough to understand the difference between an experience and a dream. Most notably, he immediately recognized the voice he heard as belonging to Jesus, even though he had never heard that voice before or since. Someone might suspiciously wonder why that voice did not speak to him when he was older, but there are cases where adults hear such voices, so it is not just children who report these kinds of experiences.

In this case, the boy was never as close to God as at that point, when his whole heart longed for divine assurance. Would the story be more persuasive if he had not desired what he reported? Legions of critics have followed Ludwig Feuerbach in using any evidence of human need for the divine as "proof" that all religious experiences are nothing more than crude fantasies of the untutored imagination. This begs the question of why God would speak to someone if God had not already prepared that person to hear what God had to say. Indeed, the very idea that God would shout down from heaven to prove God's existence to the unbelieving rightly belongs to the world of cartoons. God's Word, which always accomplishes what God intends, is covenant-generating (or, put another way, narrative-forming) and thus does not occur in random and haphazard ways (Isa. 55:11).

Many volumes, beginning with the work of William James, have been written about the nature and credibility of what can be called a supersonic supernaturalism, where sound travels on frequencies above the ear's ordinary audible limit.[3] For my purposes, there is no need to survey that literature, much of which is shaped by the quixotic quest to find a universal foundation or at least a credible cross-cultural basis for the unity of all religions. While it is true that every religion has its own sonic theology, this does not mean that it is possible to write a supersonic theology of religious sound in general. Sound is always particular and intimate, and its history must be likewise. Some scholars argue that a

2. Auditory hallucinations are most commonly associated with schizophrenia, where, according to the most widely accepted scientific theories, the brain misinterprets the sufferer's inner voice or acoustic memories. The auditory hallucinations of voice illness, which are frequent, intense, and emotionally charged (almost always negative), are thus of a completely different order from the phenomenon of hearing a voice when nobody is present. One recent study found that 45 percent of college students report having heard a voice when nobody was speaking (see Erica Goode, "Experts See Mind's Voices in New Light," *New York Times*, May 6, 2003, F1, F6).

3. For an analysis of the rhetorical voice William James uses in his great book *The Varieties of Religious Experience*, see Stephen H. Webb, "The Rhetoric of and about Excess in William James' *The Varieties of Religious Experience*," *Religion and Literature* 27 (summer 1995): 27–45.

certain word-weariness is an essential ingredient in all religions, which results in a pervasive privileging of silence over sound. Word-weariness can be found in Christianity, but not as a dominant theme. I will argue throughout this book that the biblical faith of Christianity is dependent on the claim that God has a voice and that the divine voice has a body in Jesus Christ. The biblical faith of Christianity is also dependent on our ability to hear the divine voice in the human voice of the preacher. Christianity and the fate of public speaking appear to be inextricably linked.

Revisiting Walter Ong

Though it is often observed that the God of Israel acts through the spoken word, the soundfulness of that word is rarely taken seriously. Few scholars have done more to provide a context for this observation than Walter Ong, a Jesuit historian and cultural critic. Ong's entire work can be summed up in the Pauline motto that faith comes through hearing (*Fides ex auditu;* Rom. 10:17), and he never tired of preaching about the often neglected importance of sound. The historical breadth of his knowledge was matched by a metaphysical fervor to articulate and defend the fundamental priority of the auditory over the visual. Ong was convinced that he was exploring this topic during a turning point in the history of the senses. Writing his major work, *The Presence of the Word,* in the 1960s, Ong had a sense that modernity was coming to an end while some new configuration of communicative forces was beginning to emerge. He was a scholar on a mission.

Like his mentor, Marshall McLuhan, Ong saw history as a series of media revolutions.[4] Even though McLuhan was more wary of the resurgence of orality, Ong had high hopes for the coming of what McLuhan called the "global village." Ong thought that technological innovations like television and the telephone could lead to a "secondary orality" that would make the sound of the voice more powerful than ever before.[5] Ironically, Ong's nostalgia for the past is itself a byproduct of the way

4. See Marshall McLuhan, *The Gutenberg Galaxy: The Making of Typographic Man* (New York: Signet, 1969). McLuhan, in turn, was influenced by J. C. Carothers, "Culture, Psychiatry, and the Written Word," *Psychiatry* 22 (November 1959): 307–20. Walter Ong died on August 12, 2003, just as I was making the final revisions of this book.

5. The auditory regime promised by the advent of the telephone proved false. "The telephone offers a quasi-controlled collapse of boundaries, in which the listening self can be pervaded by the vocal body of another while yet remaining at a distance from it." Steven Connor, "The Modern Auditory I," in *Rewriting the Self: Histories from the Renaissance to the Present,* ed. Roy Porter (New York: Routledge, 1997), 206.

modernity sentimentalizes everything it destroys. One of the characteristics of postmodernity is the recognition that the past can never be reconstructed in a pure or innocent form. It follows that any renewal or orality today will be indelibly shaped by the modernist trumping of the eye over the ear. This is, in fact, what we find. We talk a lot, but print has privatized and inflated the power of the word. Consequently, we are not very good at listening to each other. Moreover, the "secondary orality" Ong anxiously awaited is rapidly being replaced by yet another media revolution, the omnipresent e-mail. This technological innovation, which Ong could not have anticipated, is in some ways the second coming of the printing press, once again immersing us in the written rather than the spoken word.

Regardless of his success as a prophet, Ong succeeded in articulating what I want to call a theo-acoustics, even though he continues to be better known in communication studies than in theology. For Ong, sound, not paper, is the native medium of communication. Ong's emphasis on speech might make it appear that he shares the Protestant emphasis on preaching, but his historiography is firmly rooted in the Roman Catholic understanding of the priority of oral over written tradition. It is Trent, not Worms, that guides his thought. Ong's argument that orality is sufficient for the conveyance of truth is a translation of the Tridentine principle that Scripture and oral tradition each contain the whole of revelation, not just a part. From the perspective of Trent, the oral stands for the relative autonomy of unwritten tradition *(sine scripto traditionibus)*, which was meant as a rebuttal of the Protestant principle of *sola scriptura*. Catholic teaching on orality has evolved since Trent, but for Ong, Roman Catholicism represents the vitality of an oral community that survives into the modern world, not unscathed but still able to speak to the modern situation. Thus Ong is not only historian and prophet but also a theologian. He wants to attend to the ways in which the priority of the oral is specific to Western culture while at the same time making universal claims on behalf of the power of sound.

Ong's historiography depends on his idea of the sensorium. The sensorium denotes the way socialization involves building patterns of relationships among the senses. Ong assumes that the organizational structure of the senses that results from socialization can never be democratic. One sense always rules the others. Consequently, cultures can be compared according to the senses they privilege, but even within Western society, history can be written as the changing of the sensory guard. Recent scholarly work on the origins of modernity can provide an example of this phenomenon. At the beginning of the Enlightenment in the eighteenth century, people were exposed to a rapidly expanding amount of new information that forced them to make an unprecedented number of choices. Taste and smell became the central senses, because they are discriminating and intensely personal.[6] Taste and smell involve an immediate reaction of approval or dislike. European power over much of the world presented Europeans with a varied menu of new sensations, and thinking about those options as a matter of taste allowed them to select what they liked without losing their composure and self-control. After Europe established its dominance over much of the rest of the world, sight could return to its privileged role of inspection and clarification.[7]

Cultures specialize in one of the senses because a hierarchical organization of our perceptual skills makes the act of knowing more productive. For primitive cultures, the sense of choice is hearing. Ong prefers to call these societies oral-aural rather than illiterate, because he refuses to concede that the lack of widespread reading skills was a disadvantage. Oral-aural societies have strong social bonds precisely because their interactions are connected by the immediacy of sound rather than being mediated by print. After all, without electrical amplification, we need to be fairly close to each other in order to hear each other speak. Ong admits that the submissive character of listening tends to lead oral societies toward authoritarian forms of social institutions. Obedience to voices is blind in a way that the Enlightenment's privileging of sight was meant to overcome.[8] Every organization of the sensorium has its limitations, but Ong insists on using primitive societies as a standard for all others. This is because he believes that listening honors human dignity in a way that seeing, which objectifies and fragments, does not.

6. Drawing on the work of David Howes, Alan Corbin writes, "Smell, in particular, the sense of transitions, of thresholds and margins, which reveals the processes by which beings and things are transformed, fascinated at this period of confusion [1750–1850], whilst the sense of sight was no longer able to read the hierarchies with the same assurance." *Time, Desire, and Horror: Towards a History of the Senses*, trans. Jean Birrell (Cambridge: Polity, 1995), 182. For Howes's work, see "Scent and Sensibility," *Culture, Medicine, and Psychiatry* 13 (1989): 81–89.

7. Alternatively, one could surmise that with the rise of democracy, "public opinion" emerged to regulate individual preferences, rendering taste a social and not individual act and thus providing room for the reemergence of sight as the defining (and seductive) sense of modernity.

8. For a spirited defense of the visual power of the Enlightenment, see Hans Blumenberg, "Light as a Metaphor for Truth," in *Modernity and the Hegemony of Vision*, ed. David Michael Levin (Berkeley: University of California Press, 1993). Blumenberg notes how Philo, in his attempt to translate the idiom of Hebraic thought into Greek, changed the oral metaphors in the Bible into visual ones (see 47). For example, Philo made the giving of the law an experience of "illumination." For the best defense of light as the most appropriate image of divine revelation, see the fascinating book by Iain M. MacKenzie, *The "Obscurism" of Light: A Theological Study into the Nature of Light* (Norwich, U.K.: Canterbury, 1996).

There are problems with Ong's history of sound. Scholars today are much less inclined to identify primitive societies with purely oral means of communication. Defining another culture in terms of modern characteristics is anachronistic at best. Moreover, orality in the ancient world cannot simply be identified with rural societies while literacy is attributed to urban life.[9] Nor can orality and literacy be portrayed simply as sequential stages of historical development in a given society, with the latter replacing the former. Orality dominated the ancient world even in literate communities, while literacy never erased orality as completely as Ong sometimes implies.

The most significant problem with Ong's sequential view of history is that it leads him to romanticize orality as the foundation for all sub-sequent developments in human communication. Ong is not content to defend this point in historical terms. He provides a metaphysical foundation for his historiography by arguing that sound is the essence of personhood. "Sound," he states, "provides reciprocity and communication without collision or friction."[10] For Ong, sound binds our subjective spaces to each other in an immediate way, unlike any other form of communication. Ong could have appealed to Matthew 12:34 for support: "For out of the abundance of the heart the mouth speaks." We put our whole body into our voice.

What gives sound this unique quality of fusing subjective spaces is its relationship to time. Sound is both more evanescent and more engaging than the other senses because it "must be in active production in order to exist at all."[11] Truth in oral cultures is an event, as Ong likes to say, not a document. Prior to modernity, the spoken word could not be stored for future use or abstracted from the moment of its generation. Speaking creates relationships that are powerful precisely because they are momentary.

The idea that we are most present to each other in sound is also true about God's relationship to us. Only the sense of hearing can do justice to the way God is simultaneously with us and beyond us. Put another way, the voice of God reveals God's innermost purposes without exposing God to our objectifying gaze. Sound is the medium that best carries a supernatural message, because it delivers something external without putting us in control of its source. For Ong, hearing puts us in touch

9. For this point, see Richard A. Horsley with Jonathan A. Draper, *Whoever Hears You Hears Me: Prophets, Performance, and Tradition in Q* (Harrisburg, Penn.: Trinity Press International, 1999), 155.

10. Walter Ong, *The Presence of the Word: Some Prolegomena for Cultural and Religious History* (1967; reprint, Minneapolis: University of Minnesota Press, 1981), 124.

11. Ibid., 112.

with another person in an immediate and inward way while, paradoxically, preserving some distance between us. Of course, hearing is not always so benign. Hearing can be used for spying and eavesdropping, activities that aim at mastery and control. Listening, in its theological guise, needs to be learned. It is a moral skill, related to the virtue of patience. For Ong, the sacramental theology of Roman Catholicism instructs the faithful in the habits of an intimate and loving hearing. We are able to listen to each other only if we learn to listen to God. After all, the priest has the verbal power to transform matter and forgive sins. The spoken word elevates our merely physical presence to each other into something deeply spiritual.

The process of secularization in the West has persuaded most people that any belief in the transformative power of public speech is only a vestige of magic. Ong helps us to understand how secularization is a kind of byproduct of a certain loss of hearing. The process that social theorists have long referred to as disenchantment is really better understood as a devocalization of the universe. Disenchantment implies that we are no longer attracted to what we see. The truth is that we no longer know how to hear. Ong is eloquent even as he overstates the connection between the decline of orality and the rise of atheism: "Man is religious when the sensorium has a certain type of organization, and when it changes, he is no longer so. Religion has to do somehow with the invisible, and when the earlier oral-aural world, with its concentration on voice and sound, finally yields to the more markedly visual world incident to script and print, one may be tempted to argue, religion finally must go."[12] The key period in the transition from voice to vision is the Enlightenment, not the Protestant Reformation. The deist philosophers of the Enlightenment portrayed God as an architect who built what we can see, rather than a rhetor who spoke the world into being. The origin of modern science lies in this silencing of nature; the world is measurable due to its picturability. This is why Martin Heidegger defined modernity as "the age of the world picture."[13] The association between theory and

12. Ibid., 9–10.

13. See Martin Heidegger, "The Age of the World Picture" (1938), in *The Question Concerning Technology and Other Essays*, ed. William Lovitt (New York: Garland, 1977). Heidegger blames the emphasis on seeing for the curiosity that led to the hegemony of technological rationality in modernity. For a development of Heidegger's notion of *Zugehörigkeit*, which means "belongingness" but has *hörig* for its root, see David Michael Levin, *The Listening Self: Personal Growth, Change, and the Closure of Metaphysics* (New York: Routledge, 1989). Levin sets out to construct the conditions of an ideal listener, somewhat analogous to Jürgen Habermas's analysis of the ideal speech situation, and as this analogy suggests, Levin's project is still captured by the universal ambitions rooted in the Enlightenment's privileging of sight over sound.

visual models has broken down in science today, but its consequences have not diminished. The primacy of vision turns the world into a thing and thus endows humanity with enormous powers, but it also makes humanity a spectator, alienated and estranged from the objects of our inspection. Our world is dull and quiet—the heavens no longer declare God's glory (Ps. 19)—no matter how much we fill that void with the sights and sounds of consumerism.

In a brilliant book on the role of hearing in religion after the Enlightenment, Leigh Eric Schmidt has criticized Ong for too closely identifying modernity with the dominance of the visual.[14] It is probably true that Ong's account of how modernity armed itself with the visual in order to combat the orality of traditional societies is too linear and one-sided. Schmidt's work, however, illustrates how difficult it is to write about the relationship between seeing and hearing in the modern period without associating these senses with monumental cultural changes and taking sides with one over the other. Schmidt's main thesis concerns how the Enlightenment identified the phenomenon of "hearing voices" with religious fanaticism. He further shows how this identification led to an entire industry that debunked aural illusions by experimenting with technologies of projecting and manipulating the human voice. Schmidt does an even better job than Ong in documenting the specific ways in which modernity hinges on the relative positioning of the senses.

Of course, we cannot simply blame the Enlightenment for human failures that extend beyond the confines of a particular time and place. Our hearing is never perfect, just as we never say exactly what we think; our voice is always imperfectly related to our body. We can become mired in an inward dialogue that distracts us from the world outside. We need to hear an external sound to save us from the temptation of turning our life into a monologue. God's sound, after all, is not our own; the Word is not something we can say to ourselves. Only in God does saying perfectly correspond to being. We can use our voice to mask our true feelings; conversely, our voice can betray our feelings even when we try to hide them. God is not hidden behind God's words; God is the Word. God is a perfect community because the Father, Son, and Holy Spirit speak to each other while saying the same thing.

Regardless of questions about his historiography and his metaphysics, Ong succeeds in articulating a social theory of the spoken word that shows how the reality of sound entails a relational and transformative account of truth. We are called by the Word, just as we are brought into relationship with others through words. Hearing draws us out of

14. Leigh Eric Schmidt, *Hearing Things: Religion, Illusion, and the American Enlightenment* (Cambridge: Harvard University Press, 2000), 19–20.

ourselves in ways that gazing, inspecting, and looking do not. We have more control over our eyes, which we can quickly and completely close, than our ears, which are vulnerable to loud sounds even when we cover them with our hands. Words can reach deep inside us in ways we find hard to resist.

The Shape of Sound: A Note on Sacramental Theology

Arguably, it is the Protestant emphasis on preaching that most clearly underscores these points, and that is why I will analyze the Protestant Reformation in terms of the history of sound in chapters 5 and 6. This does not mean that a Protestant theology of preaching cannot be understood as complementing the Roman Catholic emphasis on the visibility of the sacraments. One of the great accomplishments of the ecumenical movement has been to show how much these two emphases need to be brought together. Nevertheless, their differences are still worth noting. Catholicism is truly catholic with regard to the senses, engaging all of them in a holistic presentation of the gospel. The Catholic understanding of the sacraments, therefore, can readily absorb the Protestant understanding of proclamation, but the Protestant insistence on the uniqueness of hearing is still worth listening to.

For Ong, the sacraments are a means of grace due to their verbal character, but this statement stands in need of much elaboration. Augustine set the stage for all subsequent Catholic sacramental theology by defining the sacraments as "visible words." For Augustine, working within a Greek philosophical milieu that connected knowledge and sight, the problem of revelation is how the invisible God is made visible. Robert W. Jenson has taken Augustine as his starting point in his remarkable endeavor to reunite Protestant and Roman Catholic understandings of the sacraments. One can learn much from Augustine's concept of "visible words" without agreeing with the conclusion Jenson draws from this concept—that the Word must be seen in order for it to be heard.[15] While Jenson reads Luther as supporting this claim, I will argue in chapters 5 and 6 that the Protestant Reformers taught that the invisible God is revealed primarily through the audible, not the visual. True, the Reformers can be understood as merely recovering the vocal component of the sacraments: rituals without words are empty. Thus the Reformers were especially critical of private masses, because nobody was there to hear the words of the priest. To the ex-

15. Robert W. Jenson, *Visible Words: The Interpretation and Practice of Christian Sacraments* (Philadelphia: Fortress, 1978).

tent, however, that an Augustinian sacramental theology is understood as arguing that the audible must always take the visual form of the sacraments, the Reformers can be understood as doing something much more radical.

Jenson's sacramental theology resonates with some of the themes of this book. God speaks an effective Word, which suggests that we can see what the divine voice has wrought. God's Word has a body and a name in Jesus Christ, which suggests that sound is never without shape. Furthermore, our own voices are physical expressions of who we are, which makes preaching an embodied act. Jenson goes too far, however, when he implies that sound alone is an insufficient medium for the gospel. "It can be argued that the speaking of the gospel must somehow be visible and not only audible." That "somehow" becomes in Jenson's theology a necessary connection; as a result, he can state that "every occurrence of the gospel has a sacramental aspect, a visible aspect."[16] This way of putting the issue—the Word must always be sacramental—clearly privileges the visible over the auditory. For the Reformers, the sacraments are more than verbal, but they are never less than verbal. Jenson shows his independence from the Reformers by insisting that the sacraments do not simply add a visible dimension to the sound of the Word; instead, he argues that the Word must be seen if it is to be understood. Jenson transfers the causal power of the Word to effect change from the ear to the eye. What Jenson misses is the biblical priority of hearing over seeing, since it is hearing the Word that teaches us where to look for its presence in the world.[17] It follows that Jansen's statement that the Word is always visible should be replaced with the statement that sacraments are always verbal. The Word makes the sacrament, not the other way

16. Ibid., 9, 11.
17. Jenson argues, "Confronted by the bread, the cup, and the verbal promises, as a unitary spirited and embodied address, how do we believe *this* word of God? Clearly, by eating and drinking" (ibid., 107). The presence of Christ is experienced in ritualized action that follows the visual model of the priest. Jenson is worried that putting too much emphasis on the spoken words of the sacrament makes the presence of Christ conditional, but I see no reason why sound, rather than one of the other senses, does less justice to the unconditional promise of grace in the Eucharist. The very nature of an unconditional promise entails a verbal exchange. It is no accident, by the way, that Jenson is passionate about the Eastern Church. Orthodox theology, under the sway of the contemplative tradition of Greek philosophy, tends to be Johannine and thus vision-oriented, while Western Christianity has been more Pauline and thus more auditory. For a fascinating remark on how Luther's emphasis on sound can be interpreted to support the Orthodox emphasis on divinization (*theosis,* that is, a participatory notion of justification), see Jenson's contribution to *Union with Christ: The New Finnish Interpretation of Luther,* ed. Carl E. Braaten and Robert W. Jenson (Grand Rapids: Eerdmans, 1998), 24.

around. The sacraments are an effective means of divine communication because they are the most privileged shapes of the divine sound.

Gerhard Forde does not go as far as Jenson in defining the Word sacramentally (and thus visually), but he does assign the sacraments the role of being a necessary visual enhancement of the Word. He argues that the sacraments are needed to keep the sermon from becoming a subjective event. Words are too easily internalized, he suggests. As a result, we can be left wondering whether we have really heard the sermon correctly and considered it fully. "Sacraments save because they save the Word from disappearing into the inner life."[18] From a theological perspective informed by the study of sound, this downplays the inherent power of the human voice. The spoken word, as I will argue in the context of Kristin Linklater's work in chapter 3, simply *is* the connection to one's inner life: the inner life is a soundscape that integrates body, mind, and emotion, all of which are revealed in the voice. Sound does not disappear into the inner life like light being drawn into a black hole. On the contrary, as the listener absorbs the vibrations of the speaker, sound reaches into the whole body and draws the listener and speaker together toward a new place that neither had previously occupied. There can be a visual aspect to oral communication, but the signifying power of sound is not intrinsically dependent on sight.

Sound and shape, voice and body are disconnected in fallen humanity, which makes their integration a task, not something that is given in human nature. The model here is, as always, the Trinity. God's decision to speak and the Word that God speaks are coeternal. Although our power to speak does not exhibit such creativity, the Trinity does demonstrate an ultimate connection between the freedom of the voice and the freedom of the body; one is not possible without the other. Voice and body, like the Father and the Son, are mutually implicated and dependent on each other.

Gestures can speak without vocal words—we can tell people what we want by pointing and the like—but we can also understand what someone is saying without seeing them. The point is not whether sound is always necessary for communication—it is not. Neither are visual images. The point is that everything in theology depends on how the relationship of sound and sight is conceived. Sacraments save because they demonstrate just how efficacious the Word really is.[19] The sacra-

18. Gerhard O. Forde, *Theology Is for Proclamation* (Minneapolis: Fortress, 1990), 160.

19. For Thomas Aquinas, the matter of the sacraments varies, but they all have the spoken word as their form. This word is efficacious *(ex opere operato)*. This is the primary locus for proclamation in Roman Catholicism. Proclamation exhibits its power through

ments are nothing without the words that demonstrate their relationship to faith. They do not work automatically, as Catholics and Protestants agree, precisely because they do not work silently.

Sound as the Medium of Revelation

Ong's phenomenology of sound has much to teach us about how to think about God. Speech leaves no trace in space, and so it is the perfect medium for a God who does not want to be seen. The significance of talking about God in terms of hearing, in fact, can be understood fully only by reflecting on the visual metaphors for knowledge that dominated the Enlightenment and extend back to Plato's metaphysics. Although the cave dwellers in Plato's famous allegory in *The Republic* hear sounds the source of which they cannot correctly identify, their seclusion in the dark—and their consequent *visual* confusion of shadows for reality—is the point Plato was most concerned to make. It is a point that has been well taken in the West. Talking about knowledge as illumination and ignorance as a kind of darkness comes naturally to us. To be enlightened is to open one's eyes, and to think is to clarify what we see. We so readily imagine knowledge as the broadest possible view of a topic that we rarely reflect on what we are missing when we focus on sight at the expense of sound.

Connecting knowledge to sight fools us into thinking that knowing is a private event, since you do not have to be seen in order to see. The very image of illumination conjures a quiet moment that takes place in one's solitude, since light moves without making a sound. To use Empedocles' ancient metaphor, the wise one radiates light outward, shining like a lantern. The privacy of sight is reinforced by the fact that you can see from a distance. Indeed, the farther you can see (the farther from the object you are), the more impressive is the act of knowledge.

Hearing, by contrast, establishes a more intimate relationship between source and perception. On a very basic level, this is true simply because we must be fairly close to the source of the sound we are trying to hear. Even with amplification, as all theater professionals know, we

---

its effect on the capacity of the natural to bear the supernatural. The Catholic position on the sacraments reflects a profoundly oral culture, where words are intrinsically linked to their referents. That is, words matter precisely because the Word can take material form. Words are not primarily marks on a page but instead are integrally connected to objects in the world. If this philosophy of language is less plausible today, its zealous correction by Enlightenment rationalism is no more attractive. The modern world has gone to the other extreme of desensualizing language by portraying it as an abstract system with only arbitrary connections between words and things.

understand what someone is saying better when we can see him or her speak. More scientifically put, sound waves travel slower and weaken more quickly than light waves. It is this physical limitation that makes hearing a more relational form of knowledge.

In fact, the slowness of sound, compared to the immediacy of sight, was at the heart of Greek speculation about the senses. Ancient Greek philosophers consistently explained hearing as the result of a commotion in the air. An external object must actively shock or assault the air to produce sound, and it is this disturbance that is carried to the ear. Seeing, for the Greeks, involves the meeting of visual rays that emanate from both the object and the eye in a continuous flow of light. David Chidester summarizes the most important implication of ancient Greek science for the act of hearing: "There was no presence, no connection, no continuous bond between the subject and the object of [auditory] perception."[20] Sound thus denotes distance and temporality in a way that sight does not. Rather than an inner illumination that emanates outward, hearing proceeds from the external to the internal.

The simultaneity of sight needs to be contrasted with the sequential nature of sound. We hear sounds one at a time, while we see an object all at once. This is a simplification of perception, because we must inspect an object from different angles in order to create a mental image of its entirety. There is, then, a temporal dimension to sight as well. Nevertheless, we can visually recognize what an object is all at once in a way that is not possible when we listen to a series of sounds. Even an immediately recognizable sound makes us wait to listen for what comes next. Sounds draw us out of ourselves by leading us to the source of the noise, while sight brings the image to us. Sound does not permit us to be detached from the source, as does sight, but it also does not connect us to the source in an immediate way, since sound takes time as its medium. Sound is intimate without being immediate.

Another aspect of sound that makes it a less immediate experience than sight is its inherent complexity. During the eighteenth century, it was a popular conceit that sound could be made visible. A Parisian Jesuit named Louis Bertrand Castel spent a lifetime of work trying to translate sounds into colors, so that people could see as well as hear music. His color-music show opened in 1734 and was a great disappointment.[21] The problem was that sounds possess a complexity that colors do not. When

20. David Chidester, *Word and Light; Seeing, Hearing, and Religious Discourse* (Urbana: University of Illinois Press, 1992), 7.

21. For a fascinating account of this endeavor, see Jonathan Ree, *I See a Voice: Deafness, Language, and the Senses—A Philosophical History* (New York: Metropolitan, 1999), chap. 2.

different colors are combined, they create a new color, but no matter how interesting the new color is, it is still a specific color. Sound, by contrast, is never simple. Every note emits a range of overtones that give it depth. Every sound is, in a way, multiple. The depth of sound gives it an external dimension by forcing us to strain our ears in order to make sense of its various qualities. So too the fact that so many sounds come from multiple sources makes even the simplest noise resonate with time.

That sound can be both external and intimate, as well as its basic relationship to time, enables it to function as the ruling medium for the Bible's understanding of God. We are used to thinking that it was light that broke the primordial darkness from which all life comes, but it was really God's voice that shattered the silence: "Let there be light." Sound precedes light; we hear before we can see. This is the significance of God's appearance to Moses in the fire. Moses hears the words but sees no form: "there was only a voice" (Deut. 4:12). The words illumine, not the flame. Ong makes much of the fact that the Hebrew term *dabar* means both "word" and "event." The Hebrew God is not present in the world as something luminous that attracts our gaze, either radiating from above or glowing from within. This would be the god of the pagans, who could be represented by golden (and thus shiny) idols or identified with the mysterious (but visible) forces of nature. The god of pantheism is reflected all around us and is, in the end, only a mirror of our own hopes and desires. The God of Abraham spans the apparent distance from us in the activity of speaking. Such revelation is a dramatic event, but the divine voice is also intimate and familiar, compelling us to listen intently. Indeed, the Bible is extremely modest about God's appearance—God is too holy for us to look at directly; rather than pleasing, like the glittering attraction of the pagan idols, the God of the Bible would be terrifying to our eyes—but not about God's voice. This is a voice that is forceful as well as comforting. In Psalm 29, God's voice breaks trees, flashes forth flames, and shakes the wilderness. Other psalms portray God as a shepherd calling for lost sheep. All the drama of our relationship with God can be found in God's voice.

Although cultural historians have labored mightily to explain why the Hebrews organized their understanding of knowledge around hearing rather than seeing, the simplest reason for this audiocentric phenomenon is that they thought God had chosen to reveal God's divinity to them through the spoken word. This does not mean that God never appears to people in the Old Testament. We are so used to thinking of God as a purely spiritual being that we tend to ignore passages in the Bible that describe God as having physical and bodily traits. Scholars like James L. Kugel have argued that the Hebrews developed a theological aniconism (an avoidance of divine images) only gradually, and that even after the prohibition of images was made official, many Hebrews still imagined God as having some kind of form.[22] Speculating about which parts of the Bible are the oldest and how the writers of these parts distinguished (or did not distinguish) between the physical and the spiritual is beyond the scope of this book. It is sufficient to note that even Kugel admits that the image of God inherited from the Bible by Judaism and Christianity is primarily oral, not visual.

The Hebrews were a community of listeners because they thought they heard something that no other group had. What they heard sounded unlike anything else, but it was also a voice that they recognized and thus experienced as something they had heard before. When Jacob heard a voice at the top of the ladder, he understood immediately who it was (Gen. 28:10–17).[23] The Hebrews could no doubt speak analogically about the voice of God—interpreting both natural and historical events as speaking to them of God's purposes—but this analogical language made sense to them precisely because they trusted the reports of their prophets, who claimed that God had spoken directly to their ears. "Let me hear what God the LORD will speak," cries the psalmist (Ps. 85:8). This belief that God had chosen them to listen to God's speech set them apart from their more visually oriented neighbors.

The followers of Jesus also believed that God could speak, and when they remembered Jesus, it was his voice, much more than his appearance, that they found inspiring.[24] When they thought about the authority of Jesus' teachings and the claims he made on his own behalf, they concluded that Jesus was more than just another prophet to whom God had spoken. They identified Jesus' voice with the voice of God. As Jesus said, "The one who sent me is true, and I declare to the world what I have heard from him" (John 8:26). It was not that God was speaking through Jesus, performing an act of ventriloquism. Instead, the early Christians concluded that this was the very sound of God. It was this very voice that created the world and challenged Pharaoh to free God's people.

22. James L. Kugel, *The God of Old: Inside the Lost World of the Bible* (New York: Free Press, 2003), chap. 4.

23. Zwingli uses the story of Jacob as an example of the importance of listening for the voice of God in his sermon "Of the Clarity and Certainty or Power of the Word of God," in *Zwingli and Bullinger*, ed. Geoffrey W. Bromiley (Philadelphia: Westminster, 1953), 77.

24. "Not only is there no 'accurate' visual representation of Jesus, but it is a heresy to insist that such a thing might exist." Robin M. Jensen, "Jesus Up Close," *Christian Century* (September 20, 2003), 26. Jensen goes on to explain, " The heresy is that of limiting Christ's character, nature or power by circumscribing his appearance."

The Bible thus portrays God as an eloquent performer *(Deus loquens)* exercising a commanding control over an utterly creative voice. It can even be said that God created the first humans at the point when God talked to them, for such speech called forth a response in kind. We are made, as I suggested in chapter 1, in the image of sound. By speaking to us, God grants us the ability to listen, and when we are stirred by God's voice we rise above the animal state and begin to speak ourselves. God also creates Israel by calling the people to heed God's voice. All of biblical religion can be summarized in the Shema of Deuteronomy, which begins, "Hear, O Israel."[25] When the people listen to God, they are able to answer with one voice, and Israel is born (Exod. 24:3–6). "Thus says Yahweh" is the Bible's refrain. God's speech demands obedience even as it grants us the power to respond. We can have discourse among ourselves of an egalitarian nature because all of us answer to a higher calling.

God's voice is holy, but it is less commonly pointed out that a God who speaks is a God who is revealed not only in the divine but also in the human voice. The prophets are revered in the Bible as those called to speak in God's name, since they balance God's deafening demands for justice with God's soft murmurs of mercy. The prophets demonstrate how human voices can mediate the divine plan. All speech, therefore, is endowed with potentially sacred significance. All of us can imitate God's words with our own, by talking each other out of the despair of isolation and into healthy and just relations. The Spirit moves through us like a wind as we exhale sounds into the world. Our power lies in speech too.

That God lets the prophets speak with God's own authority suggests that God's power lies not only in speaking but also in listening. That is, the prophets spoke not only *for* but also *to* God, and they often spoke on behalf of the poor and marginalized. In fact, God's hearing is not only perfect but also perfectly moral. When God tells the Hebrews not to abuse widows and orphans, God declares, "If you do abuse them, when they cry out to me, I will surely heed their cry" (Exod. 22:23). God seems compelled to respond to the sound of their misery. The Bible repeatedly depicts God as hearing the cries of those who are victims of injustice (Gen. 18:20–21; Exod. 3:7; 15:24–25; 22:7; Num. 20:16; Judg.

25. In an analysis of the role of hearing and memorization in the transmission of the Gospel materials, Samuel Byrskog argues that Matthew uses the Shema to contextualize Jesus' obedience to God and the disciples' obedience to Jesus. "Jesus' advice to hear his teaching gains its force through a confessional text implying a fundamental religious duty of obedience to Jesus." Hearing, memorization, and obedience are integrally connected. See *Jesus the Only Teacher: Didactic Authority and Transmission in Ancient Israel, Ancient Judaism, and the Matthean Community* (Stockholm: Almqvist & Wiskell, 1994), 321–22.

10:12; Ps. 12:5; Isa. 19:20; and on and on). What is remarkable is not just that the biblical writers think of God as having perfect hearing but that God seems to be more sensitive to the loud and high-pitched sounds of suffering than to other tones of the human voice.

According to Kugel, there are historical reasons for this portrait of a hearing God. "In the biblical world sound was thought to travel upward. God, situated in heaven, was thus privy to whatever sounds might be made on earth, even if He could not necessarily see from such heights everything that was happening down below."[26] From the perspective of a theology of sound, it makes sense that God is moved more by hearing than by seeing. The divine omniscience is usually conceived as a matter of seeing rather than hearing, but a God who sees everything all at once is a God who stands at a great distance from us in order to have the widest perspective. The all-seeing God is thus easily depicted as unmoved and unmoving. The image of an all-hearing God, by contrast, is of One who draws intimately close to us in order not to miss a word.

The psalms are full of requests for God to draw nearer to us, which suggests the depth to which the Hebrews imagined God to be affected by sound. The psalmist also wants to see God's face, but sound remains fundamental. Psalm 10 begins by asking, "Why, O LORD, do you stand far off?" (v. 1) and ends by asking God to "incline your ear to do justice for the orphan and the oppressed" (vv. 17–18). Psalm 102 has an intriguing account of God's sense perceptions: "He looked down from his holy height, from heaven the LORD looked at the earth, to hear the groans of the prisoners, to set free those who were doomed to die" (vv. 19–20). God looks at the earth, but the divine vision is attracted to the sounds of human suffering. The shift in imagery from looking to hearing in this psalm is subtle and sudden but overwhelmingly significant. Like us, God looks in order to hear. Notice, for example, how we glance in a certain direction in order to see if anything stands out, but when we hear something, we look more closely. Sound attracts the eye. Seeing things at such a distance that we cannot hear any sound they might make leaves us in control. We can visually examine a mute object without being affected by it. When we hear something from that object, however, we are engaged and ready for action of some kind. (To verify this, try playing a computer game with the sound off!) Even sounds from nature seem to demand a response. Gazing at clouds is an occasion for

26. Kugel, *God of Old*, 114. In fact, sound travels upward in the Bible much as does scent, which suggests that the model for how God hears us is shaped in part by the smoke and incense of the sacrificial cult. Although we can close our eyes or look the other way, when we are too close to someone it is hard to avoid their cries or their odor. See Genesis 8:21 and Leviticus 16:2.

quiet reverie, but when we hear thunder, we know to take cover. Sounds have a way of penetrating us, staying with us, and moving us to action. Perfect hearing finds its apotheosis in moral perfection in a way that perfect seeing does not.

Finally, that God listens also means that God is silent. The laments of the psalms are full of the cry "Hear my voice, O God" (Ps. 64:1). Biblical laments are eloquent testimony to the way in which God's silence is not indifference or absence. Instead, it is active and inviting.[27] The divine silence is a form of hearing, and thus it is totally unlike our own. Silence among even close friends can be uncomfortable; we rush to fill the void with words. It is as if we consider silence to have an ultimate source in something other than God. Because God speaks, God listens to what God has created, and that pause in the divine discourse is silence. Silence, then, is nothing to be feared. We can welcome silence because silence is as much a product of the Word as is sound.

A Word for the Deaf

Speaking of silence raises the topic of the deaf. Indeed, if sound should be a central theological topic, then deafness should be as well. No theology of sound can proceed without reflecting on what the deaf can teach us about both speaking and hearing. The deaf world demonstrates how a system of soundless gestures can constitute a self-enclosed language. Linguists have just begun studying American Sign Language (ASL), which is used by hundreds of thousands of people. Many advocates of the deaf argue that ASL is a natural language completely independent of English. Sign language, visual and spatial, is not pantomime; instead, it has its own syntax and grammar. The muscles of the limbs take the place of the muscles of the throat. Sign language depends on visual rather than auditory cues—reading the facial gram-

27. The strongest patristic statement on God's silence comes from Ignatius of Antioch in his letter to the Magnesians. In William R. Schoedel's translation, Ignatius identifies Jesus Christ as God's "Word which proceeded from silence" (8.1). Schoedel, *Ignatius of Antioch: A Commentary on the Letter of Ignatius of Antioch* (Philadelphia: Fortress 1985), 119. Schoedel is careful to note that Ignatius does not simply equate God and silence. Instead, he is following the Hellenistic tradition of reading silence as a portent of deep and mysterious meaning. Even in Ignatius, then, God's silence has meaning only in reference to the Word that God speaks. Moreover, Ignatius also was intent on honoring the silence of the bishop as an indication of the bishop's authority. "It is almost as though Ignatius used the silence of the bishop as an analogy of the divine silence from which Christ came forth." Virginia Corwin, *St. Ignatius and Christianity in Antioch* (New Haven: Yale University Press, 1960), 123. I will return to the question of God and silence in the last chapter.

mar of the signer is an important skill—but it still has all the properties
of a language. Indeed, the structural similarities between sign language
and spoken language are such that most of what I have to say about the
proclamation of the Word in this book can be applied equally to either
system of communication.

Signing has not always been accepted as a language. Supporters of
"the method of signs" had to struggle against "oralists" who portrayed
"gesturalism" as an inferior form of communication.[28] These debates
were highly charged, because fundamental notions about the nature
of speech were at stake. Oralists had history, as well as convention, on
their side. The Greek philosophers privileged seeing over hearing, so
they connected knowledge with sight, but they defined communication in terms of sound. To know is to see, but to communicate that
knowledge, they argued, the less reliable medium of sound is required.
The Enlightenment philosophers emphasized the role of print (which
is seen, not heard) in communication, but they also could insist on a
single and universal standard for human nature. One consequence of
this universalism was the assumption that there is only one right way
to speak. When people talk, they should talk with their mouth, not their
hands. Clear and transparent communication comes from the head,
not the hands. The Enlightenment thinkers could even suggest that
humans are not fully human unless they can make intelligible noises
through their throat.

Keeping in mind the terrible ways the deaf have been treated throughout history, a difficult point must be made that balances two concerns:
deaf individuals should not be treated like second-class citizens, but the
condition of deafness should not be treated as if it had no disadvantages.
It is difficult to maintain this balancing act when the growing field of
disability studies deplores the very term *disabled* (which replaced the
earlier term *handicapped*). For those who are suspicious of any label that
carries a negative connotation, *differently abled* is the preferred term.
Even that term is misleading, however, because we all have different
abilities. If everyone is different, and all differences are the same, then
why label some people as more different than others? The problem is
that those who advocate for a politics of identity need some set of labels
to account for the cohesiveness of the groups they represent. Advocates
for the deaf argue that they represent a distinct cultural identity, so
that the deaf are more like a Spanish-speaking minority within an
English-speaking country than a group with a physical impairment that
sets them apart from "normal" people. The idea of treating the deaf as

28. See Rée, *I See A Voice*, for the history of this conflict. Also see Oliver Sachs, *Seeing
Voices* (New York: Vintage, 1990).

a linguistic community makes sense, but the insistence on completely severing deafness from any notion of disability does not.[29] Those who take that step talk about not only an *ablist* society that does not understand the differently abled but also an *audism* that is comparable to racism or sexism. The charge of audism precludes any consideration of the voice as a fundamental aspect of human communication.

Conjuring the specter of audism has practical consequences as well. Cochlear implants, which allow the ear to process sound and send the information to the brain, are controversial within the deaf community, because surgical procedures can appear to challenge the competency of the deaf to achieve everything the hearing can do. Deaf advocates use the rhetoric of "ethnocide" in response to those who treat deafness as a medical condition that can be corrected.[30] They fear that the attempt to "cure" the deaf will wipe out their unique culture. If technology can eliminate deafness, then society will be less patient with those deaf people who refuse to join the hearing world. History supports their fears. Until the development of sign language, the deaf were cut off from society. Under Roman rule, the inability of the deaf to swear an oath precluded them from civil proceedings, rights, and duties. Civil authorities widely doubted whether the deaf could be validly married, and theologians debated whether they could be saved. Until the sixteenth century, the word *deaf* was a synonym for stupid, and until the nineteenth century, it could mean barren or empty, as in a deaf ear of corn that does not bear any grain.

While the development of sign language—which has been called a kind of writing in the air—revolutionized the social standing of the deaf, hearing loss remains a cause of isolation for many individuals. This is especially true for those who do not learn sign language, whether because their hearing loss is only partial or because their loss came after they had already learned to speak.[31] I first began noticing that I

29. For a sensitive treatment of this issue that maintains a balanced view of the relationship between deafness and disability, see Lennard J. Davis, *Enforcing Normalcy: Disability, Deafness, and the Body* (London: Verso, 1995).

30. For a provocative discussion of cochlear implants that uses the inflammatory rhetoric of "ethnocide," see Harlan Lane, Robert Hoffmeister, and Ben Bahan, *A Journey into the Deaf-World* (San Diego, Calif.: DawnSignPress, 1996), chap. 14. The authors state, "Our experiences with Deaf people have led us to view being born Deaf as a form of human variation that does not require medical intervention" (404–5). Harlan Lane has drawn on the analogy of colonization in *The Mask of Benevolence: Disabling the Deaf Community* (San Diego, Calif.: DawnSignPress, 1999), pt. 2.

31. For two fine memoirs of deaf people learning to live in the hearing world, primarily through lip reading, see Henry Kisor, *What's That Pig Outdoors? A Memoir of Deafness* (New York: Penguin, 1990), and Hannah Merker, *Listening: Ways of Hearing in a Silent World* (Dallas: Southern Methodist University Press, 2000). Also see the moving novel by Frances Itani, *Deafening* (New York: Atlantic Monthly Press, 2003).

was losing some of my own hearing when I had to lean toward people
in order to make sense of their words.[32] I became depressed about my
teaching, because I could not hear the students who sat in the back of
the classroom. Becoming hearing-impaired is more embarrassing than
having diminished vision, and the reason surely has to do with the way
sound makes us present to each other. Those who hear well often treat
the hearing-impaired with resentment and disdain. The hard of hearing
are either out of reach of our voice or crowd into our private space—or
they annoyingly ask us to repeat ourselves—but their placement with
regard to sound is never right. I wear glasses without thinking twice
about it, but the first time I put in a hearing aid, I felt shame, as if it were
my fault that I had to have help to enter the world of sound. Although I
need two hearing aids, I wear only one, which is my way of saying that
I am still of this world.

Christianity is not immune to prejudices against the deaf. Throughout
history, the Jewish and Christian emphasis on the spoken word could
easily be used to discriminate against the deaf. When St. Paul argued
that Christians receive God's grace through hearing, he meant that literally, but we know today that the deaf can receive the good news through
their other senses just as well. While the history of Christianity cannot be
told outside the history of sound, preaching can take place in complete
silence. Hearing is the gift from God that makes faith possible, whether
it is a matter of listening to voices or looking at hands.

There is something to be said, then, for Augustine's argument (which I
will address in chapter 7) that God does not need the physical apparatus
of vocalization in order to speak. Nor does God need sound in order to
hear, since the Bible clearly states that God hears the mute (4 Macc. 10:
18–19). God can speak without air or vibration because the Holy Spirit
is God's breath, a divine wind that carries sound even where there is no
air. For us, the good news about the divine speech is that it creates the
conditions for its own reception. We do not have to be without moral
fault or physical limitation in order to hear God's Word. More specifically,
we do not need ears in order to hear God's Word or tongues in order to
witness to our faith. It is no accident, then, that God commanded the
Hebrews not to revile the deaf (Lev. 19:14). This was a radical command
at a time when deaf children were subjected to infanticide. Unlike ancient

---

32. I am not trying to gain status for my analysis by pretending to be a member of
the deaf community. Indeed, the fact that hearing loss is an inevitable part of the aging
process—some level of decline is significantly under way in most people by the age of
forty—demonstrates that deafness is not an either-or condition but, for many people
anyway, a matter of degree. See the scientific analysis of this issue in Robert Jourdain,
Music, the Brain, and Ecstasy: How Music Captures Our Imagination (San Francisco:
HarperCollins, 1997), chap. 1.

Greek and modern Enlightenment philosophy, biblically based theology is able to portray speaking and hearing as the paradigmatic human (and divine) activities without thereby denigrating the deaf.

The biblical view of deafness is nuanced. The Bible does not judge the deaf, yet it recognizes deafness as a condition that is less than what God intended for humanity. Thus in the kingdom of God the deaf will have their hearing restored (Isa. 29:18; 35:5). In an echo of these prophecies, Jesus healed the deaf (Mark 7:37), a feat his followers found to be astonishing beyond measure, given the hopelessness that was generally associated with this condition. While deafness does not preclude the hearing of the Word, it is still a sign of the fact that the world is fallen and none of us are as we shall be when God restores and completes the creation. Yet those who hear cannot lord their hearing over the deaf, because we are all deaf to the divine voice. Moreover, God speaks in such a way as to heal our deafness, both figuratively and literally, so that our destiny is to hear sounds that even those of us with the sharpest sense of hearing could never have imagined.

three

Freeing the Christian Voice

Kristin Linklater and the Quest for the Natural Voice

Walter Ong's pioneering work set the stage for many advances in scholarship about orality. One of the fields that has contributed the most to this area of study is theater. The work of theater professionals should be a natural resource for the study of theology, given Christianity's fundamental stake in demonstrating the relationship between divine revelation and the sound of the human voice. For all the experimentation in the theater world and its increasing convergence with the world of film, the message of a play is still carried, for the most part, by the sound of someone talking. For this reason, I have become increasingly interested in what actors and theater teachers have to say about the human voice, and I have found Kristin Linklater's approach to be exceptionally insightful.[1]

Linklater has developed what is probably the most influential pedagogical system for teaching voice for the actor. She does not, however, expound a vocal technique that treats the voice as an instrument to be manipulated and refined according to the role that is to be played. That would merely reinforce the way our society promotes the disembodiment of the voice. Rather than impose an artificial standard on the use of the

---

1. Kristin Linklater, *Freeing the Natural Voice* (New York: Drama Book, 1976). For an example of a practical application of Linklater's work to preaching, see Jana Childers, *Performing the Word: Preaching as Theatre* (Nashville: Abingdon, 1998), chap. 3.

voice—treating it as an instrument that can be analyzed and trained apart from the body—she broadens the act of speaking by locating it not just in the vocal folds but in the entire human body. The voice can be said to embody the body, because all parts of the person, from feelings to thoughts and impulses, are expressed through the voice. Speaking, as the ancient Romans understood, is the paradigmatically public act, because the voice, coming from within, turns us inside out. Outside of old-fashioned speech departments (those that have not yet succumbed to communication studies), acting schools are probably the closest we can come to experiencing what the ancient schools of rhetoric were like. That is why homileticians have much to learn from theater professionals regarding the practice of preaching.

Linklater began formulating her approach to voice in the 1960s, at the same time that Walter Ong was making his own breakthroughs on the cultural significance of sound. It should be no surprise that her work is a product of its time. This can be seen in her analysis of the relationship of the individual to social institutions, which is replete with the utopian rhetoric of personal liberation. She makes claims about the promise of the natural voice that take a romantic and exaggerated form. "To free the voice is to free the person, and each person is indivisibly mind and body."[2] This talk of freedom through personal expression should be put in the context of the return-to-nature ideologies that were then so popular. Many thinkers in the 1960s responded to a sense of increasing social fragmentation by searching for the key that would restore a lost sense of personal integrity. Anything social was thought to be artificial and constraining, especially social institutions like formal education and the church.

Linklater too tends to accept the sixties dictum that the natural is authentic while the social is always contrived. This politics of vocal liberation leaves little room for constructive thinking about sound and the church, but theologians can still learn a lot from Linklater about the connection of voice and body. I would express this connection figuratively by saying that the body is made of sound. We know we are flesh and bone because we can speak. Even a quick glance at a baby will demonstrate the degree to which sound is connected to bodily emotion and physical gesture. We speak with our limbs as well as our throats.

The sound babies make, in fact, is important for Linklater's quest for the natural voice. Babies cry naturally, but for the rest of us, any kind of vocalization requires an effort that can be quite strenuous. The reason is that very early in our life, societal, peer, and family dynamics begin to instruct us to disconnect our voice from our body. In order not to have our thoughts and emotions laid bare, we mask our voice with

2. Linklater, *Freeing the Natural Voice*, 2.

unnecessary physical tension. We tighten our jaws and tongue, breathe shallowly, and force our speech into a narrow band of pitch. Rather than letting our body be a musical instrument, resonating with sound, we project our voice from the upper regions of our body, ignoring what lies below. Gender differences are obviously crucial in this context. Many men tend to keep away from the higher pitches of the upper parts of the body, while many women tend to avoid the lower resonators of their voice. Geography also plays a role. Linguists have noted how Americans employ less tonal variation than the French, Spanish, Italian, and even the English. This is true especially of the Midwestern accent, which tends to function as the standard for much public speaking in America. Midwesterners (I speak as one) are especially prone to disincarnate their voice from their body in an effort to be self-effacing and to fit in.

What I want to emphasize in contrast to Linklater's individualistic and utopian understanding of freedom is that the human voice is never natural. Linklater tends to see the process of vocal repression as something that supervenes upon an original (but soon lost) vocal freedom. It almost seems as if she connects freedom of the body with freedom from others. Christianity, by contrast, teaches that our voice is never free from sin, whether that is our personal sin or the social structures that tempt and oppress us. The natural is always already fallen, so that there is no voice untouched by falsity and pretension. The Christian ideal of a free voice, then, is not a nostalgic return to something primal and innocent. Instead, it is the ideal of how we sound when we gather to listen to God's Word. Our voice does not come from deep within us but rather emerges in the give-and-take of listening and speaking to others. We go to church to sing together and to listen to the Word. We go, in other words, to find our voice.

There are resources in Linklater's work to make this point. Arguably, her work is implicitly theological, even Protestant, in its insistence that speaking, as the paradigm of all acting, is the ultimate act of embodiment—the Word made flesh. Just as the voice of the trained actor needs to spring from the actor's whole way of being, the voice of God takes shape only as it is enfleshed in the Son, and it takes visible shape today in the body of the church. Linklater shows us how our body is made of sound, but Christianity shows us how this sound is not of our own making.

Nothing better demonstrates this point than the story of Mary, and few theologians have meditated more deeply on the relationship of Mary and the Word than the great Roman Catholic scholar Hans Urs von Balthasar.[3]

---

3. Raymond Gawronski, *Word and Silence: Hans Urs von Balthasar and the Spiritual Encounter between East and West* (Grand Rapids: Eerdmans, 1995), 120–27, 148–57. Also see the very helpful discussion in Edward T. Oakes, *Pattern of Redemption: The Theology of Hans Urs von Balthasar* (New York: Continuum, 1994), chap. 5.

For von Balthasar, it is Mary's obedient act of hearing that allows her to interiorize the Word. In fact, von Balthasar's understanding of the relationship of the active Word and the pliant body leads him to celebrate the passivity of all human flesh. He lifts up Mary as the perfect hearer of the Word precisely because she was perfectly passive—the humble virgin whose purity enables her to receive the seed of Christ. Mary's silence thus serves as the medium for the conjoining of the Word and human flesh. This seems to me to go too far in recommending silence as the proper form of faith. The theme of the silence of Jesus Christ is important, and I will return to it at the end of this chapter, but here I want to argue that hearing is far from being a matter of silencing the self for the reception of sound. Hearing is a dynamic relationship in sound that calls forth speech. Mary is thus more than a hollow vessel offering herself as a submissive bride. Her holy hearing—letting her body be filled with the sound of God—reverses the serpent's seduction of Eve's ear. Moreover, when she hears the Word, she responds in song, proclaiming God's majesty in the Magnificat. Rather than demonstrating the passivity of hearing (and thus the subordinate nature of femininity), Mary shows how intimately connected the Word is to the body and how Spirit-filled hearing naturally leads to proclamation. To elaborate on the unity of Word and body—the way in which women give birth to a full-bodied Word—we need to focus in more depth on the relationship of gender and public speech.

Word's Body

Any theology of sound must listen to those who have been deprived of the benefits that accrue to controlling access to the platforms of public speaking. Of course, oppression should be analyzed on both a social and a local level, because different groups can be silenced in different institutional settings. There is power in the raising of one's voice, and who gets to claim that power and on what basis can vary widely, depending on the specific situation. In the previous chapter I discussed what the deaf can teach us about speaking. In the next chapter I will examine in depth the phenomenon of stage fright in terms of the ultimate source of our power to speak. In this and the next section I want to expand on Linklater's embodied approach to voice by focusing on how women's history raises what we can call the politics of sound.

Who has access to sound's power, and who gets to define what sound is? Protestantism has traditionally preached the freedom of the Word, but it has not always lived up to that freedom by guaranteeing access to preaching for all those who are called. In fact, the pulpit frequently has been used not only to perpetuate gender stereotypes but also to preclude women from gaining practice in the speaking skills that establish social authority. If most of the stories about the trials of public speaking come from men, it is surely because men have historically had many more opportunities for public speaking than women. More important, public speaking, from the ancient world up to the present, has been one of the central arenas within which men establish their power and prestige. Revealing one's self in speech is a process packed full of meaning for men. Even draped in all the civility and etiquette of the rituals that accompany it, speaking events can be a highly charged and agonistic way of defining a man's relationship to other men, making and breaking careers.[4]

Feminists like Rebecca Chopp have focused on the question of who has the authority to speak for the speechless, rather than the problem of speechlessness itself, while feminists like Serene Jones have drawn from the category of speech to address the connection between social inequality and a variety of fundamental theological issues.[5] Perhaps the most significant contribution of feminist thinkers to this topic is the development of the notion of *voice* as a complement to the more traditional theological category of the *word*. The different connotations of *voice* and *word* are instructive. By connecting speech to the significance of the body, *voice* is a more personal, concrete, and relational term than *word*. Written words can become detached from their author, and thus the category of the *Word* sounds static and isolated. When we hear a voice, by contrast, we hear a

4. In a fascinating book, Walter J. Ong connects rhetoric to gender by tracing the history of ceremonial enmity in education. Rhetorical cultures are, he argues, essentially polemical, since students are taught to take a stand in favor of a thesis, and teachers function, in highly ritualized ways, as obstacles to their arguments. When writing replaces speaking as the model of communication, the bellowing of the male voice goes out of style.

The decline of rhetorical combat in education is thus not unrelated to the rise of co-education. See Ong, *Fighting for Life: Contest, Sexuality, and Consciousness* (Ithaca, N.Y.: Cornell University Press, 1981). In this book Ong qualifies his idea of "secondary orality" by observing that because it is founded on literacy, its basic style is irenic rather than combative. For more on the distinctive rhetoric of single-sex education, see Stephen H. Webb, "Defending All-Male Education: A New Cultural Moment for a Renewed Debate," *Fordham Urban Law Journal* 29, no. 2 (December 2001): 601–10.

5. Rebecca S. Chopp, *The Power to Speak: Feminism, Language, and God* (New York: Crossroad, 1991). Serene Jones finds the categories of drama, script, and improvisation to be most appropriate for emerging feminist theologies. It is surely no accident that, in her sensitivity to the contextual and performative aspects of feminist theologies, she has developed one of the most distinctive and personal voices in theology today. Serene Jones, *Feminist Theory and Christian Theology* (Minneapolis: Fortress, 2000). Unfortunately, her ruling metaphor in this book is that of cartography, which emphasizes a visual rather than an auditory approach to theology. Her own theological performance, however, is much more akin to listening to voices than it is to analyzing models of God.

person. Voices have timber, tone, and life. Voices can be thought to touch us, indeed to enter into us, in ways that a word does not.

The category of voice can help us to remember that the Word of God is not just any kind of sound; it is the speech of a person, that is, the Second Person of the Trinity. The incarnation, in turn, can remind us of the tactile qualities of the auditory. All sound, in fact, has a physical quality, since we hear different kinds of sounds with different parts of our body, due to the vibratory nature of sound waves. Sound and touch, as with Word and body, can work together to reveal and heal. True, the sense of touch can be a way of controlling what we grasp, which is perhaps why Jesus favored being heard over being touched (Mark 5:31; Luke 8:45). When touch is coupled with a word of grace, however, it affirms rather than restrains. The passing of the peace in church, whether it is done through the clasping of hands or the hugging of arms, is an integral part of the proclamation of the good news in the sermon.

The problem is how to order the two categories of *voice* and *word* in a way that makes theological sense. Mary Donovan Turner and Mary Lin Hudson have inquired into the phenomenon of women who lose their voice when intimidated by others and how they can learn to "talk back." They show how the term *voice* does justice to the humble quality of gospel sound. "God's power is made known through ordinary people finding 'voice.'" They also show how speaking and listening are connected to each other as well as to theology: "We must speak while hearing each other into speech. This is the way of salvation."[6] Their work demonstrates Kristin Linklater's argument that the voice is not superimposed upon the body. The voice is the vitality of the body, enabling us to reveal ourselves to each other.

Many men still have a long way to go in learning this lesson. When men think that being serious is a matter of repressing the emotions, they project their voice from their head or, more specifically, trap their voice in their throat. Many men push their voice down in order to sound as if they are in control of themselves and their environment.[7] By contrast, women's voices, according to the Western construction of gender, can fluctuate more in pitch, as if the sounds they make have as

6. Mary Donovan Turner and Mary Lin Hudson, *Saved from Silence: Finding Women's Voice in Preaching* (St. Louis: Chalice, 1999), 38, 52.

7. Walter Ong has speculated that the exclusion of women from roles of public speaking prior to the electrical amplification of sound was not unrelated to the physical capacity to project sound in large spaces. "There is a theory that the operational root of male dominance among human beings lodges less in the male's larger skeleton and muscles than in his more powerful voice—a theory seemingly supported by our earlier observation that sound is itself an indication of the active use of physical power. Without artificial amplification, the typical woman's voice simply cannot reach the thousands who found themselves enthralled by the bellowing of the old-line male orator from antiquity through

many contours as their bodies.[8] Voice stereotyping remains, even though the entry of women into all kinds of public positions has changed how we perceive the connection between voice, authority, and the body.[9] Transformations in audio perception are especially important for the church, because the proclamation of the good news is nothing if it is not worth shouting.[10] When the Word is preached as if it did not need to be inflected, that is, when it is preached as the transference of the

the nineteenth century. Before the advent of public address systems, women orators were understandably few. Moreover, the openly warlike character of the rhetorical or dialectical arena hardly appealed to most women either because of temperament or training or both." Walter J. Ong, *The Presence of the Word: Some Prolegomena for Cultural and Religious History* (1967; reprint Minneapolis: University of Minnesota Press, 1981), 249–50. Ong could have used Acts 2:14 and 14:10, where Peter and Paul respectively gather an audience by speaking in a loud voice, as examples of his argument. Authority is exhibited and recognized by many visible signs, but sound is one of the primary marks of status. When only men were permitted to speak in public, the voice of authority naturally sounded like a man's. Where Ong is misleading is in implying that lower pitches carry farther than higher ones; in fact, the opposite is the case, which suggests that the physics and the perception of sound do not always coincide.

8. For a gender reading of the Western construction of the senses, see Constance Classen, *The Color of Angels: Cosmology, Gender, and the Aesthetic Imagination* (New York: Routledge, 1998), especially chap. 3. She notes that speech is traditionally the prerogative of men, but women are traditionally portrayed as more talkative than men. "This attribution of talkativeness to women was supported by the association made between speech and the feminine quality of fluidity. Speech was imagined to flow like water, and, in the case of women, like an unending stream" (74).

9. While the men who dominated the news once spoke with booming, stentorian voices, the pitch of newscasters has become higher and lighter. After Ted Baxter's parody of the deep-voiced news anchor on the *Mary Tyler Moore Show,* a certain kind of male projection could never be heard in the same way again.

10. The more women preach, the more our sense of sound and its connotations is transformed. This observation is confirmed by the historical changes that Ann Douglas documents in her book *The Feminization of American Culture.* "The everyday Protestant of 1800 subscribed to a rather complicated and rigidly defined body of dogma; attendance at a certain church had a markedly theological function. By 1875, American Protestants were much more likely to define their faith in terms of family morals, civic responsibility, and above all, in terms of the social function of churchgoing." Ann Douglas, *The Feminization of American Culture* (New York: Doubleday, 1988), 7. The vitiation of the Calvinist tradition corresponded to the rise of women's influence on American culture. Douglas has been criticized for her portrait of how female authors like Harriet Beecher Stowe and Margaret Fuller exploited their femininity to gain cultural influence—her reading is not implausible: "Nineteenth-century American women were oppressed and damaged; inevitably, the influence they exerted in turn on their society was not altogether beneficial" (11)—and much of her analysis is limited to the Northeast. Nonetheless, her interpretation of the changing social function of the ministry helps to explain why, during this long century of disestablishment, ministers lost status and respect. Also see the important book by Roxanne Mountford, *The Gendered Pulpit: Preaching in American Protestant Spaces* (Carbondale: Southern Illinois Press, 2003).

content of one talking head to a bunch of empty heads, the result is not only a boring sermon but also bad theology.

For all that a feminist theory of voice can teach theology, there are some dangers when the category of voice is allowed to eclipse, rather than complement, the category of the Word.[11] Indeed, the case can be made that such an eclipse has already occurred in our culture. Universities are increasingly turning away from the lecture as the primary means of education. Professors and students sit in circles, or they sit in dark rooms looking at screens. The late-night rap session and the cinema are becoming the dominant models for all forms of education. Can churches afford to follow such trends? True, seeker churches have been successful at bringing the Word to the unchurched in the form of a café. Seeker churches are putting away the pews and getting out the sofas while making sure that everyone has plenty of coffee and bagels. Utilizing a variety of media can be an appropriate way to aid worship on Sunday mornings, but a book discussion or the social hour cannot replace the sermon. When that happens, the church runs the danger of becoming a salon. If the church is just another place for conversation, why not go to a coffee shop on Sunday morning instead? God is three Persons—the Father, Son, and Holy Spirit—but God speaks with one voice. The sermon is that one voice made manifest in the life of the congregation, even as it is accompanied by a variety of voices in the prayers and praises that make music to the glory of God.

The Case of the Women at the Tomb

In addition to the unique story of Mary, one of the best ways to think about the relationship of gender and the sound of God is to examine

---

11. For an example of the great potential but also the risk of a feminist homiletics, see Christine M. Smith, *Weaving the Sermon: Preaching in a Feminist Perspective* (Louisville: Westminster John Knox, 1989). She argues, "Authority in preaching has traditionally been defined as that quality of proclamation that pertains to special rights, power, knowledge, and capacity to influence or transform" (46). She laments these definitions of authority because she suspects they encourage the preacher's separateness from the congregation. She wants to weave authority and intimacy together in order to do justice to how women experience the ministry. As a result, authority becomes a form of solidarity. Consequently, any kind of hierarchy, for Smith, smacks of authoritarianism and detachment. There is much wisdom in her position, because, as the apostle Paul insists, every member of the church body has a special gift and is equally cherished by God. Nevertheless, all cannot speak at the same time. Feminist theologians who portray the sound of worship as the harmony of community without noting how that harmony is the accompaniment to the soaring solo of God's Word in the sermon risk silencing the Word with the expressiveness of the congregation.

the Gospel scene of the women at the tomb. The women at the tomb did not see anything, or, better put, they did not see what they came to find. In Mark, they did see an angel who pointed out the empty place where the body of Jesus had been laid. The angel said to them, "Do not be alarmed; you are looking for Jesus of Nazareth, who was crucified. He has been raised; he is not here. Look, there is the place they laid him. But go, tell his disciples and Peter that he is going ahead of you to Galilee; there you will see him, just as he told you" (Mark 16:6–7). The angel asks them to look where nothing is and tells them they will see what they have been told. These words of the angel not only terrify the women but also leave them speechless, as Mark 16:8 suggests. However, it is best not to take that verse too literally: "So they went out and fled from the tomb, for terror and amazement had seized them; and they said nothing to anyone, for they were afraid." Speechless at first, they must have found their voices, because if they had really disobeyed the angel's command to go and tell the disciples, how would anybody have known about the empty tomb? More likely they told only the disciples, for fear that if the news broke to the general public, they would be persecuted.

The other Gospels make this explicit. In John, Mary Magdalene tells Simon Peter, who immediately wants to see for himself. In Matthew, the women run into Jesus himself on their way to the disciples. In Luke, the disciples simply do not believe the women. "But these words seemed to them [the eleven] an idle tale, and they did not believe them" (Luke 24:11). Who would? It does not take much imagination to picture how they burst into the room of disciples with their news, and it takes even less effort to imagine how they were received. Surely they must have been exaggerating![12]

12. Origen acknowledges that some critics of Christianity dismissed the resurrection because it was based on the testimony of "hysterical females." Origen, *Contra Celsum*, trans. Henry Chadwick (Cambridge: Cambridge University Press, 1953), 109–10 (2.55). Indeed, alongside the history of the trope of hyperbole is a fascinating subtext about gender. The Enlightenment philosophers criticized hyperbole because they associated it not only with religion but also with women. Since rhetoricians traditionally identified hyperbole with frivolous embroidery of the truth—woven by those who are more at home with the decorative arts—the Enlightenment attack on this trope was to be expected. Beginning with Descartes, Enlightenment philosophers wanted their truths to be clear and distinct, whether they looked for those truths in the world of rational ideas or that of empirical facts. The connection between hyperbole and women was natural given the fact that men, in the Age of Reason, considered women to be an embellishment that made male industry more productive and male leisure more pleasurable. Whether by providing warmth to the family, deciding on decorative touches for the home, or altering textiles to add color to clothing and bedding, women's work was considered by most men to be the rhetorical equivalent of exaggeration. In their place, women played harmlessly with the

The story of the women at the tomb is strange and powerful. The entire edifice of the gospel seems to depend upon it, and yet it is told in a realistic style that refuses to silence all doubt. Given widespread assumptions about gender in the ancient world, early readers of the text would have found it radically provocative. As William C. Placher wryly observes: "In a culture where women were not considered trustworthy to testify in court, it is hard to imagine why women would be cited as those who found the tomb empty unless this recalled some historical reality."[13] The church remembers that faith was born by the voice of women, but its memory of this event is uneasy. John follows the story of the women with an account of Jesus showing his hands and side to the disciples. Thomas especially does not believe the women until he has touched Jesus' wounds. It is interesting, however, that the crucial moment in this part of the story involves breath and voice: "He breathed on them and said to them, `Receive the Holy Spirit'" (John 20:22). Jesus' voice gives life in the same way that God did in Genesis 2:7, by breathing into Adam's nostrils. More important, John ends this section of his Gospel not with a commendation of the disciples, who needed to see in order to understand, but with just the opposite: "Blessed are those who have not seen and yet have come to believe" (20:29). Assuming that women were not at this meeting, that statement precisely describes the faith of the women at the tomb. For them, as well as for those who come after the disciples, believing is hearing, not seeing.

The story of these women is evidence of how the good news of the gospel changed the nature of our hearing. Voices that were pitched too high to be credible become the very sound of faith. Of course, the gender issues in this story are complex. Marianne Sawicki, in a brilliant book, *Seeing the Lord: Resurrection and Early Christian Practices*, explains how it was appropriate that Jesus appeared to the women first. Women, after all, prepared the bodies of the dead—just as they cared for the bodies of the living—and kept vigil in their mourning. The female followers of Jesus were the ones who had the most at stake in what was happening to Jesus' body. While the men fled in panic and tried to regroup by coming up with

---

emotions while men undertook the real work of reason. The Enlightenment thus had a certain sound—a certain tone of voice that was proper and self-assured. Practicing this resolute tone of voice took discipline, but it also involved disciplining those—whether they be religious fanatics, uncivilized savages, or the fairer sex—who spoke with less self-control. As truth was defined in terms of a firm and level tone of voice, exaggeration was dismissed as unnecessary and distracting. For a theological account of the history of hyperbole, see Stephen H. Webb, *Blessed Excess: Religion and the Hyperbolic Imagination* (Albany: State University of New York Press, 1993).

13. William C. Placher, *Jesus the Savior: The Meaning of Jesus Christ for Christian Faith* (Louisville: Westminster John Knox, 2001), 168. For the best treatment of this issue, see Richard Baukham, *Gospel Women* (Grand Rapids: Eerdmans, 2002), ch. 8.

a plan for action, the women attended to Jesus' needs, even in his most passive state. It was to them that the angel spoke. They were the ones who were ready and able to hear the good news. The male disciples, however, were not nearly so ready to listen to the women, a situation at that time that would have been a humiliating disruption of their social status.[14]

Sawicki argues that the Gospels depict a battle over who owns the rights, so to speak, of the resurrection story. Even today, as scholars who study group dynamics can attest, the ideas of women are sometimes taken over by men who then claim those ideas as their own. The battle is not only between men and women but also between the perspectives of sight and sound.[15] The Gospels were written by men with at least some degree of formal education. These writers were immersed in Greek as well as Galilean culture. The Greeks privileged knowledge over belief and the visual over the auditory. The Gospel writers thus had an interest in proving the resurrection by appealing to visual sightings. Sawicki argues that the Gospel writers used their interest in visual forms of proof to take the resurrection out of the hands of women, who were more used to the dynamic of oral tradition.

Sawicki also thinks that the Gospels do a bad job of trying to cover up the role of women in the transmission of the resurrection tradition. This leads her to conclude that "a submerged tradition of *hearing* resurrection proofs now lies beneath the Greek texts, with their cultural and class bias toward what can be seen."[16] Hearing is linked to rhetorical persuasion in ways that seeing is not. To believe is to be persuaded. For the Greeks, belief, as opposed to knowledge, is the end product of a rhetorical process; it occurs in situations where one must pass judgment without the benefit of logical proof or empirical evidence.[17] Since the Greeks tended to assign a lower status to persuasion than to knowledge,

14. Marianne Sawicki, *Seeing the Lord: Resurrection and Early Christian Practices* (Minneapolis: Fortress, 1994).

15. Also see how Elisabeth Schüssler Fiorenza contrasts the two traditions of "empty tomb" and "visionary experience." She argues that men were more interested in reducing the crucifixion and resurrection to a formula of confession, while women kept the resurrection faith alive by caring for "the wretched of the earth." Elisabeth Schüssler Fiorenza, *Jesus: Miriam's Child, Sophia's Prophet* (New York: Continuum, 1995), 126. What she calls "malestream Christological discourse" sends Jesus back to heaven, where he is available only to the elite few. For her account of how women are paradigms of true discipleship, see *In Memory of Her* (New York: Crossroad, 1985), 315–34. For a powerful critique of the idea that women are pure and innocent, see Angela West, *Deadly Innocence: Feminism and the Mythology of Sin* (London: Cassell, 1995).

16. Sawicki, *Seeing the Lord*, 92.

17. See James Kinneavy, *Greek Rhetorical Origins of Christian Faith: An Inquiry* (New York: Oxford University Press, 1987).

the Gospel writers had to replace the persuasive testimony of women with the visual proof of men.

Sawicki is right to emphasize the ways in which the Gospel was speech before it was text. In the earliest years of the Jesus movement, written accounts of his sayings and his life would have been an unusual and curious innovation.[18] The idea that Mark wrote the first Gospel as a way of wresting power away from traveling prophets and teachers has much to commend it. As many scholars have observed, as the Christian community became more stable, there was a shift from charismatic wonder workers to resident teachers. The loose orality of charismatic teachers could lead to disparate stories about Jesus and conflicting rules for the young church. Nonetheless, Sawicki is wrong to argue that Mark replaced an oral tradition based on listening with a literate tradition based on reading. On the contrary, Mark initiated a battle between two different kinds of oral performance—the improvisational performances of the charismatic teachers and the scripted performances of those wanting to follow more closely in the apostolic tradition.

The argument that Mark began and *continued* in oral performance is the conclusion that has been reached by a number of scholars influenced by Werner Kelber and now led by Richard A. Horsley.[19] Mark was not written to be read silently and privately. Instead, the Gospel of Mark provided a script for a more faithful performance of Jesus' life and death. All four Gospels combined to define Jesus' voice stereophonically in order to specify who had the right to speak in his place. After all, proclamation is effective only if the one who is proclaimed can be readily identified. By turning the oral tradition of the apostles into scripts, the Gospels provided for a more permanent and thus more powerful rendition of Jesus' life, which guaranteed the confidence and efficacy of the church's spoken word.

The Gospels did not bring oral tradition about Jesus to an end. Instead, the Gospels completed a process that began at the empty tomb—a process that demanded a new form of public speech appropriate to the

18. For an overview of Jesus and speech, see Thomas E. Boomershine, "Jesus of Nazareth and the Watershed of Ancient Orality and Literacy," *Semeia* 65 (1994): 7–36. For recent scholarship on the role of writing at the time of Jesus and its impact on the transmission of Jesus' teachings, see Alan Millard, *Reading and Writing in the Time of Jesus* (New York: New York University Press, 2000).

19. Werner Kelber, *The Oral and the Written Gospel: The Hermeneutics of Speaking and Writing in the Synoptic Tradition, Mark, Paul, and Q*, rev. ed. (Bloomington: Indiana University Press, 1997; originally published 1983). Richard A. Horsley, *Hearing the Whole Story: The Politics of Plot in Mark's Gospel* (Louisville: Westminster John Knox, 2001), chap. 3. For an example of how an oral performance of Mark would change the way we read this Gospel, see Elizabeth Struthers Malbon, *Hearing Mark: A Listener's Guide* (Harrisburg, Penn.: Trinity Press International, 2002).

miracle of the resurrection. This new form of speech is what theologians call proclamation, and women were the first to be given the commission to go and put this speech into practice. It is appropriate, in a way, that Mark ends his Gospel with the women fleeing the empty tomb in terror. Perhaps what made them so afraid was less the emptiness of the tomb than the task that awaited them. They knew that the men in the Jesus movement would not believe them, yet they found the courage to speak anyway. Just as Mary was a new Eve, paralleling Jesus as the new Adam, the witness of the women at the tomb was a reversal of the fall in Genesis, where Adam listened to Eve even though he should not have done so. Women's voices are now the source of man's blessing, not his curse. The Bible has come full circle.

Jesus as the Natural Voice of God

Women certainly have been silenced by men throughout history in painful ways, but that silence does not mean they are condemned to despair. Because of their history of oppression, many women have developed skills in communicating without making a sound—skills that men sometimes do not possess. In this they are following Jesus. From the silence of the womb to the silence of the Holy Saturday mystery, Jesus could adequately express God's purposes without saying a word. Jesus also knew the power of intimidation. This is evident from his most dramatic moment of silence, when he gave no answer to Pilate's interrogation (Matt. 27:14). Moreover, Jesus knew the limits of intelligible speech, as demonstrated by his final cry on the cross. That Word-become-cry shows how God can make a sound that both shatters and contains silence, redeeming our most anguished noise. Even his ordinary speaking voice must have been extraordinary, since his disciples remembered him as the One in whose voice God could be heard. When Jesus called out to Lazarus, for example, the dead man not only heard but also recognized his voice, and he was drawn out of the tomb by its sound.

Borrowing from Kristin Linklater's work, I want to propose that we think of Jesus Christ as the natural voice of God. The Bible records God's speaking through the creation, angels, and prophets, but God finds the divine voice, so to speak, in the earthly ministry of Jesus Christ. God speaks so easily and clearly through Jesus because Jesus is the body of the Word. Recall Linklater's argument that a natural voice is possible only when there are no physical tensions or obstacles to full and free expression. That definition can help us to understand how it is that Jesus Christ is fully human and fully divine: He is the one whose body gave no hindrance to the Word. That is the significance of his teaching at the temple when he was still a boy (Luke 2:41–52). People could hear his authority in his voice.

That Jesus Christ is the natural voice of God does not mean that the Word of God is inherently masculine sounding. As I will argue in chapter 7, the Word took shape in Jesus Christ before the creation of the world, which means that God did not choose a "special" human being to be rewarded with the incarnation. If God adopted Jesus as God's Son, then God's voice to us truly would be masculine, because God would have chosen a man's voice to represent the divine sound. According to traditional Christology, however, the body of Jesus does not precede and thus determine God's voice. It is the other way around. God's Word makes the body of Jesus. Jesus' body is perfectly tuned for sound because it resonates with God's Word in the clearest possible manner. In other words, Jesus' body is a perfectly free vehicle of divine expression. This suggests that the voice of Jesus Christ has none of the limitations inherent in ordinary human voices, which are always gendered.

Does this mean that Jesus never stuttered or stalled for words? People heard God in his voice, but did they ever hear anxiety as well? As fully human, Jesus did experience something like a panic attack as a result of having to speak in spite of his reluctance. On the night when he was to be betrayed, he went to a garden on the Mount of Olives to ask his Father to take this cup from him (Luke 22:42). Yet he immediately added, "Not my will but yours be done." If he did not actively resist his destiny, then at least it seems as though he was passively resigned to it. Luke says that he was in anguish and his sweat was like great drops of blood falling to the ground (22:44). Some ancient manuscripts lack these verses. Did somebody take them out because they found it too painful to imagine Jesus in such pain? The editing of Luke suggests that there were conflicts in the early church over attributing too much anxiety to Jesus. John doesn't have the Gethsemane story, but in Mark, Jesus says, "I am deeply grieved, even to death" (14:34), and in Matthew he is agitated (26:37). In Mark and Matthew, he prays three times to God and each time finds his disciples sleeping.

It is easy to imagine Jesus afraid. The Romans could be brutal toward their prisoners. But was he anxious? We tend to think of fear as a natural reaction to dangerous and threatening situations. In the next chapter I will analyze Paul Tillich's argument that *anxiety* is a more general and complex term than *fear*. Fear is focused on a specific object, and it goes away when that object is removed. Anxiety is more troubling and less tractable. Anxiety can be defined as a fear of fear, a fear that shakes the foundations of one's faith in the world and one's trust in oneself. Anxiety is often out of proportion to the object feared. Anxiety occurs when fear overwhelms us, that is, when we allow fear to name and thus own us.

Could Jesus Christ, the Son of God, have been anxious? Could he have given in to his fear? One of the symptoms of anxiety is insomnia, and we do find Jesus wide awake in the middle of the night. He could sleep through a storm in a sinking boat, but in the garden, sleep will not come. Another symptom of anxiety is feeling abandoned, which also applies to Jesus on that night. Fear can be shared in ways that anxiety cannot. If others see the same danger, then they can react to it as well, and shared efforts can ease the fear. But with anxiety, you feel abandoned by others as well as by God. You feel as if there is nothing that can be done.

We usually think of Jesus as being afraid of the physical torment that he ultimately submitted to, but it is just as plausible to think he was anxious about speaking his mind to his Father. In fact, sermons about Gethsemane typically focus on the drowsy disciples, as if Jesus chose a late hour to go to God in prayer only in order to test their physical endurance. A close reading shows that the Gospels actually portray the disciples as a distraction to Jesus, almost a comic relief for the intensity of what he has to face. From a perspective informed by the study of voice, Jesus was worried not about the disciples—whom he easily and quickly rebuked—but God the Father. He was grieved even to death not by the cross but by the depth of this distressing act of communication. True, he wanted the company of the disciples to ease his burden, but the task at hand was not the need to give himself over to the earthly authorities. More urgently, the task was to humble himself before his heavenly authority. Jesus had to ask about the necessity of the final stage of his mission, and he had to ask it of the One who had sent him to accomplish what only he could do. Jesus would have been afraid, perhaps, of the upcoming physical pain, but he would have been in anguish over the question whether to divulge his fear to his Father.

If the Trinity can be understood best in terms of the category of sound, as I will argue in chapter 7, then Gethsemane is surely the deepest and most mysterious moment in the Son's relationship to the Father. In the beginning was the Word, and that speech was the fellowship of the Father, Son, and Holy Spirit. God risked the divine conversation by creating the world, where God's voice could be drowned out by human noise. God risked further humiliation by deigning to speak to us directly. But in the garden, God risked losing the divine voice altogether. The whole mission of the Word came down to a few words that risked everything, even though they could change nothing. If Jesus had said nothing to God that night, then his pain would have been kept inward and private. It would have been a human pain, but it would not have been pain shared by the Father and the Son. The very sound that constitutes their unity had to be filled with their separation. In order to save us, Jesus had to give voice to our alienation. If Jesus had been unable to speak, then every silence that followed truly would be terrifying. The fate of the world hung on his courage to speak.

In the end, Jesus pushed his voice to the point of hoarseness. According to the Gospels of Matthew and Mark, Jesus' last intelligible words were "Eli, Eli, lema sabachthani?"—"My God, my God, why have you forsaken me?"—which is traditionally called the cry of dereliction. This cry is often taken as the painful climax of the incarnation, when God most identified with the human condition. It is a theological commonplace, first systematized by Jürgen Moltmann, that Jesus was never more human than at that moment of vocal anguish.[20] The way Jesus shared our humanity is crucial to Christian faith, of course, so claims about the significance of Jesus' speech must be made very carefully. In my interpretation, the cry of dereliction should be understood in continuity with the prayer in Gethsemane. It was in Gethsemane where Jesus first confronted the upcoming rupture within the divinity, and it took everything out of him to give that rupture voice. The cry on the cross began, then, when Jesus wanted to ask his Father to alter his destiny, which he knew his Father could not do. The Father had to hear the pain in his voice in order to experience the depth of human suffering.

Jesus was never more divine than when he, as the Son, had to speak words to the Father that he knew would cause the Father pain. At the same time Jesus was never more human, because his voice was never more his own. Using Linklater's terminology, we could say that Jesus' voice was at its most natural pitch at the very point when he was ready to lay down his body for us. That is, he found his voice just as he thought he was losing it. And because the Father listened and gave him strength, his voice was the sound of our salvation.

20. For a creative development of Moltmann's position, see Alan E. Lewis, *Between Cross and Resurrection: A Theology of Holy Saturday* (Grand Rapids: Eerdmans, 2001).

four

Stage Fright at the Origins
of Christian Proclamation

Rethinking Paul Tillich on Anxiety

Central to Walter Ong's project is the idea that "speech is easy."[1] His very definition of speech as shared inwardness simplifies and idealizes what is frequently a task and a struggle. The ease of speech is the premise of all orality theorists who begin with Martin Heidegger's definition of modernity as "the age of the world picture." When these theorists talk about the decimation of the oral, they use the phenomenon of deafness as a metaphor for cultural trends that arose in the West after the invention of the printing press, and when they talk about the opposition of the eye and the ear, they leave out the mouth. Thus while Ong remains an essential figure in the study of sound, he needs to be put in a context that does justice to the difficulties of speech.

Few theologians have written more about anxiety than Paul Tillich, and so he can be usefully employed to uncover the theological dimension of stage fright. Tillich was famous for arguing that anxiety is the particularly modern form that the general experience of spiritual malaise takes, but that analysis has been neglected in recent theology. Tillich's existential

---

1. Walter J. Ong, *The Presence of the Word: Some Prolegomena for Cultural and Religious History* (1967; reprint, Minneapolis: University of Minnesota Press, 1981), 94.

embrace of emotional pain is one of the characteristics of his thought that make it sometimes seem outdated and old-fashioned. Not only is existentialism out of favor, but the medicalization of mental illness has also completely altered the way we talk about the human condition. We can be sanguine about anxiety today because we think of it as a curable ailment. Why romanticize something that a pill can eliminate? Those who still follow a Tillichian reading of psychological disorders bewail the loss of something distinctively human in the emergence of a Prozac nation. Even with all the breakthroughs in pharmacology, however, anxiety is an even more prevalent condition now than it was in Tillich's days. Its very "curability" has brought it to public attention in unprecedented ways.

Perhaps Tillich felt compelled to make a virtue out of anxiety because his ontological system made anxiety a necessity of human nature. More to the point, Tillich argued that anxiety is an inevitable consequence of our being creatures who are both finite and free. Fear is merely a psychological state. It attaches to a specific object, and when that object is removed, the fear is alleviated. Anxiety, on the other hand, is a byproduct of our capacity for self-transcendence, which is one way of defining freedom. Transcendence allows us to ask who we are by putting us outside of ourselves. Being on the outside of ourselves is a precarious situation; it is, in fact, a matter of being nowhere. Anxiety, then, has no object, or as Tillich sometimes says, it has nothingness as its object. It opens up the question of our very existence, which makes it an ontological, not a psychological, aspect of human nature.

As a permanent state from which we cannot escape, anxiety drives us to the question of God. We cannot solve the puzzle of being both free and bound by space, time, and the web of causation. The only thing that can save us is faith in God. Faith does not make anxiety go away. Indeed faith, for Tillich, is really better described as a form of courage. We have to muster the strength to accept our condition, but we cannot find that strength on our own. We need to participate in what Tillich calls the ground of our being in order to have the freedom to make the tensions of our life creative and productive. If there is a gracious source of our freedom that accepts us as we are, then standing outside of ourselves is not a matter of venturing into nothingness. Instead, standing outside of ourselves is the same as standing on the promises of God.

Bold and original, this analysis of anxiety dominated theological discussions of psychology for several decades. Mixing twentieth-century existentialism and nineteenth-century German idealism, Tillich could talk the language of a therapeutic culture while grounding that language in rigorous philosophical categories. Unlike Karl Barth's work, Tillich's theology was primarily apologetical. He wanted to save religious truth by

putting it on a firm foundation. Early in his career, he was associated with
Barth and the Word of God theology, and he continued to address their
concerns throughout his life. Like Barth, Tillich had been deeply affected
by World War I, and he also interpreted Germany's defeat as entailing
the collapse of the liberal theological establishment. He thus sought
new forms of religious expression, especially by connecting theology
to radical politics, but his forced departure to the United States demol-
ished his political dreams. His message became tremendously popular
in post–World War II America, because he began correlating theology
to psychology rather than politics. Indeed, he promised to explain not
only how preachers could be confident in their speaking practices but
also how psychology itself could be given a spiritual foundation. In
an era when behaviorism was dominating the social sciences, Tillich's
exploration of the spiritual basis of psychological problems found a
large audience, especially among those who could no longer accept
the traditional claims of religion yet sought a place for religion within
America's therapeutic culture.

In the postmodern period, foundationalism in all of its forms, especially the attempt to describe the basic ontological structures of existence
and then give them a religious interpretation, has fallen out of favor.
Tillich's theology, which spoke so directly and intimately to the post–
World War II generation, increasingly came to be seen as too abstract
and tidy to appeal to postmodern sensibilities. His analysis of anxiety
as inherent in human nature is too abstract to appeal to psychologists
working in a framework that connects disabling mental problems with
age-specific stages of development. In a word, he too quickly translated psychological conditions into ontological categories, which gives
the appearance that all personal problems are merely metaphors for
philosophical puzzles.

His treatment of anxiety is indicative of these limitations. By defining
anxiety in opposition to fear, he makes it too abstract and isolates it from
any social factors. For Tillich, anxiety is not primarily a problem of the
individual but more basically *the* problem that defines our individuality.
It thus plays a descriptive role in his system; anxiety is not something we
experience but something we are. Tillich comes close, then, to normal-
izing anxiety by making it the defining moment of self-knowledge. One
could use the same words about anxiety that Alfred North Whitehead
says about religion: it is what we do with our solitude. Anxiety is not so
much a problem as it is an opportunity. Learning to deal with it entails
coming to a better understanding of who we already are. Anxiety affirms
rather than problematizes our quest for freedom. Since it functions as
a clue to the structures of existence, the power that resolves it must
ultimately come from within.

Perhaps Tillich could not imagine that anxiety was a social phenomenon because he was too interested in differentiating Protestantism from Roman Catholicism to tie anxiety to the issue of authority. In other words, he wanted the answer to anxiety to be the Protestant theme of freedom rather than the Catholic theme of authority. Liberal Protestantism valorizes the principle of doubt by affirming the critical consciousness that Catholicism neglects. Tillich saw himself as working on the borders of theology, taking chances where he saw others, especially Barth, refusing to stray from the safety of traditional dogmatics. His view of faith, not unlike his view of himself, was in debt to the existentialist portrait of the heroic individual. Doubt for Tillich was good, because it frees the believer from the temptation of turning God into an idol of the believer's own making. His position, on the margins of traditional faith, necessarily leads to an immersion in anxious states of mind. How can the doubter ever be certain of faith? Courage becomes Tillich's primary virtue by necessity. By romanticizing individualism and stereotyping Catholicism, Tillich perpetuates some of the worst aspects of the Protestant Reformation.

So how does Tillich's analysis apply to stage fright? In Tillichian terms, speaking is one of the most concrete expressions of human freedom, and freedom can be terrifying. Indeed, there is a case to be made that stage fright is one of the least publicized and most crippling mental health problems that our society faces.[2] In poll after poll a significant number of people rank public speaking next to death in terms of their worst fears. Shortness of breath, fear of a heart attack, thoughts racing out of control toward worst-case scenarios, and a mouth so dry that it refuses to open can all be symptoms of the adrenaline surge triggered by public speaking. Victims of stage fright can destroy their career when they start avoiding situations that might require public speaking. The great actor Laurence Olivier, for example, wrote eloquently about his battle with stage fright. It surfaced late in his career, lasted for five years, and forced him to contemplate retiring from the stage. He interpreted it as punishment for his pride before he was able to see it as the result of uncontrolled anxiety.[3]

Tillich's theology can still speak to such situations, but he misses the fact that speaking phobia is more of a social than an individual phenomenon. This is made clear by the French philosopher Merleau-Ponty, who makes the loss of speech central to his phenomenology of perception.

---

2. For a very helpful and comprehensive medical approach to stage fright, see Reneau Z. Peurifoy, *Anxiety, Phobias, and Panic: A Step-by-Step Program for Regaining Control of Your Life* (New York: Warner, 1995).

3. Laurence Olivier, *Confessions of an Actor* (New York: Penguin, 1984), 261.

"Of all bodily functions," he states, "speech is the most intimately linked with communal existence, or, as we shall put it, with co-existence."[4] This can clearly be seen by a simple example: Victims of stage fright never have any problem speaking in a room alone. Only in front of others do we find our identity subjected to unwelcome scrutiny. When we are at a loss for words, we are alienated from ourselves because we find ourselves more fundamentally alienated from others. We lose our voice when we have a message to give to others but are unsure of our ability to deliver it. Significantly, actors rarely experience stage fright during the rehearsal process. Perhaps that is because they have a director monitoring their progress and thus are not allowed to become mired in a self-analysis that can lead to self-recrimination. Once the director departs, the actor can feel abandoned and overwhelmed, and the actor's imagination can run wild. Confronted by an unknown audience rather than the parental face of the director, the actor can hear a multitude of voices expressing doubt, judgment, and guilt. What is so carefully practiced in rehearsal can fall apart with just the thought of the curtain rising.

Even though Tillich's existentialism encouraged him to downplay the social dimension of anxiety, he often tried to put his ontological abstractions into a historical context. His reading of history enabled him to make a link between anxiety and modernity, and though he did not pursue this link in detail, it is not difficult to elaborate on his insight. In traditional societies, public speaking was strictly correlated with social standing. Those who spoke to the group did so according to the role they played in that society. They spoke for the good of the group, not for themselves. We inhabit few social roles today that are not of our own making. Displaced, uprooted, and detached from traditional communities, we often do not know what to say when we open our mouth. On whose authority do we speak? Speechlessness is symptomatic of the lack of a social structure sufficiently stable to mediate our personal identity.[5]

4. Maurice Merleau-Ponty, *Phenomenology of Perception*, trans. Colin Smith (New York: Humanities, 1962), 160. He suggests that the recovery of one's voice takes a "conversion" in which the speechless person opens herself to others through a concentrated effort of the whole body. Merleau-Ponty goes on to explain that speech is so intimately communal precisely because word and thought are one and the same; they are simultaneously constituted. Our speech does not convey our inner life; it *is* our inner life in public form.
5. Tillich's reading of history was shaped by Kierkegaard's breakthrough analysis of anxiety. Living during the golden age of Denmark, when commerce was destroying the traditional connection between family relations and social standing, Kierkegaard was the first to understand how freedom, disconnected from responsibility, can be paralyzing. See Bruce H. Krimmse, *Kierkegaard in Golden Age Denmark* (Bloomington: Indiana University Press, 1990). In the age of consumerism, our choices become meaningless. What Kierkegaard lamented, however, Tillich commended, turning anxiety into a hallmark of the creative self.

Feeling deprived of the authority to speak can heighten the way we internalize the judgment of our audience. Persons with stage fright feel exposed and vulnerable. No amount of positive imaging will help them regain their composure. Moreover, they frequently feel shame at being disoriented by such a simple activity, and they are often too embarrassed to share their pain, which appears so disproportionate to its object, with others. It takes tremendous courage to face stage fright, and most people who suffer from it become adept at hiding it behind a well-constructed mask.

Unfortunately, focusing on the fear by trying to analyze it in the moment of its manifestation only makes matters worse. Tillich's distinction between fear and anxiety can be illuminating in the sense that speechlessness entails a lack of an ability to focus on anything other than the anxiety itself. Lacking a manageable object, fear escalates into panic. That dynamic entails a hyper-awareness of oneself and a tendency to overanalyze one's state of mind as well as overanticipate the audience's reaction. Experts call this self-monitoring, and it only complicates the rush of adrenaline that fuels the panic.

What is needed is not Tillichian courage, which smacks of individualism and heroics, but plain old acceptance, a more modest term that Tillich also used frequently and eloquently. Anxiety will go away only with time; in the meantime, it must be experienced without judgment or analysis, which only exacerbates it. The fear cannot be controlled, but it can be domesticated and neutered. The only way to break out of the spiral of self-analysis is to open oneself to something external, which is probably why experts sometimes recommend such silly things as imagining one's audience without any clothes. Olivier was most anxious when he was alone in front of the audience for a soliloquy. When he played Othello he asked his Iago not to leave the stage but to stay in the wings where he could see him, so that he had someone in particular to whom he could speak. The idea is to put a stop to the rush of anxiety by shifting one's focus away from the gaze of strangers in the audience, which can trigger the debilitating acceleration of self-analysis. The problem is that this cannot be accomplished as some kind of self-conscious strategy, because trying to control anxiety only makes it worse. The courage to speak cannot be forced. It must be experienced more as a gift we accept than as an achievement we earn.

The experience of speechlessness from a medical point of view parallels and reinforces its theological interpretation. Stage fright internalizes worry about an audience's reaction to the degree that the speaker worries more about herself than about the audience. Because the fear now comes from within, the speaker feels trapped; to run away from the fear would be to abandon the task at hand in front of everyone, a solution that is no solution at all. The sufferer is left to experience a vertigo of self-recrimination and crippling doubt. This suggests that it is not the anxiety so much as its interpretation that is so aggravating.[6] The person suffering from this condition needs a confidence that is not her own. In order to speak with confidence, she needs someone standing in the wings who can prompt her with a word she cannot say to herself. This word does not take away the pain but instead makes it bearable by sharing it.

The good news is that the Word of God accepts our own words no matter how much we stammer and stall. In Tillich's terminology, when we have confidence in God's plan for our life and when we experience the empowerment of the Holy Spirit, doubt can be transformed, even though it is not replaced, by faith. The doubt remains, but not its most debilitating consequences. We are anxious, but we no longer translate that anxiety into self-condemnation.

Surprisingly enough, the Bible documents a variety of forms of aphonia, from the mute to the tongue-tied and the dumbstruck. Sometimes it is God's voice that silences any possible response (see 2 Macc. 3:29 and Ezek. 3:26 for examples). In God's presence a momentary loss of words is not unusual (Job 29:10; Ps. 22:15; 77:4). The Bible also knows of the medical condition of stammering or stuttering, which can be a cause of stage fright but is not identical with it. Isaiah claims stuttering will be cured in the coming kingdom of God (32:4; 35:6). One of the most moving passages in the Bible for those who suffer from speech impediments of any kind is Zephaniah's vision of the gathering of the nations in the heavenly city: "At that time I will change the speech of the peoples to a pure speech, that all of them may call on the name of the LORD and serve him with one accord" (3:9). Not only will we speak the same language, but we will speak it well. This climactic end to history is anticipated in the advice Jesus gives in the "missionary discourse" to the twelve he authorizes to act in his name: "When they hand you over, do not worry about how you are to speak or what you are to say; for what you are to say will be given to you at that time, for it is not you who speak, but the Spirit of your Father speaking through you" (Matt. 10:19–20; also see Luke 12:11–12). Zephaniah's vision also comes true at Pentecost, when God loosens the tongues of the Christians so that they might proclaim the gospel in a number of different languages.

Even given the Bible's comprehensive and realistic portrayal of a wide range of speaking problems, I want to focus on stage fright as

---

6. Although Donald Capps does not directly address stage fright, he is very helpful in explicating the anticipatory structure of anxiety. See his book *Social Phobia: Alleviating Anxiety in an Age of Self-Promotion* (St. Louis: Chalice, 1999).

the occasion for a profound experience of faith in God. Far from being a merely psychological problem in the mind or a chemical imbalance in the brain, stage fright actually tells us something crucial about what it means to be faithful to the Word of God. Stage fright is, in a very real sense, the way in which the Christian body processes the dynamic of faith and doubt. In the following sections of this chapter, I will trace a hidden history of stage fright in biblical Christianity. I will begin with the prophet Moses, who sets the stage for all subsequent religious experiences of this particular form of anxiety. I will move from Moses to Paul, with an interlude on Cicero and Augustine, and end with the experience of modern-day evangelicalism. I will conclude that Protestant, and especially revivalistic, styles of preaching have a unique connection with the phenomenon of stage fright. In the next two chapters I will look more closely at the Protestant Reformation's reflections on the nature of sound and the demands of public speaking.

Moses, the Reluctant Prophet

Ong was not the first scholar to point out the dominance of the visual for the Greeks and the oral for the Hebrews. The point was made in the nineteenth century and became a commonplace in twentieth-century accounts of the origins of Western culture. A prime example is Eric Auerbach's *Mimesis,* a groundbreaking study of the origins of literary realism. Auerbach documented the Hellenic affinity for the visual in this book's justly celebrated opening chapter, "Odysseus' Scar." "Clearly outlined, brightly and uniformly illuminated, men and things stand out in a realm where everything is visible."[7] Auerbach contrasted Homer with the Bible, which understands the contours of reality to be structured by sound, not light. We commonly think of the Hebrews as a people of the book, but it would be more accurate to call them a people of the spoken word. Indeed, their attribution of speaking to God gave all human

7. Eric Auerbach, *Mimesis: The Representation of Reality in Western Literature,* trans. Willard R. Trask (Princeton: Princeton University Press, 1953), 2. Nineteenth-century historian Heinrich Graetz was one of the first to distinguish the visual mode of the Greeks from the auditory sensibility of the Hebrews. See his *The Structure of Jewish History,* trans. Ismar Schorsh (New York: Jewish Theological Seminary of America, 1975). Oswald Spengler, the philosopher of history who announced "the decline of the West" after World War I, contrasted the auditory cultures of the past with the impersonal ocularism of modernity in *Man and Tecnics,* trans. C. F. Atkinson (London: George Allen and Unwin, 1932). Thorlief Borman also did early work on this topic in *Hebrew Thought Compared with Greek* (London: SCM, 1954). P. Christopher Smith makes the interesting argument that

speech added significance. To the extent that biblical culture mediates divine truth through speech, not images—God tells Moses, "You cannot see my face; for no one shall see me and live" (Exod. 33:20)—one would expect to find many stories in the Bible about how people struggle with finding the right words for their faith. This is, in fact, the case. Public speaking anxiety is a frequent phenomenon in the Bible—functioning as both a reality and a metaphor for the problem of obeying God—that goes back to the example of Moses.

The fact that Moses had a speech impediment of some sort has been ignored by most commentators on Scripture, and even when it is not ignored, scholars go to great lengths to sidestep its significance. In his highly speculative book about Moses, Sigmund Freud interpreted Moses' slowness of speech as evidence that he did not know the language of the Hebrews. Thus, it confirms Freud's suspicion that Moses was an Egyptian.[8] This is an odd argument to make, because Moses complains of being slow to speak when God asks him to confront the Egyptians, leading some scholars to the opposite conclusion, that Moses might have been complaining about his lack of proficiency in the Egyptian language. (An example of a prophet worrying about speaking in a foreign language can be found in Ezekiel 3:4–6.) Howard Eilberg-Schwarts gives a more psychoanalytic interpretation of Moses than Freud did by suggesting that the Bible's account of his speech impediment is part of a larger struggle over the nature of Moses' masculinity.[9]

In point of fact, Moses' impediment may have been nothing more mysterious than an inhibition. I would argue that this hypothesis best explains the conflicting accounts the Bible gives us about his life. Moses is described as the most modest of men (Num. 12:3), but he could also be given to fits of murderous rage. He is both heroic and cowardly, strong and weak. Sometimes he has no problems speaking at all, while at other times he panics at the very thought of public speaking. This is characteristic of someone suffering from stage fright. Outwardly there are no signs of the problem, as the person manages, through great concentration, to appear normal. At times, when conditions are right,

---

Aristotle's *Poetics* indicates the shift from an oral culture based on participatory rituals to a culture that conceives of ritual in terms of representation for nonparticipating spectators in "From Acoustics to Optics: The Rise of the Metaphysical and the Demise of the Melodic in Aristotle's *Poetics*," in *Sites of Vision: The Discursive Construction of Sight in the History of Philosophy*, ed. David Michael Levin (Cambridge: MIT Press, 1997).

8. Sigmund Freud, *Moses and Monotheism*, trans. Katherine Jones (New York: Vintage, 1939), 37–38.

9. Howard Eilberg-Schwarts, *God's Phallus and Other Problems for Men and Monotheism* (Boston: Beacon, 1994), 145.

giving a speech can be accomplished with apparent ease, even though it takes great effort and courage. But at other times the very thought of public speaking is enough to make someone want to flee, which is exactly how the Bible describes Moses' situation.

Jonathan Kirsch, in his popular biography of Moses, tries to explain the incoherence of the Bible's image of Moses by suggesting that there are traces of an anti-Moses tradition that survive the work of those who edited the Pentateuch.[10] He draws from a well-established scholarly convention that speculates about a supposed political rivalry between priestly castes that traced their lineage to either Moses or Aaron. In this hypothesis, the negative depictions of Moses would be remnants of—and perhaps the only evidence for—this intratribal conflict. But we need not assume that the biblical narrative is an inelegant hodgepodge of competing interests, for it is just as likely that the Bible's complex view of Moses is intentional. The portrait of Moses as incredibly flawed is meant to emphasize the fact that Moses is not divine. This was an important point to make, because rulers in the ancient world were often taken to be gods. The Bible is realistic about human nature, and never more so than in its depiction of Moses.

Moses is utterly human, but he is also unique among humans, because God speaks with him face to face (Num. 12:8; Deut. 24:10). Indeed, God and Moses have a complicated relationship, with strong emotions raging on both sides. Even with God on his side, Moses hesitates to assume the leadership of the Israelites. He argues with God, explaining that he has no eloquence (Exod. 4:10). He fears that nobody will listen to him, "poor speaker that I am" (Exod. 6:12). The Hebrew in that verse literally reads, "I am uncircumcised of lips," a euphemism, most scholars think, for some kind of speech impediment. As Kirsch points out, Moses' protest seems to take God by surprise. That there are no indications prior to these passages that Moses is an anxious speaker fits the profile of stage fright. The descriptions of Moses as being heavy in tongue and slow to speak suggest that he could speak once he got going, but it was difficult for him to be sufficiently self-composed at the start of a speech. In situations where he is relaxed and in control, Moses does not worry about speaking, but when he is called upon to play an important role in front of others, he panics. It is the anticipation, more than the act itself, that troubles him. Moses is thus not whining in response to God's summons, playing hard to get. He is desperate and defiant.[11] He begs: "O my Lord, please send someone else" (Exod. 4:13). To accommodate Moses' difficulties, God

---

10. Jonathan Kirsch, *Moses, A Life* (New York: Ballantine, 1998), 220.
11. See Brevard S. Childs, *Exodus: A Commentary* (London: SCM, 1974), 79.

allows him to rely on Aaron, who "can speak fluently" (Exod. 4:14), to be his representative. This arrangement works. Having Aaron in the wings seems to give Moses the confidence he needs.

The rabbinical tradition read the Bible so carefully and closely that it developed a rich array of stories to fill in the blanks in the biblical narrative. One strand of this tradition could not imagine that the great Moses was simply afraid of public speaking. To correct this impression, the rabbis tell the story of Moses as a small child being tested by Pharaoh.[12] Moses has playfully taken Pharaoh's crown, and Pharaoh's advisers are afraid that this is a premonition of things to come. To find out whether the child is wise beyond his years, the court officials place two bowls in front of him, one full of live coals and the other with onyx stones. An angel guides Moses' hand so that he reaches for the hot coals, which demonstrates to the Egyptian rulers that his swiping of the crown was nothing more than mindless play. Of course, Moses' fingers are burnt, and he immediately puts them in his mouth, thus burning his tongue as well. His maimed tongue accounts for his slowness of speech.

Another strand of the rabbinical tradition is more honest about Moses' shortcomings. In this story, God spends seven days trying to convince Moses to undertake the mission of speaking for the Israelites. God could force Moses to relent, but God wants to use persuasion instead. One excuse Moses uses is that he does not know enough foreign languages to converse with all the officials at the court of the Egyptian king. Moses then pleads his lack of eloquence. God replies, "Had I willed it so, thou hadst been a man of ready speech. But I desired to show a wonder through thee. Whenever I will it, the words I cast in thy mouth shall come forth without hesitation."[13] Moses continues to complain, and God becomes increasingly impatient. Finally, God says that he could have healed Moses of his speech impediment but will not do so, precisely because Moses has been so wordy in his complaints.

The first tradition offers an artful tale in order to maintain Moses' reputation. Drawing from the realm of legend, it resists the idea that Moses was flawed in any way. After all, it was an angel who guided Moses' hand to the glowing coals, and the angel did this only to save his life. Moses is a victim of the pharaoh's irrational jealousy. The second story accepts Moses' reluctance to speak as a given of his character and looks for the purpose rather than the cause of his condition. This story, which is thoroughly theological, is not so kind to Moses. He is

---

12. Louis Ginzberg, *The Legends of the Jews*, vol. 2, *From Joseph to the Exodus*, trans. Henrietta Szold (1920; reprint, Baltimore: Johns Hopkins University Press, 1998), 272–75.

13. Ibid., 324–25.

genuinely terrified of the very thought of public speaking, and his fear leads him to defy God. God seems to be just as stubborn as Moses. Why doesn't God just leave him alone? The story uses poetic license to make a theological point. How better to show God's power than for the God who speaks to choose a man who cannot speak to deliver God's message to the world?

The source of Moses' speaking problem will forever remain obscure in the historical record, but there is no doubt that it makes him more human by underscoring his dependence on God to give him the strength to lead the Israelites. Significantly, Moses' condition becomes a recurring motif throughout the Bible. It is played out again and again with the prophets, who, like Moses, must struggle to find the courage to speak on God's behalf. It is as if faith is functionally equivalent to the power of speech, a power that is not of our own making. Believing is not seeing—and not just hearing, either—but speaking.

It is worth pausing here to return to the case of stage fright in acting, since being a prophet is similar to playing a role in a scripted drama. Stephen Aaron, in one of the few full-length books devoted to the role of stage fright in acting, argues that speaking anxiety is not an occasional side effect of the acting process.[14] Instead it is inherent in the actor's task. Unlike most other art forms, acting means the actor uses herself as her principal instrument of expression, which is the source of her heightened vulnerability. Acting in the ancient world was less focused on the personality of the actor due to the use of masks, which date back to the origin of drama in primordial religious rituals. The anonymity of the mask completely hid the ritualist, protecting him from the evil eye of the spectators. The use of masks was adopted in ancient Greek theater, itself born from religious ritual, perhaps for the same reason, given how well the Greeks understood the objectifying power of vision.

Stripping the actor of a mask constituted a major transformation in dramatic practice. The modern actor is caught in the bind of both wearing and not wearing a mask, since her mask is nothing more than her ability to use her body to create a character. Gestures and costumes can provide some sense of masking, but even more important is how actors speak for another with their own voice. Actors, like prophets, do not function as spiritualists who channel voices from the departed; they must use their own voice but speak someone else's words. The voice is so personal, however, that as a mask it does not provide much protection from the judging stare of the audience. Under the light of such scrutiny,

14. Stephen Aaron, *Stage Fright: Its Role in Acting* (Chicago: University of Chicago Press, 1986).

all sorts of vulnerabilities can come to the surface. Stage fright is one consequence of the actor's worry that the audience will see through the mask of her character to her vulnerabilities as a human being. As the actor becomes more anxious, the worry intensifies because she fears the audience will see the symptoms of her anxiety and thus the illusion of the performance will be destroyed.

Such was the basic situation that defined Hebraic religion, except the actor's bind was infinitely tightened around the prophet's neck. Actors have to speak in the voice of their character, but how can mere mortals speak with the voice of the divine?[15] Prophets worried that God was asking them to speak with more authority than they knew they could ever possess, and the more they worried, the more they became convinced that their audience would interpret their anxiety as a sign of insincerity and doubt. If they showed their fright, in other words, their audience would suspect that rather than speaking for God they were really speaking for themselves. Prophets needed to speak with courage and boldness, but how could they, given the monumental nature of their task? Under such stress, feelings of vulnerability can feed on themselves and become a vicious circle that literally tightens around the neck to squeeze the breath out of the speaker.

The Bible's recognition of the prophetic bind is demonstrated by the extent to which the Israelites were attentive to the symbolics of the mouth, which could be a troubling source of defilement (Matt. 15: 11). Isaiah can speak for God only after an angel touches his unclean lips with a burning coal. Afterward Isaiah can say that the Lord made his mouth like a sharp sword (49:2). God's mouth too is a source of judgment. In a breathtaking image, Isaiah describes God as striking the earth "with the rod of his mouth, and with the breath of his lips he shall kill the wicked" (11:4). The New Testament continues this metaphor by having God spit sinners out of the divine mouth (Rev. 3:16).

Jeremiah eats God's words (15:16), and God tells him that he will "serve as my mouth" (15:19). Although Jeremiah was consecrated before his birth to speak for God, when God calls upon him, he protests that he is just a boy and does not know how to speak in public. God then touches him on the mouth, filling it with God's words (1:9). Even

---

15. "We are now reminded that right throughout the Old Testament, to those to whom He speaks, and by the very fact that He does speak, Yahweh gives a mission and authority, a commission and command, that they too should speak. . . . Not every man can do this. Not every man can speak God's Word. For not every man has heard it" (Karl Barth, *Church Dogmatics* 1/2, 490–91). This implies that everyone who has really heard the Word *can* speak it.

after this dramatic moment, he is tempted to run away from serving the Lord (17:16). The burden of speaking on behalf of God results in complex emotions. Jeremiah describes something like a reverse panic attack that occurs not when he is asked to speak but when he tries to hold his tongue: "Then within me there is something like a burning fire shut up in my bones; I am weary with holding it in, and I cannot" (20:9). Jeremiah was eloquent, but he was not a writer; he dictated his message to a scribe named Baruch (chap. 36).

When Daniel heard the voice of an angel, he fell to the ground, speechless. "Then one in human form touched my lips, and I opened my mouth to speak, and said to the one who stood before me, 'My lord, because of the vision such pains have come upon me that I retain no strength. How can my lord's servant talk with my lord? For I am shaking, no strength remains in me, and no breath is left in me'" (Dan. 10: 16–17). Here performance paralysis opens the way to a new depth of reverence for God. This description of what is surely the most appropriate response any human can make to a revelation of God's glory is followed by the angel's soothing words of encouragement: "Do not fear, greatly beloved, you are safe. Be strong and courageous!" (v. 19). These are words—from an angel standing in the wings—that can still comfort the afflicted today.

The Weakness of the Apostle Paul

According to Acts, the apostle Paul—who was converted by hearing the voice of the Lord, a voice so powerful it rendered his traveling companions speechless and left him blind—relied on God for the courage to speak to large and frequently hostile crowds. Acts portrays Paul as a master rhetorician, bold and persuasive in his defense of the gospel. Paul is the hero of this narrative, and the miraculous success of the church is its theme. Many scholars believe that the writer of this book, traditionally thought to be an associate of Paul named Luke, is more interested in dramatic effect than in historical accuracy. Indeed, authors' putting words into the mouth of their characters was a common convention in Greek historical writing.[16] The reconstructed speeches of Acts are thus

16. George A. Kennedy makes the case that the speeches of Acts have more in common with Jewish than Greek rhetorical traditions. See *Classical Rhetoric and Its Christian and Secular Tradition* (Chapel Hill: University of North Carolina Press, 1980), 129–32. Ronald E. Osborn, in *Folly of God: The Rise of Christian Preaching* (St. Louis: Chalice, 1999), calls Luke-Acts the "First Book of Homilies" (300). Note this comment from Osborn: Acts portrays Paul's career as "an impressive sequence of missionary journeys studded with dramatic sermons; whereas in his letters his mode of thought is thoroughly rabbinic and profess-

thought to be carefully staged scenes that serve to heighten the tension of the story of the church's early growth.

Luke had to make sense of the church's astounding success—against all odds—to a skeptical Roman audience. He did this by portraying Paul as an accomplished actor on the stages of the cities he visited. The people of Athens, for example, are portrayed as spending "all their time in nothing but telling or hearing something new" (17:21), and when they first meet Paul, they ask, "What does this babbler want to say?" (17:18). It is Luke's task to show that Paul was no babbler. Luke is so zealous in this task that he can sound defensive, as if he has something to hide. He repeatedly insists, for example, that Paul preached "with all boldness and without hindrance" (28:31). Most likely one of his goals was to safeguard Christians from persecution. It was a cunning rhetorical strategy, then, to make Paul look like a great Roman leader. That is, Luke portrays Paul as a consummate performer of the spoken word.[17]

Paul's letters tell a dramatically different story. Although his letters are models of rhetorical skill, there are suggestions in them that he was not the most polished public speaker. He portrays himself as someone who was known more for the hard work of organizing local churches and teaching small groups of new Christians than for addressing Roman citizens in temples and forums. His first letter to the church at Corinth deals with the divisions there, caused in part by the popularity of a Christian leader named Apollos. Apollos had all of the qualifications of an accomplished rhetor.[18] Paul, on the other hand, states that he was not sent to the Corinthians "with eloquent wisdom" (1:17). Paul's argument that weaknesses are really strengths and that leaders should act like servants might, in part, be a way of rationalizing his lack of speaking skills.

Indeed, he writes like someone who is urgently trying to achieve with the sharpness of his pen what he could not convey with the slowness of his tongue. He acknowledges in his second letter to the Corinthians that

---

edly non-rhetorical, here he appears as a master of the dais, pointing his speeches with apt allusion to classical literature and philosophy" (289). Paul even makes "the grandest gesture available to a Roman rhetor" (289) by appealing to Caesar.

17. Another way of looking at Luke is to view him as translating Paul's success as a persuasive and powerful letter writer into the more generally understood terms of public speaking.

18. George Campbell, in his posthumously published *Lectures on Systematic Theology and Pulpit Eloquence* (London: Cadell and W. Davies, 1807), makes Apollos, not Paul, the model of Christian eloquence. Campbell, who was the most important eighteenth-century proponent of synthesizing rhetoric and theology, argues that we cannot imitate the apostle Paul, who was filled with supernatural gifts, but we can try to imitate the very human rhetorical skills of Apollos (267–28).

he communicates better in letters than in person: "I who am humble when face to face with you, but bold toward you when I am away!" (2 Cor. 10:1). The discrepancy between the way Paul presented himself in person and the way he expressed himself in his letters had to be explained. Richard F. Ward states the situation clearly: "It appears that Paul was deemed ineffective in some form of public speech and that his inability to 'perform' in this way placed his apostolic authority at Corinth in some jeopardy."[19] Ward calls Paul's second letter to the Corinthians a "counter-performance" that was meant to compensate not only for his physical absence but also for his vocal inadequacies.

Paul's letters could offset his public speaking because they functioned as scripts for dramatic performance. Paul dictated his letters (Rom. 16:22), and they were written to be read aloud, which enabled him to have a voice in his churches even when he could not give speeches in person.[20] More to the point, his letters were his way of speaking without having to be judged by the persuasiveness of his public presence.[21] He used trusted emissaries to deliver and read his work—men like Titus, who was famous for his speaking skills (2 Cor. 8:18). These emissaries would have been authorized to do more than recite the letter; they would have expanded it through a dramatic performance of its contents.[22] Paul understood that the power of the Word was not complete until it had been properly proclaimed—even if he could not proclaim it.

The rhetorical skill of Paul's letters has been much studied in recent scholarship. During his lifetime, his obvious gift for writing was used against him. Paul knew what his critics said: "His letters are weighty and strong, but his bodily presence is weak, and his speech contemptible"

19. Richard F. Ward, "Pauline Voice and Presence as Strategic Communication," *SBL Seminar Papers*, 1990, 283. Ward speculates that Paul's opponents at Corinth would have been influenced by the "rhapsodes" who performed the Greek epics. Rhapsodes were known to be highly trained in presenting themselves and projecting their voices to their audience. Since, as Ward admits, there is no hard evidence connecting the Hellenic rhapsode and early Christian preachers, it seems simpler to me to draw the conclusion that Paul could not compete with the more eloquent missionaries because he was not a very enthusiastic or competent public speaker.

20. For a comprehensive treatment of this topic, see John D. Harvey, *Listening to the Text: Oral Patterning in Paul's Letters* (Grand Rapids: Baker, 1998). Also see the chapter on Paul in Kelber, *The Oral and the Written Gospel*. Arthur J. Dewey challenges the idea that the oral nature of Paul's theology should be correlated with conservative patterns of social authority and instead links Paul's utopianism to an orality that is much closer to the utopian accessibility of writing. See Dewey, "A Re-hearing of Romans 10:1–15," *SBL Seminar Papers*, 1990, 273–82.

21. See Ward, "Pauline Voice and Presence," 283–92.

22. See William Doty, *Letters in Primitive Christianity* (Philadelphia: Fortress, 1973), 45–46. Also see M. Luther Stirewalt Jr., *Paul the Letter Writer* (Grand Rapids: Eerdmans, 2003), 11–13 and 116–21.

(2 Cor. 10:10). His *logos* was of no account. He could feel limited by the written word, as when he wished that he could speak to his converts in person so that he "could change my tone" (Gal. 4:20). Nonetheless, writing brought out his epistolary brilliance, which was a providential boon to the development of the church. His skills in letter writing should not make his lackluster speaking skills puzzling. Many great writers have found that mastering the written word can offset personal problems with face-to-face communication. Moreover, there are indications in his work that Paul's education was inadequate in the practical skills of public oratory. Having been raised in Tarsus, which, according to Strabo, had "all kinds of schools of rhetoric," Paul would have been acquainted with all the elements of a typical classical education.[23] Yet he insists that he was "untrained in speech, but not in knowledge" (2 Cor. 11:6), which suggests a gap of some sort in his early rhetorical training.

Whatever it was that kept him from making the most of his rhetorical education, Paul was frustrated by his inability to communicate effectively while visiting the churches in Asia. This was especially the case with the church at Ephesus, where Paul was put off by members' undisciplined speculations and the ease of their theological verbosity. In his first letter to Timothy, he complains about their "endless genealogies" (1 Tim. 1:4), their "meaningless talk" (1:6), and their "morbid craving for controversy and for disputes about words" (6:4). Throughout his second letter to Timothy, Paul is preoccupied with the futility of public debate, which can have, he argues, only a demoralizing effect on the audience (2 Tim. 2:14). Profane chatter, he says, "will spread like gangrene" (2:17). After warning Christians in his letter to the Ephesians about crafty rhetoric and empty words (Eph. 4:14; 5:6), he asks of them, "Pray also for me, so that when I speak, a message may be given to me to make known with boldness the mystery of the gospel, for which I am an ambassador in chains. Pray that I may declare it boldly, as I must speak" (6:19–20).[24] The reference to chains here seems more than a gentle reminder of the imprisonment Paul faced in his travels; it also seems as if Paul was chained to a task that made demands on him that were profoundly distressing.

Paul evidently did not like to stand up and defend himself in group situations. Some scholars have connected this weakness to his personal

23. Quoted in Jerome Murphy-O'Connor, *Paul: A Critical Life* (New York: Oxford University Press, 1997), 49.

24. Some scholars question Paul's authorship of Ephesians and the letters to Timothy. It is possible that a secretary wrote them on Paul's behalf, which would account for stylistic features not found in the letters that are unquestionably Pauline. If Paul did not write them, these letters were probably written by a disciple of Paul who drew from Paul's experiences, so they still contain valuable information about Paul's attitude toward his ministry.

appearance, although we have no record of how he looked. The physical infirmity that he talks about in Galatians 4:13 has led to much speculation. One guess that makes sense of the evidence of the impression Paul made on others is that he had some kind of speech defect. His lack of ease with public oratory explains the fact that he did not use words of flattery and never received praise from mortals (1 Thess. 2:5–6). If he had been a better speaker, he would not have needed to explain and defend his authority in everything he wrote. Perhaps he stuttered, or perhaps he had stage fright. These would have been debilitating conditions—a thorn in the flesh (2 Cor. 12:7) for a man who dedicated himself to a traveling ministry. The resulting anxiety would have made him all the more sensitive about his authority and passionate in his reliance on Christ.[25]

Paul's theology of the Word is surely not unrelated to this lack of public presence. "We also constantly give thanks to God for this, that when you received the word of God that you heard from us, you accepted it not as a human word but as what it really is, God's word, which is also at work in you believers" (1 Thess. 2:13). Paul sounds relieved that he was not being judged according to the high standards his contemporaries had for rhetorical persuasion. He did not trust the "itching ears" of those who were easily turned from the truth by the soothing sounds of more verbally adept teachers (2 Tim. 4:3). He begged his congregations to listen for God's Word in the words he spoke, overlooking his personal limitations. The Christian movement was so convinced of the newness of its message that new forms of language, *glossolalia*, were breaking out all over the empire. Christians felt compelled to speak, even when they could not speak well. It is possible to imagine that the crucial insight into the liberating power of God's Word came to Paul as he struggled with the public humiliation he experienced in proclaiming the gospel.

Cicero and Augustine: Two Rhetors Seeking Greater Glory

Ancient history is full of scenes of speechlessness. That losing or finding one's voice is a recurring theme in the ancient world should be no

25. That Paul did not dwell on his speaking problem or try to find some psychological explanation for it should not be surprising. Mediterranean people were not introspective in the way we are today. It makes sense that Paul admitted his problem only in the context of discussing the social status of his authority, and he turned his problem into a theological, not a psychological, issue. On the topic of ancient understandings of personality, see Bruce J. Malina and Jerome J. Neyrey, *Portraits of Paul: An Archaeology of Ancient Personality* (Louisville: Westminster John Knox, 1996), esp. 185.

surprise. Public speaking was the primary means by which men (women were excluded from public speaking roles) made their reputations and fortunes. The ability to express oneself in public was the foundation for every other social activity. Cicero, for example, was Rome's greatest statesman largely because he was also Rome's greatest speaker. There must have been enormous pressure when someone rose to speak at a temple or in the agora. It is no wonder, then, that the great moments as well as the emotional crises of a man's personal development often involved the spoken word.

At few times in Western history has public speaking been more important than in the days of Republican Rome. It is difficult for us today to understand the significance Romans attached to rhetorical training. Roman culture was heavily in debt to the Greek literary and philosophical traditions. It was the Greek study of rhetoric, however, with its practical emphases on moral and political leadership, that appealed most to the Romans. For a young man like Cicero, who was a Roman citizen but not from one of the city's leading families, the law courts represented the best opportunity for advancement. Lawyers then were like actors today, providing one of the few means of public entertainment. In the forum, the busy center of Rome that combined shopping, worship, and the affairs of state, lawyers spoke in the open air and had to keep their audiences spellbound in order to win their cases.

In spite of the fact that Roman theater had a poor reputation among the aristocracy, Cicero was close friends with several of the leading actors of his day and modeled his style on their performances. Even so, he suffered from stage fright. "Personally," he wrote, "I am always very nervous when I begin to speak. Every time I make a speech I feel I am submitting to judgment, not only about my ability but my character and honor. I am afraid of seeming either to promise more than I can perform, which suggests complete irresponsibility, or to perform less than I can, which suggests bad faith and indifference."[26] Public speaking for the Romans was intensely competitive. If lawyers were like actors, they were also like athletes, doing everything they could in the name of victory. The consequences of legal and political speeches were grave. It was not unusual for lawyers to end up having to defend themselves as much as their clients.

Cicero left Rome just as his career was becoming established, because his health had taken a beating in the courts. He was underweight and had poor digestion, symptoms of the anxiety he daily faced. He forced himself to speak in public, and the result was an exhausted voice strained

---

26. Quoted in Anthony Everitt, *Cicero: The Life and Times of Rome's Greatest Politician* (New York: Random House, 2001), 58.

with overuse. His ambition had weakened his lungs, and he needed to find a method that would enable a smoother form of delivery. In Rhodes he worked with a distinguished speech teacher named Apollonius Molon, whose style was less florid than most Asian rhetoricians'. With a recuperated voice, Cicero found that the rest of his body was healthier as well. He was ready to return to Rome.

St. Augustine, who learned only a smattering of Greek late in his life, gained his knowledge of Greek philosophy primarily through Cicero. Except in the field of rhetoric, Cicero was not an original thinker, but his treatises on philosophy captured much of the wisdom of Greek thought. When Augustine read Cicero's *Hortensius,* which makes the case for the eternity of the soul, Augustine was persuaded to pursue wisdom as life's only consolation. When he later read Cicero's defense of skepticism against the Stoic ambition to understand the true nature of all things, he was able to make his break from the Manichaeans. Still later, in the autumn of 410, with his health failing, Augustine warned a young admirer not to flaunt his knowledge of Cicero.[27] He had come full circle to rejecting the pagan writer who had put him on the path to Christian faith. Augustine had benefited from Cicero, but he did not trust more susceptible Christians to read Cicero without coming under his undue influence. He wanted posterity to rely instead on his own work, which translated Greek and Roman concepts into a Christian key.

In the middle of his life, Augustine wrote his *Confessions* to glorify God and explain himself, especially to those who still wondered about his Manichaean past. The story of his agonizing decision to abandon his licentious lifestyle is well known, especially the climax when he hears the voice of the child telling him to take the Bible and read it.[28] What is less known is that his agony did not vanish with his conversion. Augustine had made a career selling the "services of [his] tongue."[29] He had to give up not only his promiscuous desires but also the power and prestige of his profession. Proclaiming the name of Jesus was to be a completely different activity from teaching students to defend the names of their clients in the law courts. The thought of leaving teaching was enough to make Augustine ill. He had trouble breathing, and he lost his voice for a time. Only his newly found faith could give him the courage to turn

27. Peter Brown, *Augustine of Hippo* (Berkeley: University of California Press, 1969), 299.

28. For a psychoanalytic account of the split in Augustine between his grandiosity and his sense of being injured, see Sandra Lee Dixon, *Augustine: The Scattered and Gathered Self* (St. Louis: Chalice, 1999).

29. Augustine, *Confessions,* trans. R. S. Pine-Coffin (New York: Penguin, 1961), 182.

his back on his students as well as his large income. The *Confessions* itself is evidence of how God had "rescued [his] tongue."[30]

At times Augustine can sound as if he turned his back on rhetoric completely, and for good reason. Rhetoric represented not only unbridled ambition but also unexpurgated paganism, since the classic texts that served as oratorical models were full of mythological stories about the gods. Augustine was thus drawn to Neoplatonic philosophy, which confirmed his distrust of the outer word of sound (pagan rituals could be noisy!) and enabled him to develop a theology of an inner word that speaks directly to the heart by means of divine illumination. For Augustine, our thoughts precede our words, so that thinking is essentially an inner and silent activity. (The Reformation emphasis on the vocal word undermined this assumption, as we will see.) Augustine drew this conclusion from the common experience that when we speak, what we say never perfectly captures what we think. This disjunction between thought and word is, he argued, one of the consequences of the fall; as a result of original sin, the transmission of thought into sound is full of—to use a modern word—static. This is unlike God, whose nature is unchanged in the incarnation of the Word. In other words, there is no division in God between thought and word; God says what God is. God's Word is enfleshed in Christ, but it does not undergo any change in that transmission. The signal is perfectly clear.

Although God chose to reveal the Word to us in the flesh of Jesus, Augustine does not think that God is dependent on the medium of sound to say what God has to say. God can illuminate our hearts in a more direct manner. For pedagogical purposes, this means, as Augustine declares in his work *De magistro*, that the Spirit is an inner teacher. "In order to know the truth of what is spoken," Augustine argues, "I must be taught by him who dwells within and gives me counsel about words spoken externally in the ear." Just as speaking, for Augustine, begins with thoughts that only later become vocal words, so too does learning begin with silent self-reflection before we are capable of exercising the discernment that allows us to be a "judge of the speaker."[31] As Brian Stock explains in his work on Augustine's theory of reading, "Signs speak inwardly only to the minds of those who already understand; they address persons who are instructed without any sounds, whose hearts overflow with the light of understanding."[32] Speaking is a problem for

---

30. Ibid., 185.

31. "The Teacher," in *Augustine: Earlier Writings*, Library of Christian Classics, trans. John H. S. Burleigh (London: SCM, 1953), 101, 98.

32. Brian Stock, *Augustine the Reader: Meditation, Self-Knowledge, and the Ethics of Interpretation* (Cambridge: Harvard University Press, 1996), 160.

Augustine because it is so bound to time. Reading and listening both are mere stimuli for meditation. Sounds disappear, but the memory retains the truth in a kind of timeless state.

By these arguments Augustine betrays his alliance with Platonic rather than Hebraic thought. Rhetoric is blind, he could insist in the *Confessions,* and thus the last thing rhetoricians need is more confidence in their speech. On the contrary, they need a renewal of their vision. The Word of God is not a shout that penetrates the deafness of the soul. Instead, the soul is darkened by sin, and the Word of God is the source of all light. For Augustine, God does not so much speak as shine.

Even given Augustine's adoption of the Greek privileging of the visual over the auditory, he could not completely forget his past. Rather than abandon rhetoric altogether, he baptized it. He accomplished this momentous task in the fourth book of his great work *On Christian Doctrine.*[33] Since the Latin for *doctrine* means something more like teaching than doctrine proper, the title is better translated "On the Art of Christian Teaching." Augustine had been a professor of rhetoric at Milan, so he was a master of the Greek and Roman rhetorical traditions. He argued that Christians should use the full range of those traditions in training their preachers. He did not think that Christians should accept pagan learning uncritically, but they should certainly immerse themselves in it passionately. Preachers especially should know Greek and Hebrew. Their education should have a particular focus on history, but Augustine insisted that the natural sciences should not be overlooked. And preachers should learn the art of rhetoric, although Augustine anticipated the Protestant Reformation in arguing that Christian rhetoric should emphasize the beauty of simplicity, since the truth of Scriptures and not the eloquence of the speaker is the point of the sermon.

Some of Augustine's misgivings about eloquence come out in his *De catechizandis rudibus* (On Teaching the Uninstructed), written around 405. Candidates for admission to the catechumenate, that class of Christians who were being prepared for baptism, needed to be instructed in the most rudimentary forms of the faith. These candidates first had to explain their motivation for wanting to know more about the faith. Subsequently, a catechist presented the essentials of Christianity to them in a single lecture. Augustine composed this treatise at the request of Deogratias, a friend from Carthage who was anxious about how to cover all of Christian history in one lesson, a problem that teachers of introductory classes know well. Deogratias was also worried about

---

33. The fourth book of *De doctrina* was the first of Augustine's books to be printed (in Strasbourg in 1465). In that same year, Cicero's *De oratore* was the very first book printed in Italy.

becoming predictable and stale in his lectures. Augustine's treatise is full of pedagogical advice—such as to keep to a central theme and to adapt the material to match the candidate's intelligence—that is still applicable today.

Augustine was interested in the psychology of the teacher as well as the methodology of teaching. He demonstrates in this work a remarkable sympathy for lecturers who are not confident in their speaking skills. We think of Augustine as a man who was never at a loss for words, and the fact that he dictated many of his books, including *On Teaching*, is further evidence of the ease with which he spoke. But he also was a man haunted by the ambition of his past and ashamed of the rhetorical glory he once pursued. He tells Deogratias that he understands how teachers can become weary. Our spoken words never do us justice. "Even when we like to speak," he admits, "we like still better to hear or read things which have been better expressed, and which may be given by us without costing any care or anxiety on our part."[34] Especially difficult, Augustine laments, is teaching students who have no desire to learn. In fact, Augustine treats lecturing as a burdensome obligation that takes him away from more pleasurable work. Uttering one syllable after another cannot keep pace with the speed of thought. What "is imbibed at one rapid draught of the mind" is forced in speech to "find utterance by long and devious paths through the lips of the flesh" (37). What makes speaking hard is the slowness of sound. Clearly the laborious mechanics of public speaking are, for Augustine, a sign of the fall.

Only a God who deigns to speak to us can redeem such labor. God needs no time in which to formulate thoughts, and yet God voluntarily took on the patient task of communicating to us through words. God "stoops to [our] ears," Augustine eloquently notes (37). God does not even have the pleasure that we take in speaking to the fullest of our ability, because God's speech to us is like our talking to a baby. God must speak in simple words that are hardly expressive of the depth of the divine dignity. Why does God do this? "For is it a pleasure to murmur into the ear broken and mutilated words unless love invite us?" (37). Augustine draws on the analogy of the hen that "with tired cry calls her peeping chicks to her side" (38). Overall, Augustine portrays God's descent in the incarnation as a journey in sound, wherein God searches not for

---

34. St. Augustine, *The First Catechetical Instruction*, Ancient Christian Writers 2, trans. Joseph P. Christopher (New York: Newman, 1946), 35. Parenthetical page numbers in the following paragraphs refer to this book. Also see Carol Harrison, "The Rhetoric of Scripture and Preaching: Classical Decadence or Christian Aesthetic?" in *Augustine and His Critics*, ed. Robert Dodaro and George Lawless (New York: Routledge, 2000).

the right words but for the right tone with which to woo us. Apparently even God cannot avoid the demands of rhetoric.

George Whitefield and the Evangelical Appropriation of Stage Fright

Stage fright did not disappear in the church after Augustine, but there is very little said about it and very little theological attention given to it until the sixteenth-century Reformers turned their attention to the power of public speaking. Even then, the Reformers were more concerned about articulating the theological grounds for a renewed confidence in the spoken word than about the difficulties many people feel in standing up to speak before a crowd. I want to propose that what gives modern evangelicalism its theological identity is its rediscovery of the integral connection between speaking anxiety and faithful proclamation.

Modern-day evangelicalism was born out of stage fright when the style of preaching in the eighteenth century changed from the reading of a written text to improvisation on set themes. This move can be seen most clearly in the story of George Whitefield, who was, in many ways, the founder of American revivalism. In a magisterial book entitled *The Divine Dramatist*, Harry B. Stout tells the story of how Whitefield unintentionally invented a new kind of Christianity. After stints as a boy preacher in London and a missionary in America, Whitefield became an ordained priest in the Church of England in 1739. His dream was to organize an orphanage in Georgia and to support it through an itinerant ministry. The Anglican leaders, however, did not welcome him into their churches, due to his vociferous attack on the established clergy. Consequently, he took to preaching in the open air. He was not the first to try this, but he did stamp field preaching, as it was called, with his own dramatic personality.[35]

Outdoor preaching required special skills that revolutionized the nature of the gospel proclamation.[36] Whitefield had to compete with

35. Open-air preaching was common at Paul's Cross in the sixteenth century. Because the crowds were often unruly, preachers had to develop a style that could hold their attention. See Bryan Crockett, *The Play of Paradox: Stage and Sermon in Renaissance England* (Philadelphia: University of Pennsylvania Press, 1995), 38–39.

36. Outdoor preaching also required new efforts of hearing by the audience. In 1739, Whitefield preached a sermon at Christ's Church in Spittlefields, England, that shows how much he was thinking about the act of listening. The sermon was called "Directions [concerning] How to Hear Sermons," and the text was Luke 8:18: "Take heed therefore how you hear." He exhorts his congregation not to doze like Jesus' disciples and not to listen to the preacher with their "outward ears" alone. He also suggests that congregants

both the noisy entertainment of the vendors in the marketplace and the quiet but authoritative tone of what he called the "velvet-mouthed" preachers in the established churches.[37] Behind a pulpit, notes and an outline made sense, but in the open air, in front of crowds that reached ten thousand and more, a manuscript only encumbered the preacher's ability to move freely during the sermon. Even more important than movement was Whitefield's vocal power. If he had not been able to engage those who stood farthest away—reading a manuscript casts the head downward—the whole enterprise of revivalism would have failed.[38] When Whitefield discovered the power of his voice, he also discovered a new way of embodying the Word and of organizing the church. As Stout puts it, "An unsurpassed sense of power accompanied the realization that voice and body were released to their utmost in the field" (75). The evangelical style was born in the strength and courage it took to attract and retain large crowds by exclaiming God's Word.

---

pray for the preacher "to endue the minister with the power to speak" (privately printed pamphlet, Luce Library Special Collections, Princeton Seminary). This is not to suggest, however, that listening was not the subject of ecclesial formation before Whitefield. In a perceptive study of sound in early modern England, Bruce R. Smith notes how the Church of England liturgy was designed to produce active listeners by turning the voices of the many into one. "The purpose of preaching is, then, to make Christian believers subject to God's voice, through the voice of the preacher." Bruce R. Smith, *The Acoustic World of Early Modern England: Attending to the O-Factor* (Chicago: University of Chicago Press, 1999), 264.

37. Harry B. Stout, *The Divine Dramatist: George Whitefield and the Rise of Modern Evangelicalism* (Grand Rapids: Eerdmans, 1991), 67. Revivals in Whitefield's day could be very noisy, not least because critics and skeptics would try to interrupt them with noise of their own.

38. One of the most striking noises to come out of the Great Awakening was the "holy whine," which was evidently a kind of intoning that became ritualized as a way for outdoor preachers to rest their voices. "When men spoke to crowds in the open air, on a high key, with great excitement for a long time, the over-strained voice would relieve itself by rising and falling, as a person tired of standing will frequently change position. This soon became a habit with such men, and then would be imitated by others, being regarded as the appropriate expression of excited feeling. The same causes produce the same sing-song tone in the loud cries of street-vendors in our cities. But the whine of the preacher, associated for many ignorant hearers with seasons of impassioned appeal from the pulpit, and of deep feeling on their own part, has become a musical accompaniment which gratifies and impresses them, and like a tune we remember from childhood, revives the memory of joys that are past, pleasant and mournful." John A. Broadus, "The American Baptist Ministry of One Hundred Years Ago," *Baptist Quarterly* 9 (1875): 19. This is one of those cases where we clearly would benefit from a sound recording instead of a written record. For another mention of the holy whine, see Wesley M. Gewehr, *The Great Awakening in Virginia, 1740–1790* (Gloucester, Mass.: Duke University Press, 1930/Peter Smith 1965), 114.

Whitefield could hold the attention of crowds of people who did not know each other only by capturing their imagination. He also had to provide them with a common experience that could turn a crowd into a congregation. The personal experience of a new birth in Christ became, of necessity, something that preceded rather than followed theological instruction. This shift to an individual and emotional piety in evangelicalism has been much lamented by those who regret the loss of continuity in theological tradition and the lack of religious authority that makes that continuity possible. What needs to be stressed, however, is that this subjective turn of piety was the product of a new kind of preaching that created, in turn, a new understanding of the public role of religion.[39]

Whitefield was able to transcend denominational and social barriers—and thus is the father of parachurch organizations that have no creedal statements or doctrinal requirements—by marketing religious discourse as an object of consumption that is simultaneously entertaining and edifying. According to Stout, he accomplished this by a thoroughly unprecedented synthesis of the church and the stage. From his earliest years, Whitefield had been infatuated with the theater. He wanted to be a star more than a theologian, and though he spurned the stage when he became as popular as the most famous actors, he did not abandon its techniques. Under Whitefield's influence, Scripture, in Stout's words, "became a dramatic script with a cast of characters whose lives and roles served as models for later generations to 'impersonate'" (xx). Whitefield was a one-man show, since he was capable of playing any character; he even portrayed the women of the Bible. His theatrical style would doubtless strike us as histrionic today, but it was conventional for its time. What was not conventional was using the style of the stage to advance the gospel. This kind of preaching was so revolutionary that riots and physical assaults were not uncommon.

Although he successfully blurred the lines between acting and preaching, Whitefield did not resolve the ancient rivalry between church and theater. Instead, he brought this rivalry to a new level of competitive infighting. Whitefield frequently denounced the stage even as he borrowed from it. In fact, he was able to be on such intimate terms with the style of the stage only because he was protected from criticism by his public antagonism toward it. At one point in his career, members of an actors' guild took to interrupting his sermons with the ringing of bells

39. Ironically, the commonly made charge that evangelical theology fosters a subjective piety ignores the essentially oral quality of evangelical culture. Oral cultures are more communal and less introspective than highly literate cultures. Churches that look askance at the alleged emotionalism of evangelicalism tend to be more literary in their approach to the Bible, which results in a greater individualism than in evangelicalism.

and the banging of drums. Both evangelists and actors were despised by the elite of their society, but what they did not know was how much they would come to rule the world in future years. By competing against each other for audiences that were becoming increasingly detached from established institutions, evangelicals and actors were developing the entertaining styles that put them center stage in a world dominated by the consumerism of the market.

Whitefield's experiments in extemporaneous speaking were accompanied by a great amount of anxiety.[40] His success seemed to depend on converting the fear he experienced before he began to speak into an emotional torrent of tears and pathos in the sermon. Even as a young man, he had experienced stage fright. As his popularity grew, the problem became worse. "Invariably before preaching," Stout writes, "he would feel weak or sick. Sometimes he would feel hoarse, certain that his voice was going to fail him. At other times he would be unable to catch a breath—all classic signs of the anxiety attacks faced by many great performers" (75). In the anxious transition from imagining the worst to beginning the speech, he prayed and meditated. Once the sermon began, he regained his composure, and he interpreted this experience as divine deliverance. The explosive character of his speaking was not unrelated to this interplay between the anguish of impending doom and the delight in unexpected success.

Stout observes that these panic attacks never left Whitefield during his long and productive career. The only way he could deal with his anxiety was to plunge into the very activity that he most feared. This dialectic of terror and liberation was exhausting, and "the only deliverance he could imagine was death" (76). This is a typical reaction for many people who feel trapped by their panic, even if their longing for death is only the momentary reprieve of fantasy and imagination. For Whitefield, death became not just the solution to his anxiety. It was also the key to his theology. Death would reunite him with Jesus, the source of all of his confidence. Only by dying to himself could he live to preach the Word of God.

Although Whitefield remained a lifelong Calvinist, his preaching provided the foundation for the evangelical emphasis on a personal

---

40. Stout notes, "Extemporaneous preaching had become an accepted innovation among the Oxford methodists during Whitefield's tenure there. In 1735 John Wesley discovered the method by accident, having once forgotten his notes. The ensuing extempore sermon was so powerful that he recommended it to all who could muster the courage. Sometimes the speaker would not even know his text until he rose to preach. Such preaching established a unique bond between speaker and hearer and released the full range of improvisation and inspiration. For dramatic speakers like Whitefield it was the perfect release" (*Divine Dramatist*, 43).

experience of the dynamic of sin and grace in which the listener, as well as the preacher, battles the anguish that attends the moment prior to a public confession of faith. As Whitefield found his release when he began talking, his listeners—many of whom were already in a liminal state of social marginality—would find their salvation when they answered his challenge to claim Christ as their own. The anxiety about their condition to which Whitefield brought them paralleled his own experience of stage fright, and their solution, like his, involved leaving the safe anonymity of the crowd to discover grace as the relief that comes from the public performance of faith.

After Whitefield, evangelical preaching would be more in debt to passion than scholarship and more in tune with dramatic storytelling than dogmatic or moral instruction. Even though revivalists did not need to keep up with theological scholarship, they were under an even greater pressure—the pressure to perform. Much of the subsequent history of Christianity in America can be told from the perspective of sound; simply put, some denominations permit more vocal modulation than others. African-American preachers, for example, are known for their use of variation in volume, pitch, facial expression, and movement across the stage, characteristics that have had a great impact on Pentecostal and charismatic churches but not on mainline Protestant denominations. As James Cone explains, "in black preaching, the Word becomes embodied in the rhythm and the emotions of language as the people respond bodily to the Spirit in their midst."[41] People who grow up in churches with a European lineage can remember their first visit to a black church because the worship sounds so different. Mainline Protestant churches are relatively quiet, which is surely one of the reasons they are in decline. Black sermons can be agitated and loud. They are poetic happenings that, not limited to the spoken word, include a wide array of joyful yet intelligible noises. As Cone notes, "truth is found in the shout, hum, and moan as these expressions move the people closer to the source of their being."[42] Language comes in a variety of forms, from groans to gestures, which allows the Holy Spirit to communicate the Word untethered by social convention.

---

41. James Cone, *God of the Oppressed*, rev. ed. (Maryknoll, N.Y.: Orbis, 1997), 18. The risk of Cone's theological program is that it ontologizes features of African-American existence that are more properly interpreted as historical and therefore contingent. See Victor Anderson, *Beyond Ontological Blackness* (New York: Continuum, 1999), chap. 3. Also see L. Susan Bond, *Contemporary African American Preaching: Diversity in Theory and Style* (St. Louis: Chalice, 2003), and Richard Lischer, *The Preacher King: Martin Luther King Jr. and the Word That Moved America* (New York: Oxford University Press, 1995).
42. Ibid., 21.

The relationship between evangelical and African-American churches is complex, but they share a tendency toward loudness. This makes them suspect to the churches of the Magisterial Reformation.[43] For those with refined ears, loudness is to sound as exaggeration is to truth; by going too far to be heard, it distorts the message that is being conveyed. Leigh Eric Schmidt, who documents the battle over sound in his book *Hearing Things*, notes that there was less ambient noise in the air in the nineteenth century, which would have made the din of camp meetings reverberate far across the land. Evangelical noise, in other words, was not contained in church buildings; it was very public, and to some it was nothing more than a public nuisance. This conflict was not just between good taste and bad taste, however those sides were drawn. It was a conflict in ecclesiology. The question concerned who was to speak for God, and what kinds of sounds were to be counted as divine.[44]

Before returning to the question of the future of preaching and its role in worship, I want to go back to the Reformation. Chapter 5 will document the Reformation's relationship to sound and voice, and chapter 6 will pair three Reformation theologians with three contemporary theologians in order to examine how the Reformation heritage of sound has fared in contemporary theology.

43. The acoustemology of evangelical churches is also to be distinguished from churches that belong to the Radical Reformation. Mennonites, for example, have a communal understanding of sound, which leads them to suspect strong individual voices and emphasize collective singing. For this point I am grateful to insightful and inspiring conversations with Shirley Showalter, president of Goshen College in Goshen, Indiana. It is interesting that the Quaker focus on silence stretches Christian tradition out of its recognizable shape.

44. Schmidt argues that a variety of topics were used by more liberal-minded theologians to limit the oral excesses of evangelicals: postbiblical miracles, extraordinary spiritual gifts, the authority of ministers, the disciplinary power of churches, the sufficiency of Scripture, and the use of catechesis in Christian education (*Hearing Things*, 71).

five

The Protestant Reformation as an Event within the History of Sound

Revocalizing the Word

When Ulrich Zwingli decided in 1522 to challenge the right of the Roman Catholic Church to tell the good people of Zurich what they could eat, he was set on a course that would make him one of the leaders of the Protestant Reformation.[1] Medieval Christians took it for granted that fasting was a sign of holiness and that special days honoring the saints should be set aside for meatless meals. Indeed, it is fair to say that fasting was the primary means by which the liturgical calendar was honored. Without a meatless diet, the calendar could not distinguish between holy and ordinary days. By Zwingli's time, this custom

---

1. Ulrich Zwingli, "Of Freedom of Choice in the Selection of Food," in *Early Writings*, ed. Samuel Macauley Jackson (Durham, N.C.: Labyrinth, 1987). A similar polemic can be found in Erasmus's dialogue between a fishmonger and a butcher in his colloquy "A Fish Diet," in *The Colloquies of Erasmus*, trans. Craig R. Thompson (Chicago: University of Chicago Press, 1965). Zwingli has been too harshly treated as a rationalist by High Church theologians. One of his sermons has perhaps the clearest statement of any of the Reformers of the freedom of the Word. See "Of the Clarity and Certainty of the Word of God," in *Zwingli and Bullinger*, ed. G. W. Bromiley, Library of Christian Classics 24 (Philadelphia: Westminster, 1953), 59–95. Zwingli ends this sermon with twelve rules for discerning God's voice, which shows how the freedom of the Word does not mean it lacks content or that there are no rules for its interpretation.

had lost much of its theological substance. Zwingli, for example, could not understand why meat was prohibited but not fish and eggs.[2] More important, Zwingli was also convinced that regular fasting never had much biblical support in the first place. Because he believed, as people still do today, that meat is the stuff of muscles, he decided to stand up for the manual laborers who insisted that they needed a heavier diet to sustain their strength.[3] Zwingli's sermon, however, was not just a matter of defending the common man against contrived restrictions of the Roman elite. He was calling into question the very foundation of religious and social order. The liturgical calendar structured medieval time more than the seasons did. It told laity when to fast, but it also told pastors what to preach. When the religious calendar no longer counted the days for much of northern Europe, preaching, as well as eating, became a much more spontaneous affair.

Johan Huizinga, in his classic work *The Autumn of the Middle Ages*, reminds us that the Protestant Reformation did not invent the power of the spoken word. On the contrary, the spoken word was especially powerful in the Middle Ages, he suggests, due to widespread ignorance and naiveté. He tells the story of the popular preacher Brother Richard, who preached in Paris for ten straight days. He spoke in the famous Cemetery of the Innocents from five until ten or eleven o'clock each morning. As many as six thousand people camped in the cemetery in order to secure a good place to hear him, and after his tenth sermon the people wept, according to a contemporary account, "as if they were watching their best friends being put into the ground."[4] Medieval preachers of the mendicant orders were accomplished at moving their listeners to tears by describing the pains of hell or the sufferings of the Lord. They could also launch blistering moralistic attacks on the vices of luxury and vanity. For Huizinga, this is evidence for his thesis that everyday medieval life was much more colorful and intense than life is now. "Modern man has, as a rule," he writes, mournfully, "no idea of the unrestrained extravagance and inflammability of the medieval heart."[5]

2. The question of why fish were not categorized as meat in the ancient world is fascinating. See Stephen H. Webb, *Good Eating: The Bible, Diet, and the Proper Love of Animals* (Grand Rapids: Brazos, 2001), 129–32, 223–25.

3. Fast days often functioned as holidays; this was hard on the artisans, who had their work frequently interrupted, and day laborers, who could barely afford missing their wages. Some men took the holy days as an opportunity to spend the day in the tavern.

4. Johan Huizinga, *The Autumn of the Middle Ages*, trans. Rodney J. Payton and Ulrich Mammitzsch (Chicago: University of Chicago Press, 1996), 5. Describing medieval sermons, he writes, with affection, that "no effect was too crude, no change from laughter to tears too abrupt, no intemperate raising of the voice too crass" (221).

5. Ibid., 15.

People were more impressionable because their experiences were more concrete and tangible.

The sound that most impressed the medieval mind was the bell, not the sermon. In his comprehensive history of village bells in rural France, Alain Corbin refers to them as a form of rhetoric.[6] They sent multiple messages, texturing the landscape with a sonic depth. Perhaps most important, they functioned as calendars, marking the time for births, deaths, and weddings. They also served to define the boundaries of the villages. A bell that could be heard from any place in town had a unifying effect that is hard to imagine in our noisy cities today. Parishes were acoustic spaces, and beyond the comforting sound of the bells was the wilderness. The precinct of the bell tower itself was designated as a quiet space to prevent noise from disrupting the worship service and to intensify the effect of the ringing. Taverns, fairs, inns, and children were to be kept at a distance. This gave the church an auditory prominence due to its stillness, but it also focused attention on the bells, which led to a tradition of complaints about their loudness and battles over their control. Bells were so identified with the dissemination of religion that the leaders of the First Republic sought to mute their influence by strictly regulating their use. Bells continued to ring, but they were increasingly under governmental control, sounding the alarm or summoning help in wartime, for example. Whoever controlled the bells had the power to deafen the public, silencing others and thus monopolizing public speech. That we cannot hear bells today in the way that people heard them in the past is evidence for the historical character of sound and the social pliability of the senses.

Even given the sonic prominence of bells, there is no point in arguing that words were not heard by medieval Christians in vivid and powerful ways. In fact, the opposite is just the case: words had all the power of visual illustrations, and thus medieval sermons bordered on the baroque[7] in their overuse of imagery and examples. What can be argued is that the participants in the Protestant Reformation were ready to hear a new kind of word as well as practice a new kind of hearing. Protestants did not rediscover preaching; they reformed it. They were able to set free the Word by imagining it as originating in sound, not image, and thus in need of revocalization, not illustration. As Protestants learned to focus all of their senses on speech, they increasingly turned against the pervasive dominance of the visual, which in turn further enhanced

---

6. Alain Corbin, *Village Bells: Sound and Meaning in the Nineteenth-Century French Countryside,* trans. Martin Thom (New York: Columbia University Press, 1998).

7. Of course it would be more historically accurate to call the medieval sermon "gothic," but given the literary connotations of that term, "baroque" will have to do.

the power of the human voice. As a result, there was "a very concrete shift from a world brimming over with physical, visible symbols that were open to a rather wide range of interpretations—some intentionally ambiguous—to one principally with verbal symbols that were subject to the interpretation of a carefully trained and ostensibly learned ministry."[8] If these claims about the sonic uniqueness of the Protestant Reformation sound exaggerated to our ears, there is a reason. It is hard for us today to fathom the power of the spoken word because we treat speeches as if they were texts. Reading is our normal operating mode, and thus the spoken word is a modification of discourse that requires extra focus and attention.

The Reformation was characterized by an outpouring of words in service to the biblical Word of God. This was a verbosity caused not by the need to explain an image or to make a moral point. Rather, it was a verbosity that intended to convey grace through sound. Such verbosity was not unrelated to the social turmoil of the time. As I showed in chapter 4 in my discussion of evangelicalism and stage fright, individuals can interpret the breakthrough from fear to confidence in public speaking as an experience of grace. So can entire communities. Whole societies can have their will to express themselves oppressed and thus can experience the ecstasy of breaking through obstacles in order to find their voice. Typically in such circumstances, someone will emerge to dramatize this dynamic.

In the case of the sixteenth century, many people throughout Europe were ready to hear something new as well as speak with new freedom, but the risks involved in such a transformation were enormous. That is why it took a Luther—who overcame his own religious anxiety by finding a strong and singular voice—to break through the visual blanket that was suffocating European Christianity. Luther's anxiety took the form of not being able to put his sense of sinfulness into an adequate set of words. He once confessed for six straight hours, without feeling any satisfaction.[9] What he sought was a new relationship between words and the Word. He could not preach the gospel without being able to articulate how God found his words acceptable, but if his words failed to give an exhaustive account of his own sins, how could they become the means of praise and gratitude? When Luther gave voice to his rediscovery of the justifying power of the Word, he spoke for the multitudes, relieving them of one kind of verbal responsibility and giving them a new kind of

8. Carlos M. N. Eire, *War against Idols: The Reformation of Worship from Erasmus to Calvin* (Cambridge: Cambridge University Press, 1986), 316.

9. James D. Tracy, *Europe's Reformations, 1450–1650* (Lanham: Rowman & Littlefield, 1999), 48.

verbal task. Words could spring forth as praise because God had already said the Word that releases us from our sin.

As many scholars have noted, it is hard to pinpoint the exact moment when Luther discovered the doctrine of justification by grace alone. This is because his discovery was more like a process than a single event, and a key part of the process occurred when, after the publication of his Ninety-five Theses, he was forced to defend his views in public. With the advent of the printing press, Luther's theses circulated throughout Germany, making him an overnight celebrity. Now he had to find out whether he had the strength of speech to back up his theology. He did not know that he would soon find out that his courage to speak out would radicalize his understanding of faith. In finding his voice, he would also find that God's Word to us liberates us from worrying about saying the right thing!

Luther's discovery of personal confidence in public speaking could only be interpreted as a radical challenge to the established authorities of the Catholic Church, who strictly regulated the right to speak and undermined the confidence of the laity in their own voices. The Roman authorities were right to feel anxious—even to the point of not knowing what to say—in their anticipation of the general outcry that one person could release. Once voices were freed, there would be little possibility of harmonizing the subsequent din. Noise would never sound the same.

When Luther found his voice, a new kind of sound was heard in Europe. Perhaps the closest analogy to this event in our own recent past is the turmoil that was unleashed when Bob Dylan went electric. Now that our lives are rarely without a soundtrack of contemporary music accompanying us as we shop, study, work, and relax, it is hard to imagine how radical rock 'n' roll once was. Historians like Greil Marcus have recovered a revolutionary moment in the history of sound that has since been absorbed into the noise of modern life. Dylan was not the first to play an electric guitar, of course, but he was the first folk hero to do so. When he plugged in his electric guitar at the Newport Folk Festival on July 25, 1965, it was as if he were crashing through his own Wittenberg door.[10] The cries of betrayal at his concerts during the world tour that followed came to a climax when someone yelled "Judas!" at him during

10. Greil Marcus, *Invisible Republic: Bob Dylan's Basement Tapes* (New York: Henry Holt, 1997). Just as there is a great deal of mythology surrounding Luther's nailing his theses on the Wittenberg door, there is a great deal of mythology about Dylan's Newport appearance. For an alternative account, see David Hajdu, *Positively 4th Street* (New York: North Point, 2001), 254–63. Regardless of whether their break from the past can be precisely pinpointed, Luther and Dylan initiated similar revolutions in the history of sound. For an excellent theological reflection on Dylan, see Alan Jacobs, "It Ain't Me, Babe," in *A Visit to Vanity Fair* (Grand Rapids: Brazos, 2001).

the 1966 "Royal Albert Hall" concert (which was actually recorded in Manchester), to which Dylan replied, "I don't believe you." The charge of betrayal was prescient. Like Luther, Dylan had split his audience into two. His voice resounded with the strains of a cultural war that would be played out on the musical stage.

The whole range of the social conflicts of the 1960s could be heard in Dylan's eery and edgy voice. Significantly, Dylan found his voice just when the whole country was trying to figure out what democracy really sounded like. Part of his magic was in the way he reached back through time to reprise and mix the voices of gospel music, blues, country, protest songs, and Appalachian laments. He thus continued and revolutionized the folk music that had first put him on the stage. The folk tradition that he emerged from romanticized the rural poor as being more authentic than the urban elite. The idea was to sing songs representative of the plight of the people—written, frequently, by anonymous or forgotten figures and full of the protest that the political left could co-opt and make its own. When appropriated for a political message, folk music could sound like it belonged in a museum, not on the streets. Dylan's voice rebels against curators and politicians. By setting the music free, he captured the sound of American freedom.

Dylan overcame the didactic shape of folk music just as Luther overcame the didactic nature of medieval preaching. Dylan suffused traditional music with his own idiosyncratic tastes, turning it into a medium of something more personal and mysterious. "There's nobody that's going to kill traditional music," he wrote. The protest songs popular with the antiwar crowd were "not folk-music songs; they're political songs. They're already dead."[11] Dylan did not just repeat traditional music. He discovered within the American musical tradition a strange new world, much as Luther and Barth had rediscovered Paul's voice in the Bible. He sang with a voice that was disarmingly unique—human and transcendent, awkward and melodic, flat and unapologetic, in other words, utterly American. Of course, he opened the door, like Luther before him, to a world of voices that was more fragmented and chaotic than he ever could have imagined or anticipated. Rock music would go through many stages, stages that parallel the development of Protestantism: the pietism of 1970s soft rock, the fundamentalist ranting of heavy metal, the sectarian primitivism of punk, the neotraditionalism of orchestral rock, the spiritual elitism of the latest alternative music scene, the Pentecostal ecstasy of drug music, and the tolerant, liberal pluralism of world music. Dylan had set free the human voice but could not control its destiny. Rock became commodified as the soundtrack of

11. Dylan, quoted in Marcus, *Invisible Republic*, 113.

modern life, just as Protestantism became, for a time, the civil religion of America. But for a moment, in 1965, when Dylan sang, it was as if people were learning how to hear all over again. His roots in gospel were not accidental. He had learned how to preach in a new key, and his proclamatory style was every bit as revolutionary as Luther's.

Both Luther and Dylan let loose an outburst of sound that led to lofty lyrical heights but also to the anarchic depths of rebellion. Just as rock concerts have become the occasion for all kinds of excessive behavior, the sixteenth-century sermon could incite people to riotous reactions against the religious status quo. More precisely, what has been aptly called "the stripping of the altars" was both a cause and a result of the renewed interest in preaching. The medieval church provided social cohesion through its dramatic representation of the biblical narrative, which often took visual form; the decimation of this ocular structure was a tremendous shock to most people. Protestants were reacting against the theatrical aspects of the Mass, but the crisis they precipitated made theater all the more important. The importance of Shakespeare's plays for early modern England demonstrates the significance of theater in helping people cope in times of great epistemological stress.[12] For Protestants, the sermon grew to carry a new theatrical weight. The sermon had to become more performative in order to take the place of the drama of Catholic rituals. By stripping grace of all the "superstitions" that many people found comforting, Luther left people feeling more vulnerable to the effects of sin and thus more in need of a comforting word of grace.

When Protestantism shattered the religious unity of Europe, it wanted to fill the ensuing void with its own authoritarian rule. Indeed, by making every home a church and every man a priest, it resulted in greater control of the church over everyday life. Nevertheless, Protestantism also inadvertently opened the way for radically pluralistic religious views, which made tolerance a virtue of necessity. This is the standard view, anyway, of Protestantism's accidental role in unleashing modernity and secularism. What secular historians often miss is the extent to which giving laity a greater voice in the church served as preparation for democratic forms of government. Secular historians also miss the theological point that the logic of Protestant theology drove a wedge between church and state. The social significance of Protestant theology's defiance of all epistemological foundations is immense. Protestants believed that the Word of God is its own authority, and thus, when they were being con-

12. Bryan Crockett, *The Play of Paradox: Stage and Sermon in Renaissance England* (Philadelphia: University of Pennsylvania Press, 1995), 32.

sistent, they could not appeal to authorities outside of the Holy Spirit's invigoration of Scripture for consolation and support.

A theology freed from any foundation other than its own confidence in proclaiming the truth began the process of decoupling the destinies of Europe and Christianity. The eventual result was that Christian churches were forced to devise competitive strategies for their success and survival. This was much more true in the United States, where disestablishment aligned the churches with a booming market economy, than in Europe, where established churches still relied on the protection of governments to ensure their viability. When Protestants came to America, with its open frontier, they developed a penchant, as Alexis de Tocqueville noted, for a rhetoric that could do the expansive landscape justice.[13] Of course Protestantism soon became the *de jure* established religion of America, with a church on every street corner, or so it seemed. Thus began the cycle of reformation all over again: Protestants on the margins of the mainline churches had to revert to an exaggerated rhetoric in order to capture the attention of a religiously complacent audience.

Protestantism infused sound with all the drama of the Christian faith. It was born out of the desire to shake up moribund religious tradition by appeals to a simpler and more intimate faith. But it was also polemical from the start, having to defend itself against the presumption that accompanies centuries of steady and solid tradition. By arguing that a more trustworthy faith lay buried beneath innumerable layers of superstition, Protestantism was committed to a theological project that was essentially pedagogical in nature. The Protestant recovery of the doctrine of original sin kept Protestant churches from assuming that it was enough to be raised in a Christian country. Instead, the Word had to be proclaimed anew every Sunday, in order to break the long-ingrained habit of taking the gospel for granted.

The evangelical character of Protestantism did not immediately lead to an emphasis on missions. Indeed, Catholicism during the age of Trent was much more aggressive about spreading the faith to new lands. Christopher Columbus combined the mandate to convert the heathen with the glory of the Crusades to ignite one of the most remarkable expansions of any religion in world history. As a result of his travels, the Catholic Church became the first truly transoceanic institution. Protestant churches during this period were increasingly relying on state support in order to weather the spiritual and military battles of the sixteenth and seventeenth centuries. Nonetheless, like all movements that rely ultimately on persuasion over tradition, Protestantism could not rest on

13. Alexis de Tocqueville, *Democracy in America*, trans. George Lawrence (New York: Anchor, 1969), 437–41.

past successes. Even the established Protestant denominations had to undergo periodic revivals in order to maintain their standing. Protestant theology, in its rhetorical mode, is essentially connected to missions, because even the most committed churchgoers are in continual need of hearing the Word preached as if for the first time.

Recent history confirms these points. While the more established Protestant churches have become stagnant as they struggle to regain their momentum within large institutional frameworks, less centralized Protestant traditions continue to expand at an explosive rate. Protestantism is like sound in that both have to be continuously generated or they disappear. At its heart, Protestantism is a dynamic movement, conversionistic and expansionistic, or else there is no reason for its existence.

The Medieval Sermon: A Very, Very Short History of Preaching

The changing role of preaching in the church must be put in a historical context if we are to grasp Protestantism's significance. Perhaps the most distinctive character of the medieval sermon was the way it was integrated into the role the church played in providing social cohesion. As Larissa Taylor explains, "besides its spiritual and didactic value, the Medieval sermon was an event that offered people the opportunity to socialize, flirt, debate, and catch up on the latest news and gossip. Estimates from a variety of sources indicate that people at the end of the Middle Ages attended sermons in great numbers."[14] The Mass was a drama performed by the priest, and it was not essential for the people to watch all of the details. People came and went, often talking noisily with little regard for the service.[15] Some caught up on their sleep, but disturbances were also common, as was the presence of dogs. The church would become quiet only when the congregation kneeled and raised their eyes to see the Host held high above the priest's head for all to see. This was called the sacring, and a bell was rung just before it in order to get the people's attention. The high altar was like a stage, separated from the people by a rood screen, which divided the nave from the chancel.

14. Larissa Taylor, *Soldiers of Christ: Preaching in Late Medieval and Reformation France* (New York: Oxford University Press, 1992), 226.

15. For descriptions of the noise during medieval worship services, see Huizinga, *Autumn of the Middle Ages*, 183–85. For a more positive view of popular religion in the late Middle Ages, see Eamon Duffy, *The Stripping of the Altars: Traditional Religion in England, 1400–1580* (New Haven: Yale University Press, 1992).

For most Christians during the Middle Ages, seeing the elements was the climax of the worship experience. Consuming the elements, and then only the bread, would have been an annual event, occurring on Easter Day after confession during Holy Week and the Lenten fast.

While the sermons of the Reformers can be read with great profit today, medieval sermons can be confusing to the modern ear. As Taylor explains, "the sources and authorities, overwhelmingly biblical, seem to be heaped together. The sermon is divided and subdivided, often using artificial techniques, and its main parts do not always seem to go together as well as they should."[16] The attitude of many medieval preachers was that Scripture needed to be enhanced, even embellished, in order to draw in the typical listener. Once the Reformers began putting into practice the humanist scholarship that treated texts as sufficient unto themselves, they criticized this rhetorical overkill as an insult to the Word of God. At stake was a new sense of the limits to florid rhetoric, which some scholars have connected to a rising emphasis on direct and to-the-point communication in the personal relations of a business-savvy class of merchants and organized tradesmen who expected nothing less in their relationship to Scripture.

Medieval piety could be expressed in a variety of ways, but one common thread, according to Hughes Oliphant Old, was an increasing apprehension of the Bible as a book full of obscurities. "It more and more became a book of mysteries that could only be solved by mystical contemplation."[17] One could add that as the number of people who were puzzled by the meaning of the Bible grew, preachers tried to make it look familiar by using rhetorical strategies like allegory, humor, and bawdy tales. A difficult biblical doctrine might be explained, for example, through the letters of a saint's name. Such ploys, typical of an oral culture, played to the audience's desire for drama and entertainment. The humanist and Reformation elite complained, but so did medieval preachers themselves, who grew tired of audience expectations. In fact, it was a standard homiletical strategy to criticize the audience for its lack of seriousness.

At the center of the medieval sermon was the piety of imitating Christ. Taylor once again: "The doctrinal shift from Jesus to Paul carried with it enormous implications for the ordinary believer, for the change from an affective piety that embraced the notion of the imitation of Christ to a more intellectualized form of belief and observance led

16. Taylor, *Soldiers of Christ*, 228.

17. Hughes Oliphant Old, *The Reading and Preaching of the Scriptures in the Worship of the Christian Church*, vol. 3, *The Medieval Church* (Grand Rapids: Eerdmans, 1999), xvi. Also see Paul Scott Wilson, *A Concise History of Preaching* (Nashville: Abingdon, 1992).

to physical changes on a grand scale, as representations and imagery gave way to a less materialistic, but more distant and abstract, system of beliefs."[18] Literally imitating Jesus Christ is, of course, difficult to the point of impossibility, but many scholars today downplay the idea that medieval piety placed too many spiritual burdens on believers.[19] If anything, the medieval church tried too hard to make it easy for the faithful. The church established a contractual system of penance that specified remedies for particular sins. People could easily ignore the need for inward transformation.

This brief summary is not meant to cast a spotlight on the particular weakness of medieval preaching. Until the Reformers had the foresight to usurp the educational program of the humanists, the church struggled to produce enough educated priests to keep up with its rapid expansion. This was especially true after the fall of the western part of the Roman Empire, which resulted in a decline in the number of educated clergy, in spite of the heroic effort of the Benedictines to supply enough young men who knew how to speak in public. The barbarians had no culture to replace what they had destroyed. Preachers thus played their most important role in the history of Western culture (up to the Reformation) at just the time when their numbers, as well as the quality of their training, was in decline. Exegesis was made difficult by the fact that almost nobody knew Greek or Hebrew. By necessity, the liturgy, rather than the preacher, became the true interpreter of Scripture, which helps explain why preaching could often be omitted from the worship service altogether.

Indeed, throughout the period immediately preceding the Middle Ages, the liturgical calendar increasingly organized the use of Scripture. Preaching thus became festal, with the Scripture being chosen to correspond to the feast day. The cycle of feasts was itself a form of preaching, a scheme that expounded the substance of Christian doctrine through the turning of the days. The practice was to interpret Scripture in order to explain the significance of the feast. By the fifth century, more and more worship services had a reading of the Scripture without a preaching of the Word. The long-run impact of festal preaching was to integrate and even conflate the lives of the saints with the stories of Scripture. Their legends were read during worship and interpreted in the sermon, blurring the distinction between written and oral tradition that the church had worked so hard to preserve with the closing of the canon. The leveling of the differences between biblical narrative and

18. Taylor, *Soldiers of Christ*, 230.

19. For an exception, see Steven Ozment, *The Reformation in the Cities* (New Haven: Yale University Press, 1975), 22–32.

hagiography made Scripture seem like nothing more than the pious re-
porting of miracles and exemplary lives and contributed to the humanist
quest to separate the biblical text from later encroachments.

After missionary preaching converted and pacified the barbarian
tribes, lectionary preaching became the mainstay of the pulpit. The
lectionary emerged incrementally at the end of the Roman Empire, in
the fifth through seventh centuries. As Old explains, "The lectionary in
many ways was an important aid for preserving a discipline of reading
and preaching Scripture at a time when that surely must have been
difficult, but at the same time it conventionalized Christian preaching
so that for centuries its effect on the Christian world was more formal
than vital."[20] The lectionary was useful because the church was full of
priests who could not compose a well-organized sermon. It organized
the reading of the Bible by demonstrating the relationships that obtain
among the Old Testament, Gospels, and Epistles and reducing books
of the Bible to their essential meaning. The correct Scripture had to
be read on the right day; that was more important than understanding
Scripture in any depth. As Old points out, selection itself is a form of
interpretation, so it diminishes the responsibility of the preacher to reflect on the Bible. As Old concludes, "the tragedy of it all is that as the
lectionary developed, the Church lost interest in the public reading of
Scripture."[21] Public reading became perfunctory. As long as the proper
passage was read, its content did not matter.

It is important to pause and consider the role that Charlemagne
(742–814) played in the codification of Christian worship. His genius was
to recognize that religion had to be the substance of a united European
culture forged among rival barbarian tribes. The regulation of preaching
in the liturgy was thus a political tool for his grand political plans. He
encouraged missionary work, but Christianity spread so quickly that
it was often only poorly understood. In such conditions, there was an
urgent need for catechetical preaching. People needed to be instructed
in the basics of the faith. The enforced usage of the Roman version of
the lectionary was necessary for cultural uniformity. An unintended
consequence of such uniformity, however, was a level of monotony in
preaching. As Old states, "the same sermons had been preached on the
same texts from Advent to Pentecost year after year for several centuries."[22] This trend was exacerbated by the use of homiliaries, sample
sermons that priests with little training could give, often verbatim.

20. Old, *Reading and Preaching of the Scriptures*, 143.
21. Ibid., 168.
22. Ibid., 250.

Charlemagne's reforms did not last long. By the early medieval period, preaching was the bishop's responsibility and not ordinarily expected of the average parish priest. A service without the bishop would be a service without a sermon. The reforms initiated by Cluny replaced preaching with an increasingly sumptuous liturgy, while the Cistercians revived preaching with a more simplified liturgy. In fact, there seems to be a direct correlation between the systematization of the liturgy and the decline of preaching. There was a golden age of preaching from 1125 to 1274, led by Bernard of Clairvaux and spurred in part by the demand for public address created by the Crusades. The revival of preaching was also led by the Franciscans and Dominicans. Francis learned the importance of preaching from the Bible and even was said to preach to the birds. The early Franciscans believed that preachers should practice humility and poverty as evidence of their reliance on grace. The preacher should be a witness to the words he proclaimed, not just a messenger. The Dominicans, who were known as the Order of Preachers, came to prominence in the controversy over the Cathars and the subsequent need for doctrinal clarification in southern France.

As this survey suggests, there are continuities between the medieval and the Reformation sermon. Although the freedom of the Word taken to its logical conclusion entailed if not the dismantling then at least the downplaying of the liturgical calendar, the lectionary did not just disappear. What became popular was the *lectio continua* (preaching on a book in the Bible straight through to the end of that book) as opposed to the *lectio selecta* (the lectionary proper). Lutherans, for example, following Luther's conservative approach to liturgical reform, retained the medieval lectionary for Sunday sermons, but Luther preached the *lectio continua* on weekdays and complained that the lectionary emphasized the moralistic aspects of Christianity. (It is easy to find contradictory assessments of the lectionary in Luther's writings.) The Reformed abandoned the lectionary for the *lectio continua*.

What was really original about Protestant preaching was not that it was exegetical or evangelical, traits that had been part of the gospel proclamation from the earliest centuries. Instead, I would suggest that two interrelated traits set apart Reformation preaching: a certain occasionality (a denseness in its relation to time) and, connected to this, a prophetic or exclamatory tone. First, the occasionality. Once the sermon is deregulated from the church calendar—and once the lectionary loses its hold over preaching—by default the sermon becomes determined by the occasion of its delivery. The Protestant sermon thus comes close to conforming to the nature of its medium, since sound is, as we have seen, intimate but transient. The human voice gathers together an audience, but it does so only for as long as the speech is in play. As Hans Jonas aptly states, "The duration of the sound heard is just the duration of hearing it."[23] The spoken word gains its power from this temporal limitation. We can put away or pick up a book or magazine whenever we want, but a voice beckons here and now, and if we do not listen carefully, then we find ourselves like the movie patron asking our neighbor what the actor said only to be answered with a hush. If we define rhetoric as the art of listening to an audience so that the message can be adapted even while it is being delivered, then the Protestant sermon becomes an example of pure rhetoric to the extent that the preacher trusts in the Holy Spirit for the success of its delivery.

Second, the prophetic tone. Because it is the means by which God extends salvation to those who have the ears to hear, the Protestant sermon is urgent, intense, and passionate. These traits might appear to contradict my contention that the Protestant sermon is "pure rhetoric." After all, the reliance on rhetoric to shape the sermon came into prominence only after the church decided to restrain charismatic prophets, like the Montanists, who spoke "naturally" and spontaneously. This confuses, however, the study of rhetoric, which can be formal and abstract, with the practice of rhetoric, which can range from the nearly formless to the totally prescribed. The Protestant sermon is intimate and personal, which is what I mean by occasional. At the same time, it is provocative and demanding. It both invites and summons. That there is some degree of tension between these two traits is not a problem for Protestant preaching. On the contrary, the Protestant sermon gains much of its power by combining attention to the intimacy of sound with an emphasis on an exclamatory tone. Another way of putting this is to say that the Protestant sermon is too serious to be sophistic but too conversational to become ornate and pretentious. Of course, this balance is possible only because the preacher is echoing a Word that is not her own—a Word that is as magnificent as it is unadorned.

The Printed Voice

The emphasis on the printing press in Reformation historiography has often detracted from the more important role of the pulpit. What this emphasis obscures is the extent to which the Protestant Reformation was a matter of speech, not text. Even the texts of the Reformation period had all the vividness and vigor of the spoken word. True, the Reformers took advantage of the advent of printing to mount an ambitious

23. Hans Jonas, *The Phenomenon of Life: Toward a Philosophical Biology* (New York: Harper & Row, 1966), 137.

program for lay literacy. The publication of countless pamphlets and an enthusiasm for sermons are evidence for the often repeated observation that piety shifted from the visual and sacramental to the verbal and pedagogical. But the printing press did not suddenly change the oral nature of European culture. The rise in literacy rates did not immediately translate into a habitually book-reading public. Although the long-term impact of a print culture would transform the nature of religious tradition by splintering the ties of collective memory, the short-term effect enhanced the spoken word by making sermons and preaching manuals more available than ever before. People still read aloud to each other, but now they had more books to read aloud from. This goes against the thesis popularized by Marshall McLuhan that Gutenberg typography silenced the human voice. Print is subordinated to the image today, but it was still a vehicle of sound in the sixteenth century.

While Walter Ong's defense of oral over written tradition is decidedly shaped by his Roman Catholicism, his reading of the Protestant Reformation is more subtle and nuanced than McLuhan's. Ong admits that the Reformation was, in terms of its location in the history of the senses, complex and confusing. Although he blames the printing press for reducing the power of the spoken word, he rightly argues that Protestants took advantage of this technology to promote preaching. The elevation of the sermon was thus a means of delaying rather than accelerating the shift from an oral to a textual culture. As Ong explains, "in making the text of the Bible more physically accessible by sheer multiplication of copies, print heightened the attention accorded to words themselves by comparison with the attention accorded other elements in the Christian heritage (such as nonverbal symbolism, liturgical gesture, and the like) and thus opened the way to develop further the Christian (and Hebrew) feeling for the power of words, especially of God's word."[24] Until the written word was devocalized in the modern period, printed texts remained conduits of sound.

What the printing press did change, as Ong is perceptive in pointing out, was the nature of theological argument. The printed word fixed religious divisions in immovable ways, hardening different emphases until they became viewed as absolute oppositions. In the most comprehensive and insightful treatment of this topic, Elizabeth Eisenstein suggests that printing reinforced the iconoclastic tendencies of Protestantism by dispensing with the mnemonic use of images. The Protestants were very aware of the argument that images were the books of the illiterate, but they used the second commandment to argue that the illiterate should be

24. Walter J. Ong, *The Presence of the Word: Some Prolegomena for Cultural and Religious History* (1967; reprint, Minneapolis: University of Minnesota Press, 1981), 282.

taught to read rather than be given graven images. Yet even this analysis has its limits, because printing made images more available throughout Europe than ever before, and Protestants and Catholics both exploited this fact by using cartoons and caricatures to criticize each other.

Rather than disputing the relevant roles of print and sermon, it might be useful to think of sound as the category that brings together these means of communication into a single mode. Even in print, the message of the Reformers was urgent, personal, and transformative, so that we can talk about the use of pamphlets to convey a printed voice. Likewise, sermons absorbed much of the seriousness that can be associated with print. As Eisenstein points out, before printing took over the gathering and circulation of the news, sermons had been "coupled with news about local and foreign affairs, real estate transactions, and other mundane matters."[25] Relieved of these pressures, preachers found their voices as their sermons became more theological.

For a while, anyway, printing reinforced the Protestant insistence that truth comes in the form of a voice. At the heart of the Reformation is the recognition that the Word of God is the subject of a speech act that culminates in the act of hearing, rather than a priestly ritual whose climax, for the kneeling congregation, is the elevation of the Host for all to see. This dismantling of the "shared repertoire of symbols, prayers, and beliefs which crossed and bridged even the gulf between the literate and illiterate"[26] could lead to confusion and demagoguery. There is no doubt that Luther ignited a rhetorical explosion, much to his own dismay. There were times when the loudest voices were the most likely to be heard. Nevertheless, the situation was as creative as it was chaotic. Reflecting the humanist impulse to be true to the classical texts, theologians multiplied words in order to do justice to the indivisible (as well as invisible) fecundity of the one true Word of God.

The Protestant recovery of a soundful Word constituted a shift from the visual to the verbal, and the result was a massive critique of the Greek sensorium that ranked the eye above the ear. Every society regulates and manages the senses, but the Reformation was radical in the importance it gave to the perceptual practice of listening. Not until the Enlightenment's "devocalization of the universe,"[27] when a God who speaks came to be seen as an offense to the hegemonic voice of reason, did Protantism experience the profound loss of the centrality of hearing in the life of the faithful. Pietism, rather than being a distor-

25. Elizabeth L. Eisenstein, *The Printing Revolution in Early Modern Europe* (Cambridge: Cambridge University Press, 1983), 93.
26. Duffy, *Stripping of the Altars*, 3.
27. Ong, *Presence of the Word*, 72.

tion of the Reformation, can be interpreted as an attempt to revive the art of religious hearing. Pietistic Christian circles were characterized, as Leigh Eric Schmidt points out, by "the devotional ordinariness of hearing voices, the everyday reverberation of spoken scriptures, and the expectedness of a conversational intimacy with Jesus (as well as angels and demons)."[28] Today evangelical Protestants orchestrate the most vocal attack on the tonelessness of Enlightenment humanism by continuing to privilege the auditory over the ocular.

Nevertheless, just as it is possible to go too far in connecting the Reformation to the printing press, it is also possible to go too far in focusing on the polemical attack against the role of the visual in religious representation. The story of Protestantism, in other words, cannot be told simply in terms of the opposition between the visual and the verbal. Every religious tradition is too complex for that, and recent studies on the role of material objects and images in Protestantism suggest the need for caution when it comes to general historical schemes.[29] Protestantism had great ambitions for social transformation, and visual cues were employed for that purpose. Although iconoclasm was a real danger of the Reformation, the task of the Reformers was not to pluck out the eye but rather to recontextualize the relationship between image and word.

The End of Enthusiasm? An Enthusiastic Crusade against Enthusiasm

The story of the eclipse of sound climaxes with the Enlightenment, although this claim must be nuanced. It is too easy to blame the Enlightenment for every fault in theology, and, to complicate matters, there was no single thing called "the Enlightenment" anyway, since that philosophical movement took different forms and had diverse agendas depending on its national setting.[30] There is a need for geographical specificity in this discussion, and because much of the character of

28. Leigh Eric Schmidt, *Hearing Things: Religion, Illusion, and the American Enlightenment* (Cambridge: Harvard University Press, 2000), vii.

29. See Collen McDannell, *Material Christianity* (New Haven: Yale University Press, 1998). Also see Peter Matheson, *The Imaginative World of the Reformation* (Minneapolis: Fortress, 2001), and David Morgan, *Protestants and Pictures: Religion, Visual Culture, and the Age of American Mass Production* (New York: Oxford University Press, 1999).

30. The American Enlightenment, for example, was significantly different from its European counterpart. See Henry F. May, *The Enlightenment in America* (New York: Oxford University Press, 1976), and J. R. Pole, "Enlightenment and the Politics of American Nature," in *The Enlightenment in National Context*, ed. Roy Porter and Mikulas Teich (Cambridge: Cambridge University Press, 1981).

American religion was shaped by developments in England, that country can serve as a test case for a close look at the actual mechanisms used by a wide range of thinkers to discipline the power of speaking that the Reformation unleashed. To be even more specific, we have to look at the period prior to the Enlightenment to see how the stage was set for the quieting of the Protestant voice.

The distinctiveness of the English Enlightenment can be summarized in one sentence: England had no Voltaire because it had no Jesuits. That is, the established church in England was less powerful than Catholicism in France, so there was less to rebel against. The Enlightenment in England avoided the bitterly anticlerical rhetoric that was common in France, because religious indifference, especially after the Toleration Act of 1689, was greater. Economic prosperity and Lockean empiricism combined to make the marketplace, not revolutionary slogans, the engine of social change.[31] The calmness of the philosophical weather in England was not produced solely by material forces, however. More significant was the rhetorical effort to contain the storms of religious exuberance that were created by the various religious wars of the Reformation period. The English civil wars of the middle part of the seventeenth century had opened the floodgates to religious extremism of every variety. The backlash that ensued led to the restoration of the monarchy in 1660.

The Restoration changed not only the politics but also the culture of England. Conservative forces led a revolt against what was commonly called *enthusiasm*, a catch-all term that the defenders of reason used to denigrate any nonconformist behavior that smacked of irrationality and passion.[32] Enthusiasm was connected not only to religion but also to the arts. The connection between the two is that enthusiasts of either the religious or the poetic variety made claims to be divinely inspired. Enthusiasts spoke a word that originated from within rather than being heard from without. All romantics are enthusiasts in this sense because they believe that inspiration is ultimately a private, soundless affair. Luther, with his ear for the vocal nature of faith, was the first to draw this connection between enthusiasm and the internal word.

31. For a good discussion of the national settings of the Enlightenment, see James M. Byrne, *Religion and the Enlightenment: From Descartes to Kant* (Louisville: Westminster John Knox, 1997), chap. 2.

32. For the best historical survey of this term, see Michael Heyd, *"Be Sober and Reasonable": The Critique of Enthusiasm in the Seventeenth and Early Eighteenth Centuries* (Leiden: E. J. Brill, 1995). He argues that, while enthusiasm was not an easily identified phenomenon, the reaction to it was. Heyd focuses on the religious and scientific, rather than literary and rhetorical, dimensions of enthusiasm and its critics. He argues that it was debates over enthusiasm on the eve of the Enlightenment that led to the increasing reliance on reason as a necessary antidote to the unruly nature of the passions.

All this is the old devil and old serpent who made enthusiasts of Adam and Eve. He led them from the external Word of God to spiritualizing and to their own imagination. . . . In short, enthusiasm clings to Adam and his descendants from the beginning to the end of the world. . . . Accordingly we should and must constantly maintain that God will not deal with us except through his external Word and Sacrament. Whatever is attributed to the Spirit apart from such Word and Sacrament is of the devil.[33]

Enthusiasm is not just bad theology, for Luther; it is also, from the perspective of the established order, bad politics. When the Word is devocalized, religious mischief and poetic extravagance are the results. The boundaries of decent prose, it appears, are not unrelated to the boundaries of reasonable behavior. When the external Word is separated from the institutional church, which authorizes preaching as a communal and not an individual affair, words proliferate and disseminate without any regulation at all. Although Luther himself could shout louder than anyone, he recognized the dangers of mouthing religion outside of the body of Christ. By the middle of the seventeenth century, rhetorical overkill had led to the shedding of much innocent blood. Consequently, there was a swing in the other direction, toward plain speech and objective reasoning. Preachers and poets alike were not to be overcome with passion.

The revolt against enthusiasm was not uniform or systematic, but it was widespread and especially set the tone for English literature and philosophy. It had its foundations in the via media established by Queen Elizabeth, which was not a theological position in itself but a rhetorical strategy meant to stifle the extremes of both Protestantism and Catholicism. Several factors were at work in the return to balance in the seventeenth century. Restorationist literature did not necessarily deny the emotions and the imagination, but it did see them as likely causes of disturbances to the rule of reason. There was a new respect for temperance and suspicion for anything that was, in the words of Francis Bacon, "high flown and forward fancy."[34] There was also a new respect for simplicity in style that reflected a renewed interest in science. Thus Meric Casaubon could write in the first book to be published against enthusiasm in 1655 that "Tertullian had never been an Heretick, had

33. From the Smalcald Articles 3.8, in *Martin Luther's Basic Theological Writings*, ed. Timothy F. Lull (Minneapolis: Fortress, 1989), 530–31. Luther goes on to note that "John the Baptist was not conceived without the preceding word of Gabriel, nor did he leap in his mother's womb until Mary spoke" (532).

34. Quoted in George Williamson, "The Restoration Revolt against Enthusiasm," in *Seventeenth Century Contexts* (London: Faber and Faber, 1960), 221. This essay remains the best analysis of the literary response to enthusiasm.

he been a better Naturalist."[35] Religion was, in the words of one literary critic, "trimmed up with too many Tropicall pigments, and Rhetorical dresses."[36] Too many people were claiming revelations from God; theologians began to argue that preaching should be an acquired, not an inspired, talent.

The problems with enthusiasm, which itself was a caricature of the prophetic and occasional form of Protestant preaching, do not mean that its critics had all the right answers. In fact, the excesses of enthusiasm prepared the way for the excesses of the Enlightenment. More specifically, the critique of enthusiasm served as a bridge between the iconoclasm of the Reformation period and the intensification of iconoclasm in the Enlightenment. In other words, the Enlightenment inherited but also transformed the Protestant battle against superstition and irrationality. The Enlightenment philosophers, however, did not have to undertake the onerous duty of policing religious discourse themselves. Instead, religious insiders who had internalized Enlightenment ideals jumped at the opportunity of regulating religious rhetoric. As Schmidt notes, "while the Enlightenment posed a massive challenge to the revelatory voices and devout hearing of popular piety, the faithful necessarily worked all along on their own ways of delimiting what the ear was allowed to hear."[37] It was important for Christians who wanted to assimilate to the new intellectual regime of moderation and perspicuity to define themselves in opposition to the more preposterous actions of the less liberally educated of their faith.

That Enlightenment philosophers had a strategy of muting excessive sound similar to that of some Protestant groups does not mean they had the same ultimate aim. The Enlightenment philosophers attacked religious exuberance because it did not fit with their idea of the dignity of human nature. Protestants were more interested in the dignity of God. Consequently, their similarities in terms of stylistic preferences for restrained language are superficial. The Puritans are a good example of this crucial difference. The Puritans were trying to find a radically simplified rhetoric that could speak the Word anew, while Enlightenment philosophers tried to subject the Word to a more universal language based on reason, civility, and common sense.

One should not be fooled, then, by the so-called plain style of preaching that the Puritans first practiced and perfected. They rejected the idea that the Word needed human shaping in its presentation based on their confidence in divine, not human, authority. They were thus more

35. Quoted in ibid., 216.
36. Ibid., 209.
37. Schmidt, *Hearing Things*, 72.

in debt to Augustine than to Bacon. Although Augustine had been the regius professor of rhetoric at Milan, he insisted that his own eloquence in the pulpit be subordinated to the *eloquia Dei*. In fact, he had been put off by the unsophisticated style of the New Testament until he came to realize that the sublime can be found in the simple, the perfect in the apparently plain. For Augustine, clarity itself is the highest form of beauty, because beauty takes verbal shape only when words convey the truth. The preacher need not strain after God with a florid array of figures; instead, the discourse of the sermon can be relaxed in the confidence that saying less can say so much more.

The very term *plain style* can be misleading. Puritan preachers were not trained to be insensitive to the needs of their audiences. On the contrary, their efforts to do justice to God's Word encouraged them to sample a wide range of rhetorical strategies. The "metaphysical" preachers of Shakespeare's day were often accused of vain showmanship for their extravagant use of figures of speech, but the Puritans themselves could employ an impressive mix of rhetorical strategies, albeit limiting them to a more direct association with biblical images. Even their disdain for scripted sermons only indicates how much work Puritan ministers put into the thoughtful preparation of their messages, which were far from spontaneous in the sense of being improvised on the spot. This is clear from the title of what is often called the handbook of Protestant plain style preaching, *The Art of Prophesying*, by William Perkins.[38] Perkins calls the sermon premeditated but warns against writing and memorizing it, because that would take away from its natural rhythm and flow. Artifice should be avoided, but not good craftsmanship.

The basic principle of the Puritan sermon was the freedom of the Word of God. The Word of God is its own authority, a principle that precedes and anticipates the postmodern rejection of epistemological foundationalism. Just as postmoderns hold that what we call rationality is one form of speech among many, and that it cannot be justified except in terms of social conventions and practices, Puritans understood that nothing can guarantee the authority of the sermon except the presence of the Holy Spirit. In practical terms, however, they verified that presence by holding the preacher accountable to the faithful explication of Scripture. The result was a rejection of the baroque style of preaching, common in late medieval Catholicism, that highlighted the virtuosity of the speaker. In theory the Puritans also rejected many of the charms and claims of rhetoric. But such preaching remained loyal to one of the firmest of classical rhetorical principles—the idea that the most excellent

38. William Perkins, *The Art of Prophesying*, rev. ed. (Edinburgh: Banner of Truth Trust, 1996). The original Latin edition was published in 1592.

speaking skill is the ability to conceal the speaker's art. The naturalness of the sermon, then, was a carefully crafted aim.[39]

Admittedly, it is hard to hold together a natural speaking voice and an appreciation for the various "tricks" to be learned from the art of rhetoric, but this is what actors do every time they walk onto the stage. The very point of Kristin Linklater's work is to train actors to speak in a natural voice that is nonetheless dramatic. Religious and poetic enthusiasts strained after an elevated tone that sounded overheated and false to those who were wary of prolonged theological debates. Enlightenment thinkers chose to speak instead with the disembodied voice of universal reason.

It is my argument that the Protestant practice of proclamation, with its emphasis on the freedom of the Word and its occasional and prophetic characteristics, can accommodate a variety of speaking styles, and a truly plain style would be one of them. To speak plainly is to be charged with telling the truth in the moment. The plain style puts the emphasis on a natural voice, but it does so with great enthusiasm for the drama of the Word.

---

39. See Hughes Oliphant Old, *The Reading and Preaching of the Scriptures in the Worship of the Christian Church*, vol. 4, *The Age of the Reformation* (Grand Rapids: Eerdmans, 2002).

six

Soundings

Listening for Echoes of the Reformation

What has become of the Reformation emphasis on sound and voice? In this chapter I will focus on the three greatest sixteenth-century Reformers, pairing them with three important modern theologians, one belonging to the twentieth century and two who are carrying their work into the twenty-first. I am not trying to argue that these duets are the only possible arrangements of Reformers and contemporaries. Nor am I claiming that these pairings comprehensively cover the whole field of theology! Instead, I am trying to create some synergy by listening to how theologians of the sixteenth century talked about the speaking and hearing of the Word compared to how theologians talk about the same subject today. In that process I hope to enhance our understanding of both the past and the future of Christian proclamation. The following sections, then, are offered as a theological call and answer, mixing theologians with similar voices in order to hear something new about the sound of God.

Erasmus/Tracy

Erasmus was not a rebel, but if he can be said to have rebelled against anything, it was scholasticism. Scholasticism dominated medieval thought. What made it so cohesive was its style and method rather than its doctrine or philosophy. This might be surprising, because we typically think of the scholastics as being so logical that they did not have much style. We get this stereotype of the arid and rigid scholastics from their books, which are full of abstruse metaphysics and complex logic. The problem is more with us than with them, however, because we do not know how to read these books, which were produced by an educational system for which reading and writing was not the central activity. The scholastic style was essentially oral, more specifically polemical. Scholastic schools had required readings, but for the most part, instead of being read privately by students, these texts were read out loud by licensed masters. These lectures (the Latin *lectio* also meant reading) would include the master's own commentary on the texts, so that reading was not only public but also argumentative.

Scholastic education thus reflected a love for language that was not stifled by their love for metaphysical speculation. As R. J. Schoeck has noted, "there was a tendency to attribute 'reality' to words as not only the symbols but even more as the perfect expression, the veritable translation of things into another mode of existence."[1] Words had a significance for the scholastics that is hard for us to imagine today. Their central pedagogical technique was the oral disputation, which was carefully regulated but vital and lively nonetheless. Only the form, with little of the vitality, ends up in the written documents the scholastics produced, which accounts for our lack of appreciation for their pedagogy. Perhaps the closest students come to this form today is in high school debate programs, which have the same combination of being strictly controlled and passionately intense.

High school debates can become exhausting when they turn into a game where debaters use the rules to try to outsmart each other. Something similar happened with the scholastics. Characteristically, the scholastics used logic to push ideas to their very limit, rather than, as in our day, to unveil the structure of everyday utterances. This zeal represented a pinnacle of intellectual consistency and honesty, but it could also be ruthless and annoying. The rules for disputations were gathered from Aristotle's *Topics*, which was studied in the first year of the university curriculum. By the time Erasmus began his career, there was a weariness of theological debate—especially the unending dispute between realists and nominalists—and a sense that something new was needed. The humanists longed for intellectual exchanges that

---

1. R. J. Schoeck, *Erasmus of Europe: The Making of a Humanist, 1467–1500* (Edinburgh: Edinburgh University Press, 1990), 172. Schoeck is borrowing here from R. W. Southern's idea that medieval thinkers were defenders of a kind of *Sprachlogik*.

would be shaped by a close reading of ancient texts—*ad fontes*, back to the sources, was their hermeneutical rule—rather than obtuse and specialized metaphysical abstractions.

Erasmus, who pokes fun at theologians in his satire *The Praise of Folly*, had nothing but disdain for the scholastic style and method. He prided himself on being a grammarian rather than a theologian, and he shared little with the scholastics except their love for language. *Folly* (to which he gave the title *Moria*) has a conversational tone absent in the scholastics. "Like its author and the humanism he transmitted, the *Moria* is ambiguous, formally complex, and *vocal* in the best sense—that is, poetic."[2] Erasmus's style was literary rather than philosophical—he was a polished writer rather than a debater, although much of his writing retains the qualities of a conversational mode—and his use of humor set him apart from the theologians who raged all around him.

It is one of the ironies of history that just when Erasmus thought he was leading the way beyond the pedantic disputations of theological argument, he would become caught in Christendom's greatest theological controversy, and his own disposition would keep him from understanding the magnitude of the transformation that he helped ignite. He was surpassed by someone who also had no patience for Aristotle, but Luther's zeal for argument—and the polemical, disputatious nature of nearly all his writing—makes him much closer to the scholastics than Erasmus. Erasmus and Luther shared a passion for textual integrity, but the directions they wanted to take restored texts diverged dramatically.

Even though Erasmus was left behind when Luther charged ahead with theological reform, Erasmus never relinquished his position as the leader in the push for classical education based on original texts. His zeal for scholarship did not make him a dry and abstract theologian. Indeed, his contemporaries in the Ciceronian controversy accused him of having an eclectic style that lacked the purity of true imitators of the ancient masters. Erasmus, however, never practiced imitation for its own sake. Rather, his interest was in using Latin models as vehicles for modes of speech that would meet the particular needs of his contemporaries. Nevertheless, while Erasmus is known as one of the greatest scholars of the church, especially for his contributions to the recovery of the Greek New Testament, he is frequently unappreciated

---

2. Thomas O. Sloane, *Donne, Milton, and the End of Humanist Rhetoric* (Berkeley: University of California Press, 1985), 67. Sloane suggests that *Folly* needs to be read out loud to be appreciated fully.

(or downright dismissed) as a creative thinker whose theology can still speak to us today.[3]

Erasmus is the epitome of theological disappointment—the scholar who raised greater hopes than he ever could have fulfilled. To some he was a heretic whose theological ideas, such as they were, have received the fate that they deserve, but not before they opened the door to the splintering of Christendom by undermining confidence in church dogma. To others he appears to be weak and vacillating, unable to fathom the drama in which he played a major role and unwilling to act on the strength of his own convictions. He thus managed to be both too close to and too distant from Luther and was often condemned for being both at the same time! Indeed, comparisons to Luther were rarely to his advantage. Luther's defiance at Worms could only make Erasmus look equivocal, which was reinforced when he chose the hermeneutical strategy of finding both freedom and determinism in the Bible in his argument with Luther over free will. Those who look upon him with favor today often portray him as one of the very first of modern men, someone who stood for the autonomy of the individual and the liberation of freedom of thought from the terrible weight of tradition. The idea that Erasmus was a secret warrior for the forces of secularization seems even less persuasive than the depictions of Erasmus as a theological loser. What all of these portraits miss is how much Erasmus was like Luther and Calvin in the ways he tried to rejuvenate and reform Christianity through a reclaiming of the power of speech.

His project, however, was not born out of an anxiety about speaking the right word. He was a public theologian, in the sense that he wanted to craft the right discourse for the public good, but there is little of personal anguish in his work. Thomas Sloane has brilliantly connected this aspect of Erasmus to his Ciceronian heritage. "Ciceronian man recognizes the battleground but is less convinced that truth lies within or is to be found by exclusively contemplative means. On the contrary, he substitutes for the anguished and intense interiority of Christianity the public quest for probability."[4] Erasmus was never at a loss for words. Indeed, he was a master of what the humanists called *copia*, a free-flowing style, full of an abundance of examples to illustrate any and every point. Speakers fear stopping midsentence, whereas writers do not have to cope with this problem. Speakers assuaged this fear by

3. For a history of the reception of Erasmus, see Bruce Mansfield, *Phoenix of His Age: Interpretations of Erasmus, c. 1550–1750* (Toronto: University of Toronto Press, 1979). I have also drawn from Cornelius Augustijn, *Erasmus: His Life, Works, and Influence*, trans. J. C. Grayson (Toronto: University of Toronto Press, 1991).

4. Sloane, *Donne, Milton*, 128.

cultivating commonplaces, adages, proverbs, or apothegms that could be easily introduced into the flow of a speech. These were the speaker's stock in trade, and Erasmus spent a lot of time and energy collecting and publishing such sayings. By publishing them, of course, Erasmus was changing their original intent; he stood between the oral culture of the Middle Ages and modernity's emphasis on the written word.

Erasmus's discovery of speech as the central category of theology would be better understood and thus more celebrated today if it were not for our misunderstanding of his concentration on philology. In fact, Erasmus was more fascinated with language as such than either Luther or Calvin. In an almost postmodern vein, he showed no trace of anxiety over the plasticity of language and the instability of its referential power. He made the most of this fascination by using grammatical erudition, in the form of a disciplined service to the text, to replace the unrestrained ambitions of the scholastics with a more modest pursuit of knowledge. His linguistic researches, which favored cutting through centuries of commentaries to a new beginning in thinking about the Bible, thus constituted an indirect attack on the established order.

This is far removed from the modern notion of grammar as the analysis of the formal properties of sentences, especially the relationship between meaning and syntax. Erasmus follows the traditional understanding of grammar as the analysis of writing that complements the rhetorical analysis of speech. For Erasmus, learning grammar requires an immersion in the best classical authors that leads, necessarily, to correct speaking and moral development. Rhetoric was thus an alternative to philosophy. It provided the skills of creating "voice on paper."[5] The result was a subtle but daring assault on philosophy, in which exegesis replaces the role that logic played for the scholastics.

Because Erasmus worked in the humanistic tradition that laid down a smooth set of transitions from the narrow work of the scholar to the wider responsibilities of the public intellectual, he was one of those blessed theologians whose religious piety found a perfect expression in his rhetorical practice. Indeed, he had a refined sense of the propriety and decorum he considered appropriate to the distinctive subject matter of God.[6] Moderation for Erasmus was not only a hermeneutical

5. Ibid., 87.
6. See Marjorie O'Rourke Boyle, "Rhetorical Theology: Charity Seeking Charity," in *Rhetorical Invention and Religious Inquiry* (New Haven: Yale University Press, 2000). Boyle argues that the dialectic of the scholastics found its completion in faith, while the rhetoric of the humanists leads to charity. She also connects rhetorical theology to the hyperbolic style of the mystics, and she makes the fascinating argument that the mystics, rather than violating the conventions of propriety, extend those conventions to God. The proper way of talking about God just is hyperbolic. Since the love of God is boundless, our love for God

virtue but also a way of life, and this practice of hermeneutical charity made him a target of both sides of the religious factions of the sixteenth century.[7]

Rhetoric was more than a means of communicating the faith for Erasmus; it was also a lens through which the whole arc of God's activity could be viewed. Christ is the speech of God, accommodated to our needs, and the theologian is foremost a rhetor, inspiring others to listen anew to the divine words of a God who stoops to speak. As with moderation, Erasmus raises imitation, which is the guiding principle of rhetoric, to a higher, theological power in the *imitatio Christi*. In fact, the imitation of Christ enables the Christian to affirm life from a peaceful center that is accommodating and hospitable, and thus imitation and moderation reinforce each other. Rhetorical theology seeks the forbearance of charity more than the judgment of understanding. Marjorie O'Rourke Boyle might go too far in indicting alternative theological methods: "The rejection of rhetoric as the proper theological method betrays a servile fear, the fear of punishment, of damnation, that error and sin provoke."[8] But she does help explain why Erasmus was free to play the fool in his satirical works. He did not seek the dialectical certitude of the scholastics, wherein, he thought, true folly was to be found.

Boyle, the most historically grounded rhetorical theologian writing today, has been able to show how Erasmus's understanding of language informs his understanding of theology by focusing on his critical edition of the New Testament.[9] The Novum Instrumentum was meant to be an improvement on the Latin of Jerome by a more thorough investigation of the Greek texts. Many theologians, however, thought that the Vulgate, which had provided the language for church councils as well as the liturgy, was sacred script. The ensuing contro-

---

should be likewise. "This exaggeration of language is evident in the mystical predilection for hyperbole and exclamation and for the imagery of eroticism and intoxication, as in the commentaries on the Song of Songs" (92).

7. See Manfred Hoffman, *Rhetoric and Theology* (Toronto: University of Toronto Press, 1994).

8. Boyle, "Rhetorical Theology," 92. She uses the phrase "servile fear" in the sense of a medieval ascent to God from fear to love and associates the fear of error with a need for certitude and thus a theological predilection for logic over grammar, an association she especially finds in Luther.

9. Marjorie O'Rourke Boyle, *Erasmus on Language and Method in Theology* (Toronto: University of Toronto Press, 1977). This brilliant book is one of the best treatments of the general theme of rhetoric and theology. For a historical overview of religion and rhetoric that reveals Boyle's constructive theological position, see her entry, "Religion," in *Encyclopedia of Rhetoric*, ed. Thomas O. Sloane (New York: Oxford University Press, 2001), 662–72. I have benefitted not only from reading Boyle but also from generous private correspondence with her.

versy settled on a single word. Erasmus had altered the opening of
the Gospel of John from "In principio erat verbum" to "In principio
erat sermo." Boyle brilliantly shows how this single alteration—he
made many others—demonstrates the genius of his thought. I would
only add that it also shows his limitations. Erasmus knew that he was
within his rights because the change was correct grammar, but he also
knew that he was making a theological statement. The Greek noun
logos can signify several different words in Latin. The advantage of
translating it as *verbum* (which means word) is *verbum*'s specificity,
because it denotes the singularity of the revelation of Jesus Christ.
For Erasmus, however, that specificity is a shortcoming. The Logos
suggests to Erasmus that the Son is the speech of the Father, not just
a single word that the Father utters. Erasmus is on good theological
grounds here, because the Logos says everything that God wants to
communicate. The Logos is, to use rhetorical terminology, the copious discourse of the Father, and thus Erasmus translates it as *sermo*,
or speech. The Word is not just a word but the entire grammar that
organizes our speech about God. Indeed, God is eloquent, which means
that God says just enough—and in the right way—to persuade us to
the divine truth.

The choice of *sermo* over *verbum* marked a significant departure from
the Augustinian tradition that had dominated the theology of language
up to that point. For Augustine, as we have seen, the Word that God
speaks is heard internally before we give it an external voice. Augustine
works by analogy: Just as God does not need sound to speak, we think
silently before putting our thoughts into words (although, of course,
we have a hard time putting our thoughts into words, which God does
not). Consequently faith, like thought, begins in the interior recesses
of the heart, where it is silent before it makes sound. If Augustine
was drawn to this theory of language because of his own misgivings
about the temptations of rhetorical verbosity—he came to prefer the
one word over the many—Erasmus had no such reservations. Indeed,
Erasmus would have translated *logos* with *oratio*, but this is a feminine
Latin noun, and thus Erasmus thought it would be incongruous. (For
Erasmus, theology should never go against propriety.) Nevertheless,
oratio is what he thought *logos* meant. Jesus Christ is the speech of
God, not the pronouncement of a single word. And like Augustine,
Erasmus works with an analogy between God's speech and our own.
Just as the Logos is the Son enfleshed in language, we too come to
know ourselves—and God—in actual words, not just silent thought.
Erasmus acknowledges that God's speech transcends our own, but he
insists that the Father is made known through the words of the Son,

just as vocalization is the means by which we know ourselves as well as each other.

Christ is not only God's oration but also an orator himself. This should not be taken, as it often is, to mean that Erasmus portrays Christ as a mere teacher. Christ is the perfect speech of God; for Erasmus there can be no higher compliment. Nonetheless, this does not go high enough for most orthodox theologians. Because he portrays Christ as the discourse of God, rather than God's singular Word, Erasmus opened himself to the charge that he locates revelation in Jesus' teachings and not the incarnation proper. What Erasmus really opened up was the possibility of a radical rethinking of the Trinity. As Boyle points out, medieval theology articulated the sufficiency of Christ by the formula of the *verbum abbreviatum*. The single Word of the Son was sufficient to reveal the will of the Father. The prophets had to speak copiously about God, but the superiority of the New Testament is in the brevity of its Word. Christ is the concentrated, not the copious, Word of God. Erasmus takes the risk of identifying Christ with the entire range of the sound of God and not just a timeless pronouncement. This is a risk because the portrait of God as eloquent can make God appear to be polymorphous rather than triune. Erasmus did not have the conceptual tools he needed to elaborate on precisely how God is self-constituted by the divine conversation, so that it is in speaking, and not just in a once-and-for-all word, that God is triune. I will take Erasmus's insight further in the next chapter.

Along with trinitarian problems, there is something of hubris in Erasmus's alteration of the Vulgate. By saying that the Logos is eloquent speech, Erasmus falls into the very temptation that Augustine sought to avoid. This is not to say that Augustine's devocalization of the Word is better theology. Erasmus's mistake is in subordinating the rhetoric of the Word to classical standards. As a good humanist, he insisted that style is a matter of imitating the masters, and he incorporated this same point into his theology of language. The result is that he portrays the divine condescension as a means of encouraging our own rhetorical sophistication. God became eloquent oration in order to enable us to speak with the same grace. This gave Erasmus too much confidence in language. Because Erasmus believed that God saves us through language, he also believed that theologians should be able to reconcile their differences—and in the process, save Christendom—through Christlike speech. The study of rhetoric had, after all, civilized the Greeks and the Romans. This was the greatest sin of the scholastics, whose disputations he called *logomachias*, that is, contending against the Logos. Boyle gives away the game with a revealing quote from his *Apologia* to the Novum Instrumentum. Erasmus says that God "hates proud eloquence, I allow; but much more, the supercilious and arrogant inability to speak."[10] In fact, for Erasmus, God loves eloquence, which has the power, when properly articulated by the grammarian, to save the world.

To be fair to Erasmus, his form of pride was subtle. He was ordinarily not given to outlandish claims on his own behalf, because that would have been a violation of the classical decorum he so admired. His muted pride in his own eloquence is thus of one piece with his inability to appreciate excessive elements in religious language and life alike. As one scholar has written, "Erasmian piety is marked by optimism and a certain superficiality. It is a piety of the lowlands rather than of the mountains, intimate rather than passionate."[11] Nowhere is Erasmus's piety more evident than in his understanding of freedom. Freedom, for Erasmus, includes the largesse of charity but should be disciplined by a strong sense of authority, just as the art of rhetoric must be practiced within the confines of the imitation of nature and a close attention to classical texts. Indeed, his natural skepticism reinforced his defense of authority, rather than the reverse, because without a philosophical basis upon which to decide theological disputes, church hierarchy had to be given its due.

Erasmus's view of freedom was complex, and for that very reason it was bound to lead to misunderstandings with Luther, who valued clarity over complexity. Boyle has argued that their debate over the will was a clash of genre as much as theology. Erasmus did not want to define freedom but rather set about juxtaposing the various options that circumscribed the debate. He wrote in the tradition of skepticism, seeking the most probable solution to the conundrum but denouncing nothing and inquiring into everything. Boyle insists, "The calculation of probability was no evasion of the truth, as Luther would charge, but rather the kind of decision Erasmus considered appropriate in disputed questions."[12] Of course, the first rule of rhetoric is to know one's audience, and in this case Erasmus's pursuit of consensus blinded him to the needs of a church in crisis.

Freedom was not the only topic that was to separate Erasmus from Luther.[13] Erasmus was fond of using the figure of the circle to depict

10. Quoted in Boyle, *Erasmus on Language and Method*, 57.

11. Cornelis Augustijn, *Erasmus: His Life, Works, and Influence*, trans. J. C. Grayson (Toronto: University of Toronto Press, 1991), 200.

12. Marjorie O'Rourke Boyle, "Erasmus and the Modern Question: Was He Semi-Pelagian," *Archive für Reformationsgeschichte* 75 (1984): 76.

13. See Marjorie O'Rourke Boyle, *Rhetoric and Reform: Erasmus' Civil Dispute with Luther* (Cambridge: Harvard University Press, 1983). Also see her splendid essay "The Chimera and the Spirit: Luther's Grammar of the Will," in *The Martin Luther Quincentennial*, ed. Gerhard Dünnhaupt (Detroit: Wayne State University Press, 1985), 17–31.

the perfect harmony of Christ. Christ reconciles all the quandaries of existence, and it was Erasmus's attempt to convey this spirit of reconciliation to his contemporaries that set him apart from Luther's more confrontational style. Indeed, Erasmus continues to be a hero to all those who fear the ideological repercussions that follow the blazing trails of excessive figures who define faith in singular terms.

This is not to say that Erasmus was always temperate and judicious in his arguments. His polemical attacks could betray the moderation that was at the heart of the classical virtues. His customary practice was to be affable in the pursuit of persuasion over accusation, but he could also be relentless in wielding irony against ecclesial abuses. Nonetheless, his irony was stable rather than unstable. His classicism led him to season his polemic with just the right amount of forbearance and restraint. When his elegance was translated into political activity, a certain gradualism, even a conservativism, was the result. Although Luther was politically conservative in his own way, the public performances of their social criticisms could hardly have been more different. Luther's rhetoric was as unstable as Erasmus's was stable, and Luther's prophetic prose led to a very different theological, if not political, reaction to the failures of church authority.

Near the end of his life, in 1525, Erasmus composed a remarkable homage to his lifelong love for language, *Lingua* (The Tongue).[14] He was not happy with the course of events in Europe and felt persecuted by all sides. From his vantage point of sophistication and moderation, Europe had descended into barbarism, with theologians leading the way. *The Tongue* is in the tradition of monastic meditations on the sins of excessive and inappropriate talking, and Erasmus must have longed for the quiet of the cloister after having fought so many theological battles to no avail. In this book he turns his literary skills against the very verbosity that is his own weakness. In fact, this text is not a successful piece of rhetoric. It is brooding, rambling, and uneven, and worst of all it is pedantic, with too much display of his classical learning. This is ironic, because the pagans tended to glorify the tongue, while this work overflows with its condemnation. It barely masks the bitterness of a scholar who has been scorned by the object of his devotion, revealing the extent of Erasmus's disappointment.

Although Erasmus suggests in this work that the tongue can both poison and heal, it is its destructive power that receives most of his attention. Indeed, he considers the unbridled tongue to be the worst disease

14. Erasmus, *The Tongue,* trans. Elaine Fantham, in vol. 29 of *Collected Works of Erasmus,* ed. Elaine Fantham and Erika Rummel (Toronto: University of Toronto Press, 1989). This is the first English translation of this text.

of the mind. He castigates the religious and political authorities for not doing enough to control the frenzy of public speech that is threatening social order. He even admits that he need not address himself to women, "who commonly are reproached on this score" (264), because they seem subdued compared to the unrestrained bickering of theologians. It is not just the Protestants that he is protesting. Against the false modesty of the monks he writes, "Their belly rumbles from hunger, but their tongue is tipsy. They abstain from consuming flesh, but at the same time do not hesitate to gnaw the flesh of their neighbor. They restrain their teeth from biting on animals, but they plunge a serpent's fang into their neighbor. They spare cows and sheep, and do not spare their brother, for whom Christ died" (358). With words like this, it is easy to see how the Christian ideal of remembering the sacrifice of Christ by a vegetarian diet came to stand for the height of hypocrisy and eventually faded away in history.

In contrast to such petty grumbling, Erasmus longs for a more classical approach to rhetoric: "Pleasant speech, shrewd and serious, flowing when the occasion demands it but brief and concise when necessary, can win a man great distinction if it is adapted to the subject, circumstances, and persons involved" (271). At times Erasmus speaks eschatologically of the spirit's new tongue, utterly different from the tongue of the flesh (371), but he always returns to more practical matters. He wants an economy of speech that would reflect an honest commerce among persons. A bit wistfully, he suggests that God has given us speech "to make the relations of men more pleasant" (277). What the present situation lacks is a sense of the mean in all matters, but especially speech. A relentless loquacity—to be distinguished from the serene mastery of a copious style—stirred up by Luther clearly frightens Erasmus. Just as the Jews, he writes, have an uncircumcised heart, too many Christians have an uncircumcised tongue (405).

To detect excessive speech, nature has given us visible signs, such as stuttering, stammering, and lisping (381). Stammering, in fact, is one of Erasmus's favorite charges against the scholastics, whose logical obfuscations kept them from speaking eloquently. Referring to Matthew 6:7, Erasmus observes that "the Lord condemns stammering even in prayer" (409). Indeed, Jesus "sometimes answered the unspoken thoughts of the Pharisees before they could reveal their intentions" (384). Such clarity, swiftness, and confidence in speech are what Erasmus considers to be the work of the Holy Spirit, although he also praises the prudence of the speaker who feels "great anxiety in case he should say anything improperly through lack of great care" (387). Stage fright—"the most eloquent men were barely willing to rise and speak and were nervous at the opening of their speech"—helps to distinguish between true and false confidence.

Only at the very end of this treatise does Erasmus begin drawing from the Bible to speak more positively about the tongue. He appeals to the example of Christ, who said we must render an account of every idle word we have said at the day of judgment. His final appeal is to the succinctness of God. "Now as God speaks most seldom and most briefly, so he speaks a truth both absolute and powerful" (323). God gave birth to the Word through speech and created the world through the Word, and God spoke through the prophets and the Son. That is a lot of speaking, but God does not speak in an unseemly manner. As if in apology for his decision to translate *logos* as *sermo*, Erasmus argues that the Son is a modest expression of the Father's wishes (405–6). Erasmus bows to tradition in accepting that Jesus is the Word, not a multitude of words. He adds that the perfect relationship between the Son and the Father should serve as an inspiration to us to make our own tongue obedient to our heart (315). God, Erasmus seems to be saying, does not waste any words, speaking only when there is need. Indeed, the genius of Christianity is that it eliminates "the infinite talkativeness of forms and rituals," since the Gospels reveal the truth so simply (323).

Erasmus's exaggerated attack against human speech was meant to be part of a larger work attending to the study of preaching, a counterpart to the fourth book of Augustine's *De doctrina christiana*. Erasmus began this book, *Ecclesiastes sive de ratione concionandi*, in 1523 and finished it just before his death.[15] This book, which appeared the same year as the first edition of Calvin's *Institutes*, is neither polemic nor commentary, and thus it is one of Erasmus's most theological treatises. Although Erasmus himself never preached, he defended the dignity and importance of the preacher, calling Christ the *Sermo Dei*. His primary concern in this book, however, is to provide preachers with the hermeneutical tools necessary for interpreting the Bible. He also offers an outline of sermon topics. The purpose of the preacher is to establish peace in the heart of the listener through reflecting on the philosophy of Christ, just as the magistrate establishes peace in the commonwealth.

Erasmus's emphasis on peace is surely commendable, given the passions that were then building to a breaking point. Perhaps only someone who did not believe that the fall had ruined language could have been a pacifist in such a tumultuous period. Nonetheless, by correlating the peace of Christ with the harmony of the established order, he attenuated

15. My account of this text is shaped by Robert G. Kleinhans, "Ecclesiastes sive de Ratione Concionandi," in *Essays on the Works of Erasmus*, ed. Richard L. DeMolen (New Haven: Yale University Press, 1978), 253–66.

the transformative power of the sermon. Indeed, he advises preachers to focus on the law of God and the virtues of Christ. The word of the sermon, as well as the Word of God, is primarily an intelligible communication that can be grasped by the mind and enacted by the heart. It is typical of Erasmus to think not only that preachers should be scholars/educators but that a textbook in homiletics could significantly contribute to church reform. Although he clearly shares with the Protestants a desire to reform preaching, it would have been hard for Erasmus to have gone further out of his way to sidestep the Reformation doctrine of justification by faith alone.

Perhaps the closest theologian we have to Erasmus today is the Roman Catholic scholar David Tracy.[16] He has the intellectual range of this Renaissance figure (which is remarkable given the greater complexity of academic disciplines today), and he also displays something of Erasmus's grammatical genius in his capacity to understand the intricate relations among theological and philosophical positions. Moreover, he shares Erasmus's insistence that grammatical rigor need not be separated from the high standards of eloquence.

While it is true that Tracy's early work in *Blessed Rage for Order* on the transcendental foundation for the recovery and regulation of religious language is not dissimilar to the scholastic metaphysics of the sixteenth century, in reality he is in basic agreement with Erasmus's nuanced attitude toward both the possibility and the limitations of our knowledge of God. Tracy never tires of exploring the various paths theologians have constructed toward understanding God, yet he is sensitive to the basic human limits that make faith extend beyond what the mind alone can grasp. His representational Christology is a good example of how he uses philosophy to make the case for Christ and yet portrays Christ as offering us more than philosophy will ever know. Christ represents the innermost possibilities for good that are the evidence of God's grace, yet the idea of Christ is beyond what we could reasonably hope to expect. This is not very far from Erasmus's *philosophia Christi,* which is frequently caricatured as a merely moral portrait of redemption. For Erasmus and Tracy alike, Christ evokes the truth in an aesthetic appeal to our imagination, drawing together the good, the beautiful, and the true in a way that is superior to every (other) philosophical system.

There are also significant differences between these two that make their similarities all the more interesting. Most fundamentally, Tracy is a modern-day Erasmus who has crossed over the postmodern divide. Like Erasmus, Tracy is the premier rhetorical theologian of his age, but

16. See Stephen H. Webb, *Taking Religion to School: Christian Theology and Secular Education* (Grand Rapids: Brazos, 2000), 40–41.

Tracy plays the leading role in the revival of rhetorical theology today precisely because he is sensitive to the ways in which religious language must be fragmented, twisted, and stretched in order to do justice to God. He is postmodern in that he treats every act of interpretation as an occasion for ambiguity and pluralism; language is opaque, while meaning is never stable. Tracy's rhetorical theology has a large dose of Luther's exuberance and intensity, as Tracy's recent fascination with Luther's notion of the hidden God demonstrates.[17] Dialectic and paradox heighten the tension of his prose. It is as if Erasmus and Luther could have found common ground after all.

Nevertheless, for all his postmodern proclivities, Tracy still cherishes the category of conversation—an updated version of Erasmus's criterion of consensus—over any other mode of communication, and thus he is prone to a moderate and charitable tone in all that he writes. He is always careful to appropriate figures of religious excess in a deliberate and cautious manner, ever seeking to reconcile positions that are traditionally opposed, so that his analogical imagination is much closer to Erasmus's wide-ranging humanism than to Luther's prophetic hyperbole. This attempt to be fair to everyone, coupled with his privileging of rhetoric over ethics, accounts for Tracy's benign relationship to Rome. Like Erasmus, he represents a liberal or progressive Catholicism, yet he is even more cautious than Erasmus in avoiding direct battles with church authorities. Instead, he tries to show what an open and pluralistic theology might look like—just as Erasmus envisioned a revival of classical culture imbued with Christian aims—if it were to be embodied in the full dress of Roman liturgy and tradition. As for Protestantism, he shares with Erasmus a polite lack of interest in evangelical forms of faith.

Tracy is justly known for his analogical imagination, the title of his greatest work in constructive theology. In that book, he defines revelation in general terms as a paradigmatic representation of the whole of reality that has the character of an event. Such representations occur when human existence is confronted by basic limit situations that render our ordinary means for coping useless and irrelevant. Religious symbols thus refer not to generic experiences but to an intensification of the particular, where the general wisdom of the day breaks down. At this point in his analysis, Tracy makes a distinction between two terms that are crucial for understanding his "analogical imagination."

17. Lois Malcom, "The Impossible God: An Interview with David Tracy," *Christian Century*, February 13–20, 2002, 24–30. Indeed, Tracy's radicalization of the ambiguities inherent in language tends to undercut the confidence of his analogical imagination and thus parallels Erasmus's turn, at the end of his career, to a more pessimistic view of language.

Manifestation (his term for sacrament) is what he calls the disclosure in which we experience a radical sense of participation in reality as a whole (or God). *Proclamation* (his term for the Protestant emphasis on preaching) is the same experience dominated by a radical sense of nonparticipation. Although Tracy weaves the two together in nuanced recognition of their dialectical interplay, his connection of proclamation to distancing downplays the way sound can be the source of an intimate and unifying experience even more than sight.

By defining proclamation in terms of distancing, Tracy is able to mix praise and criticism of Protestant theology. Proclamation enables us to see the profane as the field of faithful action. While manifestation blurs boundaries and overwhelms separate identities, proclamation insists on personal responsibility and social justice. Indeed, Tracy goes on to identify manifestation with the mystical and proclamation with the prophetic. The paradigm of manifestation is visually oriented, so that the sacred illuminates all of nature. The paradigm of proclamation, by contrast, leads to a disenchantment of nature and thus an appreciation of history as the realm of God's agency. So conceived, the dialectic between the two is uneven. In a sleight of hand, Tracy assigns the intimacy of speech to manifestation and the power of silence to proclamation. By dividing the power of speech in this way, he is able to argue that proclamation is dependent on manifestation. "Whenever any Christian word loses its roots in real manifestation, it can continue for a time—even for a long time—to live by the power of the Word. Yet an exclusively word-centered Christianity is always in danger of becoming either fanatical or, more likely today, arid, cerebral and abstract."[18] To be an effective means of divine communication, the spoken word must be firmly rooted in symbolic (and therefore preverbal) representations of the divine.

All of this is another way of saying that Tracy's analogical imagination does not do justice to the vocal dimension of the Word. An analogical imagination envisions reality as essentially connected, whole, and one. Tracy is overly influenced in this regard by Mircea Eliade, with his doctrine of the *coincidentia oppositorum* and his belief that all religious symbols return us to an immediate participation in the sacred over the profane.[19] Eliade defines the sacred in terms of space rather than time—history erodes the memory of sacred places—which indicates, given my argument about the connection of sound and time, a thoroughgoing preference for sight over sound. Tracy too thinks pri-

18. David Tracy, *The Analogical Imagination: Christian Theology and the Culture of Pluralism* (New York: Crossroad, 1981), 214.

19. Mircea Eliade, *The Sacred and the Profane* (New York: Harvest, 1968).

marily in terms of vision over speech and seeing over hearing.[20] His remarkable ability to plot the coordinates for every theological strategy is evidence of a panoramic aesthetics that can survey the broadest intellectual terrain. It is also evidence of a profoundly eucharistic imagination: Tracy can make analogical judgments about the various ways in which we relate to God because he believes that words are meaningful to the extent that they disclose the presence (or, better, both presence and absence) of God in all things. At its best, this makes Tracy's theology genuinely, even radically, ecumenical. The danger is that analogy is, in the end, a serene and untroubled aesthetic. Tracy's analogical imagination surveys the scene of religion from a single, all-encompassing perspective. No matter how sweeping our vision is, however, something is always left out. Tracy is as blind to the rapidly spreading evangelical rhetoric of our day as Erasmus was to the similar rhetoric of his time. In both cases, one has the sense that the most powerful theological mind of their time is limited not by a narrow vision but by one that is too broad.

Luther/Niebuhr

There is nothing polite about Luther. In contrast to the refined Erasmus, Luther did not hesitate to use gross language when he was dealing with perceived threats to the gospel. His polemical style demonstrates the degree to which he was an essentially oral thinker. In his defense, it should be said that while some readers thought him uncouth and even un-Christian, he thought he was simply employing the most appropriate metaphors and images for the task at hand. And in contrast to Tracy, who never abandoned the training in Thomistic rigor that he received from the great Canadian theologian Bernard Lonergan, Luther spent his life vehemently rejecting his own early immersion in Aristotelian logic. The university he attended in Erfurt at one point required twenty-two books for the B.A. examination, seventeen of which were on logic and none on rhetoric. What he did pick up from his study of nominalism was a mistrust of metaphysics. The nominalist objection to universal terms left him with a lingering suspicion of the tendency of rationality to overstep its bounds.

20. Tracy's *Analogical Imagination* was conceived as the hermeneutical sequel to the transcendental argument of *Blessed Rage for Order,* to be followed by a practical theology. Tracy's lack of a third volume in this projected trilogy—an ethics—is indicative of the theoretical (theory=sight) nature of his rhetoric.

Luther's overwhelming convictions about the true source of God's grace instilled in him an accusatory spirit that would brook no disagreements. He was especially intolerant of anyone who lacked his brilliant sense of doctrinal clarity, which put him on a path of unresolvable opposition to Erasmus's sensitivity to the distinction between the certain and the merely probable. Indeed, Luther's cunning criticisms have succeeded to this day in portraying Erasmus as a superficial and uninspiring theologian. In Luther's mind, Erasmus's concern for consensus and moderation proved that he was hardly a theologian at all. He thought Erasmus was a mere rhetorician, one who trusted in human words to do the work of God rather than one who was grasped by the one true Word that can only be proclaimed.

And proclaim Luther did, although it should be no surprise that, judged by the standards of classical rhetoric, he was hardly eloquent. As Hughes Oliphant Old points out, Luther "made no attempt to be a great orator."[21] His God was less patient and reasonable than Erasmus's, and so was his rhetoric. He put his trust in the natural language of the people rather than the examples of the Greek and Latin classics. In his *Table Talk*, Luther described speech as "a great and divine gift. It's with words and not with might that wisdom rules men." "To think," says Luther, "that Satan, that proud spirit, may be put to flight and thrown into confusion by such a frail word on human lips!" It is clear that Luther equates the power of speaking with the power of faith, but his reading of aphonia is highly gendered. He was a product of his time in thinking that the faith of women should be expressed in other ways. "Eloquence in women shouldn't be praised; it's more fitting for them to lisp and stammer."[22] Stammering, for Luther, demonstrates a feminine piety that is humble and quiet, whereas preaching—and cursing Satan—represents the highest pitch of male vocal power.

Like Erasmus, but in a less systematic fashion, Luther developed a theology of language to convey his theology of the Word. All of his theology was, in a way, a reflection on the mystery that salvation comes through the proclamation of the gospel. Preaching is not merely preparation for worship; it is worship. Consequently, all preaching is evangelistic. Luther had a favorite dictum that wherever there is public worship there should be preaching—a radical claim for his day. For Luther, a priest might be more but should not be less than a preacher.

---

21. Hughes Oliphant Old, *The Reading and Preaching of the Scriptures in the Worship of the Christian Church*, vol. 4, *The Age of the Reformation* (Grand Rapids: Eerdmans, 2002), 5.

22. Martin Luther, *Luther's Works*, ed. and trans. Theodore G. Tappert, vol. 54, *Table Talk* (Philadelphia: Fortress, 1967), 317–18.

"He who does not preach the Word, although called by the church for this very thing, is certainly no priest."[23] All of the sacraments, especially baptism, Communion, and intercession, are forms of proclamation.[24] Proclamation is just what Christians do, so in a way it characterizes every Christian activity.

When it came to the Eucharist, Luther insisted on the "real presence" of Christ in the elements, even as he argued that the words of institution ("This is my body," 1 Cor. 11:24–25) are the instruments of Christ's presence. He was afraid that, if the Lord's Supper were turned into a memorial meal, Christian worship would be all talk. If Jesus is the speech of God, then his words are absolutely trustworthy. He accomplishes what he says, which suggests that the words he used to institute the Lord's Supper must be more than metaphorical. Luther's theology of sound thus led him to a basic agreement with Catholic tradition that in the sharing of this food Christ is truly present. This basic agreement kept Luther from supporting any radical liturgical innovations, although he did propose the abolition of daily full Masses in favor of Scripture readings, sermons, prayers, and hymns. He also criticized the sacrificial

---

23. Quoted in Brian A. Gerrish, *The Old Protestantism and the New: Essays on the Reformation Heritage* (Chicago: University of Chicago Press, 1982), 97.

24. Just as a Mass without a sermon was a distortion of the role of the Word in medieval theology, a sermon without the Eucharist is a common distortion of the Word in many Protestant churches today. Christ gives us two primary gifts to continue his presence after his ascension: his body in the Eucharist and his voice in the sermon. We can touch, taste, smell, and see Jesus in the elements, but we hear him in the preaching of the Word. If the Word is the voice of Christ and the Eucharist is Christ's body, then proclamation should be accompanied by Communion, just as a wordless Communion would be meaningless. Proclamation finds its completion in the consumption of the elements, which demonstrates that the words of revelation are made effective by the Spirit when they enter our mouths. Communion consists of the tactile and visual signs that make it clear that the words of the sermon are not only audible. The Eucharist is thus, among other things, a reminder that the Word is never *asarkos*, that is, without flesh, just as it is the destiny of all flesh to enjoy the sound of God forever. The elements are mute, however, unless we give them a voice. After all, the Eucharistic liturgy is given to us in Scripture; we know what to do only because Jesus told us. The sacrament thus requires preaching to beget faith; the mumbling of a formula accomplishes nothing (*Institutes* 4.14.3). This is why Paul conceptualizes the Lord's Supper as a form of proclamation (1. Cor. 11:26; 2:1; 9:14, Phil. 1:17-18; Rom. 1:8). Christ's body is on the table, but his voice is in the minister. If proclamation and sacrament are intertwined, then they should occur together in the context of worship. The logic of the Reformers, even if not their actual practices and their heritage, calls for a weekly Communion. Calvin favored weekly Communion, although his 1541 proposal for monthly Communion was rejected by the Genevan Council in favor of a quarterly celebration. Even though it did not practice a weekly Communion, the Reformed tradition gave birth to a very strong sense of the power of Communion. This is probably due to the emphasis the Reformed put on the verbal nature of the event, turning it from a passive time for meditation to a time for celebration and evangelization.

interpretation of the Mass, because it placed too much power in the hands of the priests.

Luther never published a blueprint for a distinctively Lutheran rite. In one of his brief writings on the topic, from 1523, he lamented the silencing of the Word by reading and singing in churches and explains that as a result "a host of un-Christian fables and lies, in legends, hymns, and sermons were introduced that it is horrible to see." He was direct in how to reform the Mass: "Let everything be done so that the Word may have free course instead of the prattling and rattling that has been the rule up to now."[25] Of course, Luther could be guilty of his own verbosity, and he never carried his sweeping statements about the freedom of the Word to their logical liturgical conclusion. He was not a systematic theologian, even though he was a genius at making his own psychological tensions productive by reflecting on them in the light of the perennial mysteries of the faith.[26]

Luther was an earthy thinker, and there is plenty of evidence scattered throughout his writings that he did not downplay the material qualities of God's Word. True, he could follow Augustine in talking about an "outward word" that is useless unless it is animated by the Holy Spirit. But the difference between Luther and Augustine on this point is crucial. Luther did not mean that the true Word of God is an inner illumination of the heart that can dispense with sound altogether. Such was the thinking of the spiritualists who raised Luther's ire. The outward words that God uses to communicate the divine will really are God's words. The purpose of these words is to penetrate the heart, but their physical reality cannot be ignored. As he declared in the *Church Postil* of 1522, "The church is not a pen-house but a mouth-house."[27] The words recorded in the Bible are true sounds, and God truly speaks through them.

An example of Luther's auditory emphasis can be found in his lectures on Hebrews, where he flatly declares, "For what Christ has said about heaven and the life to come is grasped only by hearing, since it transcends not only all understanding, be it ever so deep, but also the capability of desiring, be it ever so extensive."[28] God is received in no

25. Martin Luther, "Concerning the Order of Public Worship," trans. Paul Zeller Strodach, in *Luther's Works*, vol. 53, *Liturgy and Hymns*, ed. Ulrich S. Leupold (Philadelphia: Fortress, 1965), 11, 14.

26. This is not to say that Luther's theology can be readily reduced to his personality. As Stanley Hauerwas has suggested to me in personal correspondence, part of the wonder of Luther is that he was such a good theologian in spite of his personality.

27. Quoted in Theodore S. Liefeld, "Scripture and Tradition, in Luther and in Our Day," in *Interpreting Luther's Legacy*, ed. Fred W. Meuser and Stanley D. Schneider (Minneapolis: Augsburg, 1969), 30.

28. Martin Luther, *Luther's Works*, vol. 29, *Lectures on Titus, Philemon, and Hebrews*, ed. Jaroslav Pelikan (St. Louis: Concordia, 1968), 145.

other way than through hearing, it seems, because hearing is the most obedient and least corrupted of the senses. Our ears are not as subjected to the excesses of desire as our eyes and tongue. Luther goes on to say, "This is the one, and the greatest, thing God requires of the Jews, yes, of all men, namely that they hear His voice."[29] The mystery is not that God speaks but that we, even given the gift of lidless ears, still close them to God's Word.

Luther deals with that mystery with typically graphic rhetoric. He is fascinated by Psalm 40:6, which states, "But thou hast perfected my ears." He notes that Jerome translated this passage as "But thou hast dug out my ears." He likes the metaphor. God digs at our ears as we dig up the earth, in order to plant seeds that will bear fruit. Although he does not refer to the parable of the sower and the seeds, Luther does refer to Mark 7:34, where Jesus says, "Be opened," and comments, "No one listens to Christ except when the Father digs out and opens his ears."[30]

Then comes a remarkable summation of his theology of the Word. God no longer requires the feet or the hands, he says, implying that we need not make pilgrimages or do the work of liturgy for our salvation. "For if you ask a Christian what the work is by which he becomes worthy of the name, 'Christian,' he will be able to give absolutely no other answer than that it is the hearing of the Word of God, that is, faith. Therefore, the ears alone are the organs of a Christian man, for he is justified and declared to be a Christian, not because of the works of any member but because of faith."[31] *Solae aures sunt organa Christiani:* surely there is no clearer explication in all of Christian theology of the idea that faith comes by hearing.

For Luther, then, sound is the natural milieu of Christian faith. It is certainly true that Luther uses *ear* metaphorically to emphasize the unmerited quality of God's grace, but at the same time he can be quite literal in his insistence on hearing as the organ of faith. We find this difficult only because we are so removed from a culture immersed in orality. The gospel for Luther quite simply is oral. It should "really not be something written, but a spoken word which brought forth the Scriptures, as Christ and the apostles have done. This is why Christ himself did not write anything but only spoke. He called his teaching not Scripture but gospel, meaning good news or a proclamation that is spread not by pen but by word of mouth."[32] Luther goes so far as to

29. Ibid., 149.
30. Ibid., 223.
31. Ibid., 224.
32. *Luther's Works,* vol. 35, *Word and Sacrament I,* ed. E. Theodore Bachman (Philadelphia: Muhlenberg, 1960), 123.

say that the Old Testament alone bears the name Holy Scripture, since the Gospels are sermons more than they are texts. Even the Old Testament, however, is meant to be heard, not read. Thus the Bible belongs to the sermon, just as the sermon belongs to the Bible. Indeed, Luther's meditations on the "hidden God" could be labeled the "unpreached God." Emanuel Hirsch was right to say that the Gospels were a "living voice" for Luther *(lebendige Stimme)*, which makes the Bible not a "reading book" *(Lesebuch)* but a "listening book" *(Hörebuch).*[33]

The idea that reading the Bible is an act of hearing does not mean that Luther claimed to directly hear God's voice when he read the Bible. This was the danger of those whom Luther called "fanatics," who were filled with private revelations that abrogated ecclesial authority. Sound is more complex than that, and Luther was well aware that voices can blend and harmonize to create resonant effects. Luther certainly did believe that God once spoke, quite literally, to the prophets and others. But for us today, he argued, the Word is ordinarily mediated by a human voice, whether it is the voice of someone who is reading the Bible out loud or someone preaching the gospel. Such mediation, however, does not keep us from hearing God's voice *in* the voice of the reader or preacher. In an act of theological imagination, shaped by how the Bible identifies God through its narrative of the divine character, we can hear the divine in the human, just as we hear the voice of a novelist in the characters she creates. God does more than just authorize the Bible as God's Word; God actually speaks to us through the Bible, to the extent that we are open to hearing its words as God's own.

In order to hear God speak through the Bible, the theological ear needs to be trained. Reading Scripture is not enough; memorization and meditation are essential.[34] Luther was so immersed in the Bible that he did not quote it so much as speak it. By meditation, Luther meant that one should "always repeat the oral speech and the literal word in the Book and compare them with each other, not only in your heart but also outwardly."[35] Part of his motivation for translating the Bible into German was to teach the German people how to hear the gospel afresh. Of course, his translation spoke with not a little bit of his own voice. "His German translation, itself a resanctification of the vernacular, secular

33. Emanuel Hirsch, quoted in William A. Graham, *Beyond the Written Word: Oral Aspects of Scripture in the History of Religion* (Cambridge: Cambridge University Press, 1987), 147.

34. See Paul J. Griffiths, *Religious Reading: The Place of Reading in Religious Practice* (New York: Oxford University Press, 1999). This book offers a wealth of material on orality; note, for example, the description of composition as dictation, using Thomas Aquinas as an example (56–57).

35. Luther, quoted in Graham, *Beyond the Written Word,* 149.

tongue, attempts to capture the colloquial force of the sacred yell."[36] Even when it is read softly, the Bible has the power of a good shout.

By defining the Bible in terms of sound, Luther did not mean to reject religious images altogether. In fact, he backed down from his earlier criticisms of ecclesial art and even at times grouped words and images together as equally necessary as outward or material signs of the inner working of the Holy Spirit. This same mixture of the radical and the reactionary can be found in Luther's ideas about education. During his early, more optimistic years, Luther raised the expectation that the majority of the people could break through the inflated and embellished piety of the late Middle Ages to a more direct relationship to God. Protestant leaders fought the persistence of popular superstitions among the largely illiterate peasantry by joining a theological emphasis on the Word of God—both written and spoken—with bold initiatives in public education. They wanted all believers to be equipped with communicative skills sufficient to revive the church and proclaim the gospel.[37] While he was working on his translation of the Bible, Luther defended an unlimited and voluntary access to the Bible, and he saw the family as the natural place for such instruction. Events soon made him change his mind. The Peasants' War, the rise of Anabaptism, and the popularity of spiritualists who rejected formal education convinced him that religious instruction needed to be in the hands of the secular authority. Luther's success in making religious doctrine an essential part of the curriculum produced the first Protestant school system. Nevertheless, his training in nominalism, as well as his two-kingdom theology, made him pessimistic about the possibility, so fervently pursued by the scholastics, of integrating faith and learning.

Such irresolution gives rise to a tension between the church and the world that fosters a deeply ironic imagination. The stubbornness of

36. Ernest B. Gilman, *Iconoclasm and Poetry in the English Reformation* (Chicago: University of Chicago Press, 1986), 36. This comment is in reference to Luther's calling the gospel a "gut Geschrei."

37. None of this would have been possible if the Protestants had not allied themselves with pedagogical innovations that were products of the rise of humanism. A curriculum based on the "new learning" was first developed in the fifteenth century in northern Italy, and it soon spread throughout Europe. The humanists emphasized the study of classic texts—the Latin poets, playwrights, historians, and especially Cicero, with his emphasis on rhetoric—as models of good speaking and writing. The primary pedagogical tool of the *studia humanitatis*, which dominated Western education up to the nineteenth century, was imitation, in the forms of recitation and memorization. Rhetoric in the ancient world was not primarily a technique; instead it was an ideal. Its goal was to cultivate moral character and promote civic responsibility. The most fully formed student was the one who could stand up before an audience and exercise the power of persuasion for the public good. Protestants adopted this ideal but changed the goal to witnessing to the gospel.

the world's rejection of the gospel can lead the church to an attitude of sectarian defeatism or premature triumphalism, but it can also lead to a cautious realism that finds expression in an ironic posture. Irony enables one to appreciate unexpected incongruities, as when the best intentions end up with the opposite outcome.[38] If theologians do not often employ this trope, it is because irony has to do with the vocal qualities of language. It is expressed stylistically through tone, inflection, and rhythm. A theologian has to have a distinctive voice in order to convey irony, which is one reason Luther could be such an effective ironist.

At its best, irony can enable the church to take a long view of the world and the ways the ultimate victory of Christ must be accomplished through many detours and delays. At its worst, when Christian irony loses the joy that comes from trusting in God, it can become indistinguishable from plain old cynicism. Cynicism results in a pessimistic skepticism about the possibility that the ways of the Lord can become the ways of humankind. When Luther's ironic view of history turned dark and gloomy, he was closer to Erasmus than he would ever have imagined. Both men initially tried to create a new world of faith through their linguistic genius. Both expected the old world to fade away as their words gained power and reality. Both became increasingly disillusioned with the results of their efforts. Even before he became bitter in his later years, Luther learned to compromise with the secular authorities in order to preserve what gains his theology accomplished. Conservative political instincts made Luther panic at his own audacity, and he scrambled to replace the authority of Rome with the power of the German princes.

The trajectory of Luther's ironic view of history is a lesson in the limits of this trope. Luther's attack on ecclesial hierarchy not only authorized the emergence of new religious voices but also created a new understanding of the significance of the individual's voice. His bold personality held together a complex mixture of radical and reactionary elements, but the Enlightenment dissolved the intimacy he established between the believer and the Bible, renewing anxiety about the status of religious authority. Under pressure from the epistemological challenges of the Enlightenment, Protestant theologians were tempted to appease this anxiety with appeals to universal truths and scientific methods. Such foundationalism took the form of twin extremes—a liberal quest for the authenticity of religious feeling and a fundamentalist insistence on the inerrancy of Scripture. Both of these extremes can be found, in incipient form, in Luther, but he cannot be blamed for the sterile development that finds them hopelessly polarized. Nonetheless, it remains

---

38. For more on the theological use of irony, see Stephen H. Webb, *Re-figuring Theology: The Rhetoric of Karl Barth* (Albany: State University of New York Press, 1991), chap. 5.

the case that his battles with Rome paved the way for an increasingly rationalized and secularized public sphere that quarantined his new language of faith.

The use of irony is always contextual, and though the heritage of Luther's ironic imagination in Europe is problematic, in America irony—as opposed to cynicism—can be in short supply. Mark A. Noll has pointed out how little Lutheranism has influenced American culture and politics. "The dominant pattern of political involvement in America has always been one of direct, aggressive action modeled on Reformed theories of life in the world. Like the early leaders of Calvinism on the Continent and the English Puritans, Americans have moved in a straight line from personal belief to social reform, from private experience to political activity."[39] Noll suggests that Americans would do well to develop a greater sense of irony in working toward political and social change, and that Luther's theology of the cross is a good source of an ironic imagination. Irony enables an alert eye for the unintended consequences of our quest for progress and improvement. We rarely succeed in achieving the good we set out to accomplish, and even when we do, we often end up creating accidental harms.

Nobody has better employed Luther's irony in modern theology than Reinhold Niebuhr. It has become common in recent years to criticize Niebuhr for perpetuating the very liberalism that he fought against, but such criticisms are shortsighted.[40] Indeed, Niebuhr's ironic imagination is more effective than Luther's because it is shorn of the exaggerated sense of certainty that fuels many of Luther's polemical attacks. While hyperbole is the figure of mystics, irony is the trope for moralists, and this explains Niebuhr's strengths and weaknesses. He was not a systematic or philosophical theologian. His focus on anthropology neglected many church doctrines, especially ecclesiology, but it is important to note that the church he was addressing had compromised with secular culture for so long that, in a way, he had to address secular culture in order to reach the church. In other words, Niebuhr did not have a well-developed ecclesiology because he was working against the only ecclesiology he saw all around him, which was the idea that the church—in cooperation with the state—should be an agent of social progress. His great accomplishment was in importing a heavy dose of Luther into an American

---

39. Mark A. Noll, "The Lutheran Difference," *First Things*, no. 20 (February 1992): 38.

40. For the best account of Niebuhr's theology, see Langdon Gilkey, *On Niebuhr: A Theological Study* (Chicago: University of Chicago Press, 2001). For a defense of Niebuhr against the criticism that he was "too liberal," see Gabriel Fackre, "Was Reinhold Niebuhr a Christian?" *First Things*, October 2002, 25–27.

theological scene that was overly optimistic about the possibilities of human achievement and control. Moving the locus of Christian ethics outside of history was a useful rhetorical strategy to debunk the prevailing orthodoxy of liberal optimism. We should appreciate Niebuhr for criticizing the church he saw rather than lament his lack of a vision for what the church could come to be.

Niebuhr wrote at a time before theology became so professionalized that theologians had to decide whether they wanted to write for a broad or a specialized audience. He was less an original scholar than a creative prophet who criticized American culture by retrieving its very own Christian foundations. This is most evident in *The Irony of American History*, which was published in 1952.[41] Niebuhr wrote this book while he was still under the influence of neo-orthodox theology, but he was struggling to find ways to articulate an increasingly conservative (or "realistic") political voice that would influence a generation of public policy analysts. Irony, for Niebuhr, helps explain both the greatness and the tragedy of nation-states, since it is only through their blindness that nations can believe in their own ideals. In the case of America, our innocence about the international arena saves us from acting like a typical imperial power, although our commitment to individualism prohibits us from articulating a moral vision that would do justice to our own accomplishments in the arena of social progress and equality. Only a transcendent perspective can permit us to reconstruct the ironies of history, but even then we have to be careful not to let our claims of knowledge transgress the limits of human nature.

Luther's two-kingdom theology tended to evacuate theology of political meaning while granting the secular realm a divine mandate. Niebuhr, by contrast, shows how an ironic view of history can be sensitive to the intertwining of grace and sin in the history of nations as well as individuals. Power can be used for great good, just as the good can be used as a means of legitimizing the powerful. Christians with the best intentions often cannot tell whether good is being used for evil or evil for the good. Yet Christians—and nations influenced by Christianity—must be responsible for the power they have by acting to pursue the good as they understand it.

At his best, Niebuhr used irony to demonstrate how the biblical view of human nature generates the most persuasive narrative of both individual and collective life. Like Luther, however, Niebuhr could let his irony degenerate into a kind of cynicism, where Christianity contributes nothing to politics that the politicians do not already know. In its degenerate form, an ironic view of history means merely that

41. Reinhold Niebuhr, *The Irony of American History* (New York: Scribner, 1952).

governments should be organized according to a balance of power and that governments should have a realistic assessment of the need to use force in international affairs. Transcendence becomes an empty cipher designating the way people are often mistaken about their own interests and thus need to be self-critical and modest. Likewise, nations should deploy their power with humility, patience, and charity. In this way, Niebuhr's irony became translated into principles regarding the importance of experience over dogma, the practical over the theoretical, and the democratic over the authoritarian. All of this is good advice, but the less connected to theology it becomes, the more cynical it seems, as if Christian faith teaches nothing more than common sense and prudence, even though, ironically, it promises so much.

Calvin/Hauerwas

Calvin preached almost daily, and more than two thousand of his sermons survive. Hughes Oliphant Old notes that he was neither a dramatic speaker nor a magnetic personality, yet people listened intently to his words. "He seems to have had an intensity which he focused on the text of Scripture which was so powerful that he drew his hearers into the sacred text along with him."[42] Perhaps he was able to keep the focus on the text of the Bible because he spoke without notes or a manuscript. His preparation included a thorough study of the biblical passage, but he composed the sermon while he was presenting it. He also never flaunted his learning but used the French language with an unusual degree of clarity and precision. Simplicity for Calvin was a mark of sincerity.

This does not mean that Calvin lacked style. It is not enough to repeat God's own declarations, because sinful ingratitude has made us deaf to the divine voice (*Institutes* 1.6.4). Thus Calvin advocated a liveliness in sermons. John H. Leith notes, "He made use of drama, of personal address, of antithesis, of gradation of emphasis, of exclamations, of appeals to the absurd and irony."[43] All of this was in service, however, to the actual content of the biblical lesson. Like a good actor, Calvin used his own voice, without any false theatrics, to make the text come alive. He called this the familiar style. As T. H. Parker explains, "*Familière* might be better rendered by the word 'personal,' used in the colloquial modern

---

42. Old, *Reading and Preaching of the Scriptures*, 4:129.

43. John H. Leith, "Calvin's Doctrine of the Proclamation of the Word and Its Significance for Today," in *John Calvin and the Church: A Prism of Reform* (Louisville: Westminster John Knox, 1990), 221.

sense—to make the message of Scripture a personal matter, not just a collection of historical ideas."[44] Calvin, however, used no anecdotes or personal stories to achieve this end. Rather, he kept to the script. In his third sermon on Jacob and Esau he clearly stated the purpose of the sermon: "When the Gospel is preached in the name of God, this is as much as if he himself did speak in his own person." He went on to say: "I speak, but it behooves that I hear myself being taught by the Spirit of God."[45] The preacher should hear, even in his own words, the sound of someone else.

Indeed, Calvin often talked about God in terms of voice, as the following sample quotations show:

> Thus again it ought to be borne in mind that God has proposed to speak to us by the apostles and prophets, and their lips are the mouth of the one true God.[46]

> There is no other way of raising up the Church of God than by the light of the word, in which God himself, by his own voice, points out the way of salvation.[47]

> I think he [the apostle John] calls the Son of God "the Word" simply because, first, He is the eternal wisdom and will of God, and secondly, because He is the express image of His purpose. For just as in men speech is called the expression of the thoughts, so it is not inappropriate to apply this to God and say that He expressed Himself to us by His speech or Word.[48]

Calvin's skillful communication of the gospel was nothing less than a form of imitating God. The God he preached was a God who preached. As Dawn DeVries has argued, the Word for Calvin is not only the source and norm for faith and doctrine. It is also the instrument of grace.[49]

---

44. T. H. L. Parker, *Calvin's Preaching* (Louisville: Westminster John Knox, 1992), 139.

45. Calvin, quoted by Leith, "Calvin's Doctrine of the Proclamation," 227.

46. John Calvin, *Calvin's New Testament Commentaries: The Epistle of Paul the Apostle to the Hebrews and the First and Second Epistles of St. Peter*, trans. William B. Johnston (Grand Rapids: Eerdmans, 1963), 254.

47. John Calvin, *Commentaries on the Twelve Minor Prophets*, trans. John Owen (Grand Rapids: Eerdmans, 1950), 257.

48. John Calvin, *Calvin's New Testament Commentaries: The Gospel According to St. John, 1-10*, trans. T. H. L. Parker (Grand Rapids: Eerdmans, 1961), 7.

49. Dawn DeVries, *Jesus Christ in the Preaching of Calvin and Schleiermacher* (Louisville: Westminster John Knox, 1996). DeVries's larger project is an attempt to salvage liberal theology by arguing that its abandonment of history is already entailed in Calvin's understanding of preaching. DeVries acknowledges that Calvin was a biblicist in ways that academic theologians cannot be today. But she thinks that he also made room for a

Calvin can be said to sacramentalize the Word *(Sacramentum verbi)* because he believed it quite literally dispenses Jesus Christ.

Calvin's prose has a settled quality that Luther's lacks. Brian A. Gerrish has noted how Calvin was sufficiently removed from Luther that he could accept Luther's theology without approving of his rhetoric. Gerrish offers the example of one Albert Pighius, who had deplored Luther's gross exaggerations concerning the depths of human depravity. In his 1543 reply defending Luther, Calvin states, "I grant it, but still say that there was good reason that drove him to such exaggeration. He saw the world stupefied by a false and pernicious confidence in works, as if by a fatal lethargy. What was needed to awaken it was not voice and words but the trumpet blast, thunder, and lightning."[50] Calvin blamed Luther's opponents for forcing him to sound so violent at times. More significant, Calvin understood that the historical context of Luther's work shaped Luther's rhetoric, just as he understood that Luther's context was no longer his own. Calvin could speak in a much more restrained and moderate tone precisely because Luther had shouted loudly enough to awaken the most slumbering of Christians. For Calvin, the Reformation was not so much a singular event as a work in progress, which suggests that theological styles would have to change in order to meet the needs of new circumstances.

Calvin's rhetoric could also push him further than he wanted his theology to go. He compares humankind to a "five-foot worm" (suggested to him by Ps. 22:6) and says that people are unfit to be ranked with "worms, lice, fleas, and vermin."[51] Nevertheless, he was much less patient with paradox and less proficient in irony than Luther; he wanted his language to be as clear and straightforward as his theology.

Calvin was such a gifted writer that one can only conclude that his more modest rhetorical tone was a choice calculated to obtain some distance from Luther's influence. He did not have much of Luther's boisterous loquacity, but his grasp of rhetoric was as confident and

---

subjective doctrine of grace that paved the way for modern liberal theology, beginning with Schleiermacher. For DeVries, Calvin allows liberal theologians to sidestep the question of the historical Jesus by locating the presence of Christ in the moment of proclamation, not the duration of history. She thus reads Bultmann back into Calvin. What she misses is that for Calvin God is present in the divine voice as that is heard in Scripture and only subsequently in the voice of the preacher as the preacher embodies that voice. Moreover, God's presence in the divine voice is made possible by the incarnation. That is, God speaks to us because God made the decision to take our place and thus to assume a human identity; an exchangist atonement and the power of proclamation are more integrally linked than DeVries allows.

50. Quoted in Gerrish, *Old Protestantism and the New,* 38.

51. Ibid., 151. See *Institutes* 1:56 (1.5.4) for the first quote. Gerrish notes that this smacks of hyperbole.

masterful as Erasmus's. His contributions to the development of clarity and concision in the French language have been much discussed. Given his intellectual background, it should be no surprise that Calvin provides a more refined model for rhetorical theology than Luther. Like many ambitious young men of his time, Calvin early on decided to pursue a legal career, and his training immersed him in the art of classical rhetoric. He soon became more intrigued with humanistic scholarship than the technicalities of the law. His love for learning indelibly shaped the goal of his theological labor, which was the cultivation of a "wise and eloquent piety." He is often portrayed as a dull but systematic theologian who was as disciplined in his work as he was with the morals of the citizens of Geneva. This portrait negligently overlooks his rhetorical sophistication.[52]

In contrast to Luther, Calvin understood that theology must be persuasive instruction before doctrinal clarity can prove profitable for the faithful. He was influenced by Cicero's insistence that the goal of every orator is to serve the public good of the polis. He thus attacked scholasticism by arguing that theology should be profitable and practical rather than self-indulgent and speculative. Calvin is not interested in theological disputes for their own sake. Instead, the discussion of doctrine should strengthen believers by leading directly to the dispositions that are proper to faith.

The theologian should practice good pedagogy, which often means that less is more. God does not give us more information than we need. To develop his doctrine of revelation, Calvin employs a technical term, *accommodation*, that has a long and rich history in the rhetorical tradition. In a classic essay on Calvin's doctrine of accommodation, Ford Lewis Battles demonstrates the extent to which Calvin was thoroughly immersed in ancient rhetoric. Cicero had emphasized how the rhetor must be aware of the audience and accommodate to it, and Origen and Augustine (as well as Erasmus) had also used this term. In the classical period, the educational gap between speaker and audience would have been great, and rhetors thus had to learn the skills of accommodation. In fact, since speaking always involves reading one's audience, accommodation could be considered the very essence of rhetoric. So described, it can also be considered the very essence of God's relationship to us. That is exactly how Calvin used the term. Calvin transformed accommodation into a theological category. As Calvin repeatedly argued, God is of a completely different order of being from our own, and thus God must stoop to our level in order to make the divine nature knowable.

52. See Serene Jones, *Calvin and the Rhetoric of Piety* (Louisville: Westminster John Knox, 1995).

God is a rhetorician, which makes the incarnation the greatest act of persuasion in the history of humankind.

Implicit in Calvin's doctrine of accommodation is an entire theology of language. Battles points out that in the *Institutes of the Christian Religion* Calvin never uses the noun *accommodatio* but rather the verb *accommodare*. This is a significant observation, because accommodation for Calvin is an action or strategy made necessary by the demands of a particular situation. Our words are insufficient to bridge the gap between God and humanity. God thus must take the initiative, which explains why Calvin's favorite images of the divine are father, teacher, and physician. The natural and the political order speak of God's providential design for our salvation, and Calvin is fond of using the theater as a metaphor for how God sets the stage for our salvation. Nonetheless, we are blind (*Institutes* 1.8) even to the most spectacular of God's special effects—Adam could "read" nature in ways that we no longer can—which leaves us with hearing as the primary means by which God works the most powerful divine rhetoric. Scripture expresses God's voice more directly than nature, but what enables us to listen to the Bible is the clearest divine speech of all—God's willingness to condescend to us in the incarnation. God will go to the greatest extreme in making the divine Word effective. As Battles states, "as in the law court, the advocate seeks to sway the judge either to mercy or to punishment, so God has to deal not only with inexperience and ignorance but with willful stubbornness and disobedience. The divine rhetoric then becomes a rhetoric of violence, or exaggeration, of unbelievable heightening."[53] God is forced by our deafness to shout the good news; hyperbole is the usual tenor of the divine voice.

The biblical narrative has a pedagogical, rather than a philosophical, coherence, yet we remain deaf to its lessons (just as we are blind to the divine glories of nature). Because God is such an effective communicator, however, there is no excuse for those who continue in their disobedience. There is also no reason that God's communication skills should not lead, once we are justified, to our sanctification. Calvin thus held up the spiritual growth he saw in the people of Israel as an example for Christians. He could also picture the church as a kind of school wherein Christians learn how to practice God's Word. In sum, God's voice takes on different tones according to the task God sets out to accomplish. Nonetheless, the thrust of Calvin's position is that God must shout in order to get our attention.

---

53. Ford Lewis Battles, "God Was Accommodating Himself to Human Capacity," *Interpretation* 31 (1977): 21.

Does this mean that all divine rhetoric is "mere exaggeration"? In other words, isn't there something deceptive in Calvin's portrait of divine speech as "unbelievable heightening"? This might be the case if God were trying to manipulate us for a purpose that was not in our own best interest. God's Word, however, is what we were created to hear. Its form perfectly matches its content. It is the good news and thus can rightly be proclaimed with unprecedented joy and urgency. God must exaggerate to get our attention, but it is an exaggeration that conveys the fundamental truth of our dire situation and the unexpected grace of our undeserved destiny. The divine hyperbole is extravagant precisely because we could never possibly imagine what God has in store for us.

Hyperbole captures only one aspect of the divine rhetoric. It is suggestive of Christ's role as a prophet who comes to speak the truth, no matter what. God's voice has other depths. Indeed, in one of his sermons on the deity of Jesus Christ, Calvin observed, "Surely we need not stop simply at words, but we cannot understand the teaching of God unless we know what procedure, style and language He uses."[54] The style God uses is, of course, none other than the humble carpenter from Nazareth. That style is not like the polished and ornate speeches of the Greek and Roman rhetors. Why would God need to prove that God is a classy speaker? God did not become incarnate in a person of great public importance who could assume that audiences would respect his privilege and power. Instead, God became incarnate in a person who spoke in much more humble tones. This does not contradict Calvin's contention about God's exclamatory rhetoric, because the ancients did not hold hyperbole in high regard.

In fact, God seems to lack the moderation that the ancients so highly prized. God either speaks boldly, through events like the exodus, the shrill declarations of the prophets, and the boldness of the incarnation itself, or God speaks softly, in the person of Jesus Christ. Although God can impress us with the divine rhetoric, the divine purpose is to save us, not edify or entertain us, and that involves taking on our burdens. The divine speech thus has no need to follow the classical rules of style, but it has a style nonetheless. "In fact, if we heard God speaking to us in His majesty, it would be useless to us, since we would understand nothing. So, since we are carnal, He must stutter. Otherwise we would not understand Him."[55] This is a remarkable statement. The form the divine accommodation takes is not just any kind of speech but one that is analogous to a speaking impediment. In the very next passage Calvin

54. John Calvin, *Sermons on the Deity of Christ*, trans. Leroy Nixon (Audubon, N.J.: Old Paths, 1997), 13.
55. Ibid., 18.

explains what he means. "By that, then, we see that we must understand that God made Himself little to declare Himself to us. And if it were not so, how would it be possible to express anything of the Majesty of God by speaking the language of men? Would it not be too great a step to take?" If God were to declare Godself in all of God's glory, we would be so overwhelmed that we would be left speechless. God thus stutters in order to demonstrate solidarity with us. God shares in our burden of speech, meeting us where we fail to say what we mean. God gives us the gift of speech by not saying everything, which would leave us with nothing to say.

Calvin found plenty to say, but he never said more than he thought was appropriate, as demonstrated by his masterwork, the *Institutes*. This triumph of the Reformation is not systematic in the modern sense of that term—there is no single unifying principle that organizes his treatment of Christian doctrine—precisely because it is so attentive to interpreting the Bible according to the contexts of different audiences and purposes. For example, the *Institutes* begins with the question of where wisdom is to be found. Should we begin with ourselves and proceed indirectly to God, or jump right into reflection on the divine? Calvin's answer to this query is not as clear as some readers would like. Significantly, he is operating in a rhetorical and not a philosophical mode. If his aim were analytical clarity, he could not both appeal to self-knowledge and also declare such knowledge null and void. What could be confusing logically, however, works rhetorically. Calvin appeals to the reader's self-knowledge only to insist that such knowledge invariably leads away from the self and to knowledge of God. His qualified rejection of natural theology is thus meant to prepare for his readers the proper attitude they will need to think about God.

That attitude is obedient listening. Indeed, Calvin had a quite literal understanding of God's voice. The credibility of Christianity depends upon our understanding of God as the author of Scripture, and that cannot be proved but only heard. "The highest proof of Scripture derives in general from the fact that God in person speaks in it."[56] Calvin goes on: "The same Spirit, therefore, who has spoken through the mouths of the prophets must penetrate into our hearts to persuade us that they faithfully proclaimed what had been divinely commanded."[57] Calvin does not explain how this happens, but he is clear that "the beginning of true doctrine [is] a prompt eagerness to hearken to God's voice."[58]

56. John Calvin, *Institutes of the Christian Religion*, ed. John T. McNeill, trans. Ford Lewis Battles (Philadelphia: Westminster, 1960), 1:78 (1.7.4).
57. Ibid., 1:79 (1.7.4).
58. Ibid., 1:81 (1.8.5).

What makes this pious listening hard is the utter humanity of the messenger. "If God spoke from heaven," Calvin notes, "it would not be surprising if his sacred oracles were to be reverently received without delay by the ears and minds of all. . . . But when a puny man risen from the dust speaks in God's name, at this point we best evidence our piety and obedience toward God if we show ourselves teachable toward his minister, although he excels us in nothing."[59] We must learn to listen to God's humble messengers just as they learned to listen to God. When prophets or their successors, the apostles, are "called to office, it is at the same time enjoined upon them not to bring anything of themselves, but speak from the Lord's mouth."[60] The preacher must be self-effacing in order to enact God's Word.

Calvin certainly succeeded in bringing little of himself—"a puny man risen from the dust"—to the office of preaching. He remains an enigmatic figure because he almost never wrote about his early formative period in any revealing way.[61] Although Calvin had to flee France, his theology, unlike Luther's, does not presuppose, as the subtext for all that he wrote, a radical break from the past. Perhaps this is due to the fact that he never felt the need to renounce his French education in the classical arts. His reluctance to talk about his conversion experience, however, was more than an incidental aspect of his psychological profile. It was an intentional rhetorical move; he wanted to keep the focus on God, not himself. Although he had an overwhelming conviction that he was called to speak for God, he also knew that God called the weak and the needy, so he deplored any cult of personality. He had many health problems that kept before him the fragility of this fleeting life. He was sensitive to the needs of his audience, but it was their need for divine truth, not personal anecdotes, that he wanted to satisfy. By making the sovereignty of God the center of his theology, he gave his work something of the timeless quality of its subject.

In contemporary academic theology, the critique of "personal experience" is all the rage, perhaps because it is a convenient way of undermining secular society's tendency to equate religious piety with private emotions.[62] This equation disconnects religion from the institutional church as well as

59. Calvin, *Institutes of the Christian Religion*, 2:1054 (4.3.1).

60. Ibid., 2:1150–51 (4.8.2).

61. See Alister E. McGrath, *A Life of John Calvin: A Study in the Shaping of Western Culture* (Oxford: Blackwell, 1990), 14–16.

62. For a careful sorting of the issues, see George P. Schner, "The Appeal to Experience," *Theological Studies* 53 (1992): 40–59. Much of the criticism of personal experience in religion comes from narrative theologians. The appeal to narrative, however, is not the opposite of experience but a particular kind of experience. Many of these theologians do not write in a narrative form and in fact make frequent appeals to their readers' personal experience.

historical tradition and thus leaves Christianity vulnerable to the forces of the market and the practices of consumerism. Arguing against what one theologian has called "experiential expressivism"[63] can thus go a long way toward revealing the various pathologies of Christianity in America.

Few theologians are as adept at brandishing this rhetorical topos as Stanley Hauerwas. Hauerwas is a great theological performer, and much of his rhetorical power comes from his criticisms of the various ways in which the American church has become too American.[64] Hauerwas argues that being a Christian is a matter of being subsumed into the biblical narrative, so that one becomes a character in that grand story. The Christian narrative does not overlap with the American story, he insists, nor does it encourage believers to indulge in emotional states of grace. It has its own plot, which should not be expanded to accommodate us; rather, we should accommodate it.

Ironically, Hauerwas draws from his own experience more than most theologians. His voice is unmistakably individual and personal. He combines Luther's relentless hyperbole with Erasmus's charming sarcasm in a singularly Texan idiom that could not be further removed from Calvin's sober manner.[65] He shouts first and makes distinctions later. What he shares with Calvin is a social understanding of piety. For Calvin and Hauerwas, the church is more than a sign of what is yet to come. It is a model that reveals significant aspects of God's ultimate plan for the world. The church functions best as a model community when it becomes a world that is utterly different from the rest of fallen creation. Indeed, the world of the church is nothing less than a miniature version of the kingdom of God. Hauerwas thus chastises American Christians for dwelling on their private religious experiences. Instead, he wants Christians to submit their individuality to the communal norms of the church. Only thus can the church be an active and even aggressive presence in the world.

Contrary to the tone of some of his rhetoric, the church that Hauerwas imagines is sacrificial, not triumphant.[66] He follows Erasmus in insisting

63. George Lindbeck, *The Nature of Doctrine* (Louisville: Westminster John Knox, 1984).

64. Hauerwas, however, remains deeply American. See Stephen H. Webb, "The Very American Stanley Hauerwas," *First Things*, June/July 2002, 14–17. For more rhetorical analysis of Hauerwas, see Webb, "A Voice Cursing in the Wilderness," *Reviews in Religion and Theology* 10 (February 2003): 80–85.

65. Reinhold Niebuhr did a better job of distancing himself from his German background than Hauerwas has done in taming his Texan heritage. If Niebuhr grew up in an age of assimilation, Hauerwas reflects the current ethos of pluralism by taking delight in the Texan shaping of his theological style.

66. There is a tension in Hauerwas's rhetoric between his proclamatory/hyperbolic style and his emphasis on the genre of narrative and the subsequent argument that conversion

that peace is the fundamental Christian message. Indeed, Hauerwas far surpasses Erasmus by insisting on pacifism as a prerequisite for full and faithful discipleship. For Hauerwas, the church is the sacrament of sacraments, the presence of Christ's body on earth, whose only labor is the patient expectation of the end. That end is the victory of Christ, which the church already celebrates, so that it need not do battle with the forces of this world on their own terms.[67] The church can be pacifist and countercultural because it already knows how the story will end, and it is on the winning side.

At this point Hauerwas's ecclesiology departs pretty dramatically from Calvin's. Hauerwas thus brings an Anabaptist voice to the Reformation table. For all of his talk of patience, he is impatient that the church should become the kingdom of God. By contrast, for Calvin the accent is not on the church as a place to maintain a decisive distance from the world. Instead, the church is the place where Christians prepare themselves to work for the common good. This follows from Calvin's belief that God's Word accomplishes what it commands. It is covenantal speech, active and full of life. Even in its stuttering, it has the power to give what it asks. God's Word called the world into being, and it continues to uphold the world through the speech of the Spirit-filled church. The Word thus takes the form not only of grace but also of the law, and the law is more than a means of punishment. The law directs us to the good by disciplining our desires and demonstrating God's intentions. Christians can affirm the law because the law recognizes that the kingdom is "not yet" and in the meantime measures must be taken to deal with its patient postponement. Both Hauerwas and Calvin understand the church to be a polis—a community that thoroughly defines who we are—but Hauerwas tends to make the church a counter-polis (counter to the secular world) while Calvin makes the church an exemplary polis (the one institution that shows the world what it too should be).[68] Calvin would never sever

---

is a process of socialization/sanctification. He thus gives simultaneous expression to both the Radical and the Magisterial Reformation.

67. Pacifism is the ethical outcome of Hauerwas's theology of patience. We need to learn to wait upon God and not force situations to fit our immediate needs. Yet pacifism also seems to run counter to the virtue of patience by insisting that the peaceful end of all things be used as a strategy for dealing with all conflicts right now. Perhaps the role of patience in Christianity can be understood best through a comparison of Christianity and Judaism. When that comparison is made, it is easy to see that there is an impatience built into Christianity, but it is an impatience that can lead to a variety of ethical outcomes. For a consideration of Jewish-Christian dialogue on this topic, see Stephen H. Webb, "The Rhetoric of Ethics as Excess: A Christian Theological Response to Emmanuel Levinas," *Modern Theology* 15 (1999): 1–16.

68. Hauerwas does not use the term *counter-polis*, because he thinks the church should not be defined by that which it rejects. The church is the polis; it is the world that

the history of Christianity from the responsibility to pursue a political order appropriate to the life of waiting for God's rule.

Hauerwas appears to revel at times in the irresponsibility of his position. He argues that secular political philosophies can only hope to manage political differences through the virtue of tolerance, but such hope is wishful thinking because political regulation is inevitably coercive. Secular political philosophies end up rationalizing the dominance of nation states. Hauerwas refuses to elaborate a political theology, because he does not want to legitimate the inevitable violence of nation-states. The only politics he supports is, following the work of John Howard Yoder, the politics of the cross.

Although Hauerwas's approach to politics is not philosophically based, it does have a firm foundation in the biblical narrative. As one of the framers of narrative theology, Hauerwas portrays faith as a mostly gradual process of becoming socialized in the practices of an interpretive community. Reading the Bible and hearing the Word preached are possible only in the context of learning how to act like a Christian. The practices of the church speak louder than the words of the Bible. "When *sola scriptura* is used to underwrite the distinction between text and interpretation, then it seems clear to me that *sola scriptura* is a heresy rather than a help in the Church."[69] There is no text outside of its interpretation. Meaning, following Wittgenstein, is determined by use. In a most remarkably anti-Protestant sentiment, Hauerwas states, "The Bible is not and should not be accessible to merely anyone, but rather it should only be made available to those who have undergone the hard discipline of existing as part of God's people."[70] Hauerwas recognizes that the biblical narrative needs to be retold, so that spiritual power lies in the words that respond to the Word and not just the social practices that sustain community. But he also argues that the Bible gains its authority from the church. Consequently, it is the church's invitation to citizenship in a counter-polis that is crucial, not the altar call of repentance for a broken and renewed self.

Unfortunately, Hauerwas's account of conversion-as-socialization, which sustains his metaphor of church as counter-polis, does not do justice to the alien power of the Word to make all things strange and to speak to our estrangement. As distinctive as is his own theological voice—and as careful as he has been in urging the church toward a more

---

is counter to it. Nonetheless, the term does capture his meaning of a church that stands apart from the world.

69. Stanley Hauerwas, *Unleashing the Scripture: Freeing the Bible from Captivity to America* (Nashville: Abingdon, 1993), 27.

70. Ibid., 9.

effective ministry in the world—Hauerwas's emphasis on virtue and narrative has the effect of downplaying the rhetorical power of proclamation. To put the matter sharply, Hauerwas argues that the church gains its authority from the virtues that it teaches. Moreover, those virtues are necessary for a correct response to the Bible. Only by properly practicing the faith can we effectively preach and share it. It is our deeds that give our words meaning. What Hauerwas misses is how preaching disorients us before it instructs us in the virtues of faith. Preaching is not an expression of ecclesial practices; instead, it is a rhetorical practice that will always find our moral practices wanting. Our practices can never be sound unless they echo the sound of the Word.

The most important aspect of the Christian narrative for Hauerwas is its emphasis on an original peace that precedes the violent ways of the world. All Christians can agree that peace is at the heart of God's plan for creation, but the difficulty comes with articulating how the church is to mediate that peace to others. Hauerwas can quickly translate the peace of Christ into a program of pacifism because he connects peace to the category of narrative—as something given in the Christian tradition—rather than to the category of rhetoric—as something that needs to be achieved through artful persuasion. The church plays a pedagogical role in demonstrating the possibilities of the peaceful kingdom, but sinful humanity must be persuaded to embrace those possibilities. The question is what form that persuasion is to take.

Because it aims at the ultimate good of its audience, the rhetoric of the church should strive to be nonviolent, but because it does not aim at the immediate good of its audience, Christian proclamation is not always a gentle form of speech. Indeed, the power of words is such that it is frequently impossible to draw a hard and fast line between forceful acts of persuasion and literal acts of violence. The ideas of peace and tolerance can be imposed upon any discourse, of course, but this just results in an artificial restraint of the scope and style of the speech. If proclamation makes its own peace, then secular standards cannot be used to judge when and how Christian witness goes too far and strays outside the boundaries of good taste, tact, and decorum. As human language, Christian proclamation is never completely free from the taint of sin. As the Word of God, preaching can never conform to worldly standards. We hear God's Word as both a force that condemns and a truth that liberates because it is a sound that grates in our ears and makes us shudder.[71] Of course, it is a Word that we ourselves speak, and so our rhetoric must be appropriate to the ultimate mission of the

71. The Enlightenment tried to articulate the conditions for a political rhetoric that would be so rational as to be acceptable to all people, regardless of where they live or what

Son, which is peace. And we must remember that God will have the last word, which will be the same Word God has spoken throughout eternity, the Word that became flesh and dwelt among us. Nonetheless, we should not judge proclamation on the basis of a preconceived image of peace; instead, proclamation sets its own standards for what peace and violence might mean in the midst of a fallen world.

Moreover, the church exists in and takes advantage of a world where peace is made possible here and now only through the threat and use of violence. The Christian message of peace must be proclaimed with due appreciation for the role of the state in maintaining social order. Social order is surely a part of God's plan. Note Paul's defense of secular authority in Romans 13:1–7. God works providentially through secular governments as well as the church. God gives every society, no matter the time or place, an ability to restrain the consequences of sin. Undeniably, some forms of government do a better job than others at ensuring a balance between freedom and stability. If secular authorities are authorized by God to carry out functions that are necessary for the Christian mission but cannot be accomplished by the church itself, then the church must carefully deliberate about the social and political conditions that are most conducive to the transmission of its message.[72] This deliberation is inevitable, given that Christian theology has as its telos a comprehensive form of life that includes the social and political, so that it is impossible to keep the church completely out of the affairs of state. Given these considerations, the church cannot take an absolute stand of indifference to the clash of nation-states.

Contrary to Hauerwas's emphasis on the church as a prototype of the peaceful kingdom, I would put the emphasis on the premise that just as

---

they believe. This dream of a completely transparent political rhetoric is obviously utopian, and its failure demonstrates how every discourse that presumes to order our lives and arrange our beliefs is coercive and authoritarian. Protestant proclamation is no exception. Indeed, Protestant rhetoric is especially forceful because it cannot appeal to some feature of human existence higher than itself. Proclamation relies on the authority of the Spirit to attest to its truth; its authority is internal to its own speech act, and thus, as Kierkegaard understood, one can never fathom its demands in terms of public morality and universal reason. Christians hope that their actions—especially their acts of sacrifice—will lead to a harmonious world, but they do not know that to be the case, and Christians cannot judge their own actions by secular notions of peace and prosperity. The gospel makes its own peace, which can look, at times, awfully like violence. For more on this topic, see the brilliant book by Theo Hobson, *The Rhetorical Word: Protestant Theology and the Rhetoric of Authority* (Hampshire, U.K.: Ashgate, 2002), and my review of this book in *Reviews in Religion and Theology* 10 (February 2003): 44–46.

72. See the debate sparked by the work of Oliver O'Donovan in Craig Bartholomew, ed., *A Royal Priesthood? The Use of the Bible Ethically and Politically* (Grand Rapids: Zondervan, 2002).

God became incarnate in human flesh, the divine mystery can continue to be spoken in a trustworthy word *(sermo)*. Preachers are authorized to proclaim the good news of the incarnation; their authority about how best to promote peace in the world is less clear. The church must be judged on its ability to communicate God's Word effectively, which means confidently and forcefully. Salvation is what the proclamation of the gospel offers; peace comes only after the Spirit has filled us with the Word. Theology, as Karl Barth argued, should be in the service of preaching, not character formation. Indeed, more than any other modern theologian, Barth has continued the Reformation emphasis on the formative power of the divine and the human voice. His theology of the Word will be the focus of the next chapter.

seven

The Sound of God

The Return of the Inward Word

It is a staple of stereotypes of fundamentalists that they grant the Bible oracular authority. Ever since the Enlightenment set out to debunk the appeal to voices as carrying evidentiary weight, religious groups that continue to treat the Bible as an oral text have been increasingly marginalized as backward and eccentric. To be fully modern, one must be at least a little bit deaf. As the Jesuit scholar Michel de Certeau writes, "Before the 'modern' period, that is, until the sixteenth or seventeenth century, this writing [Holy Scripture] speaks. The sacred text is a voice. . . . The modern age is formed by discovering little by little that this Spoken Word is no longer heard, that it has been altered by textual corruptions and the avatars of history. One can no longer hear it."[1] In reaction to the perception that fundamentalists have a simpleminded approach to seeking the voice of God in Scripture, theologians across the liberal-conservative spectrum have gone out of their way to develop theories about how the Bible "really" speaks to us. The list of candidates to replace God's voice is rich and varied: the human author's intention, the traditional doctrine of the church, the present congregation with all of its practices and assumptions, an abstract set of propositions that can be inferred from the text, or what remains of the text when ideology

1. Michel de Certeau, *The Practice of Everyday Life*, trans. Steven Rendall (Berkeley: University of California Press, 1984), 137.

critique has stripped it of its prejudices and limitations. Some theologians suggest that we should always hear the voice of the poor in the biblical text, or the voice of women, or the voice of whoever happens to be reading it at the time, since all reading is contextual and thus socially constructed.

While it is true that the Bible is full of many voices—it is the paradigmatic example of what postmodernists call a "multivocal" text—the one voice that is silenced by these theologians is the very voice of God. God might authorize our use of the text—which means that we need elaborate and complex hermeneutical theories to guide our interpretations of the Bible—but God does not speak in the text. If God did, then whoever heard God would be hearing voices that were not there, and this would be a sign of mental imbalance, not theological insight.

Modern hermeneutical method, which articulates the conditions necessary for valid textual interpretation, emerged with Friedrich Schleiermacher and the reaction to the Enlightenment's silencing of God's voice in nature and the Bible alike. Hermeneutical method tries to answer the question: If God no longer speaks to us, then how do we tell what God is trying to say? More specifically, if God no longer speaks a vocal word, then how do we hear God's Word at all? Given the difficulties of thinking about God's voice in the post-Enlightenment world, it should not be surprising that much of modern Christianity treats God's Word as an inner awareness of the divine that has no external objectivity. Many social theorists have observed that mainstream Christianity has become a largely private affair in America. Christians define faith as a matter of preference or choice, which makes tolerance the highest public virtue. The attempt to convert others to one's faith is thus treated as a lack of manners and tact. Faith in the modern world is a matter of self-expression, not proclamation. This state of affairs surely is connected to the muting of the Word. When we ignore the vocal character of the Word, it becomes hard to distinguish between Christian piety and the cultivation of subjective emotional states. Sound asks to be traced to its source. When the Word is silenced, it becomes something we say to ourselves, rather than something only God can say to us.

Protestantism has come a long way from the classic formulation of the Second Helvetic Confession, which was written by the Swiss Reformer Heinrich Bullinger in 1561 and later adopted by the churches of Switzerland and beyond. "The preaching of the Word of God is the Word of God," it states. This confession recognizes that God is not bound to the outward word, just as it recognizes that the completion of true instruction depends on the inward illumination of the Holy Spirit. Nonetheless, "inward illumination does not eliminate external preaching."[2] God can do whatever God wants, but according to the Bible, God ordinarily chooses to accomplish the work of salvation through the spoken word. Everything thus depends on the right ordering of the external and the internal.

The Radically Rhetorical Barth

Karl Barth's entire theological career was one long commanding rhetorical performance. The Word of God simultaneously silences us and empowers us to speak, and how it does that is Barth's foremost theological preoccupation. The explosive expressionism of his commentary on Romans eventually gave way to a more sober style, but even in the *Church Dogmatics* he overwhelmed his readers with a ceaseless use of rhetorical questions, ironic reversals of common assumptions, and repetitive restatements of his thesis. Although he defined the dogmatic task as critical reflection and therefore a secondary order of religious language, his own dogmatic practice sounds very much like first-order proclamation. In a way, the *Dogmatics* is Barth preaching to the preachers. His writing has an urgent and restless quality that reflects his own doctrine of God as One who is revealed in the decision to act. The *Dogmatics* also shows Barth to be a master of using multiple voices, especially in the small-print sections. Here he dons the hat of the scholar-teacher, pausing to catch his breath. In these sections, where he directly addresses his audience, he grants himself the luxury of polemical digressions, often scolding his readers for neglecting long-forgotten episodes in the history of theology. He seems always on the verge of exploding with scorn for those who call him a conservative even though *they* are the ones who keep doing theology as if the twentieth century never happened. Barth is the premier theologian-actor of the modern age—the one theologian who understood that the theoretical dilemmas of the nineteenth century could be resolved only by a radically dogmatic rhetoric, that is, by a performance capable of returning Protestantism to its foundations in the drama of the spoken Word. It is ironic, then, that Barth is so often accused of casting rhetoric out of theology. This accusation is sometimes based on a lack of familiarity with Barth's work, as if he substituted a rather wooden and stilted orthodoxy for mainline Protestantism's progressive and dynamic participation in the contemporary social and political milieu.

2. "The Second Helvetic Confession," in *The Book of Confession*, pt. 1, *Book of Confessions* (Louisville: Office of the General Assembly, Presbyterian Church USA, 2002), 53–54.

In a slightly more sophisticated version of this accusation, Barth is paid the dubious compliment of having single-handedly brought about the decline of rhetorical studies in homiletics. His emphasis on revelation and the Bible, according to this charge, took the study of preaching out of the hands of speech professionals and put it deep in the pockets of theologians and biblical scholars. Although the power of Barth's theology is hard to exaggerate, this accusation does exaggerate the impact of his theology on seminaries in America. Thomas G. Long sets the record straight when he writes, "As the twentieth century dawned, interest in rhetoric as an academic discipline waned drastically; active research all but ceased."[3] Intellectual trends were at work that dwarfed Barth's influence. Throughout the twentieth century, fields in practical theology that were related to the social sciences grew in prestige, but homiletics was convicted of irrelevance due to its association with rhetoric. If rhetoric was already in trouble—being replaced, in an increasingly literate culture, by hermeneutics[4]—then Barth did not need to push very hard to dissolve its marriage to homiletics.

What is remarkable is not that the study of public speaking went into decline but that rhetoric is now making such a decisive comeback. Today rhetoric has made a remarkable recovery in many academic disciplines—often in the guise of performance or communication studies—and is once again staking its claim to be the rightful helpmate to preaching. Before theologians rush to return rhetoric to the seminary curriculum, however, it would be prudent to inquire into what Barth really said about rhetorical studies and what his approach to preaching can still teach us today.

The criticism concerning Barth and rhetoric can be most damaging when it suggests that Barth put so much emphasis on Jesus Christ as the sole Word of God that he left no room for preachers to apply that Word by speaking on God's behalf. For David G. Buttrick, one of the theologians most responsible for restoring rhetorical studies to homiletics, Barth undercut the social relevance of preaching and thus "in some ways all but destroyed preaching in the name of the Bible."[5] Buttrick

3. Thomas G. Long, "And How Shall They Hear? The Listener in Contemporary Preaching," in *Listening to the Word: Studies in Honor of Fred B. Craddock*, ed. Gail R. O'Day and Thomas G. Long (Nashville: Abingdon, 1993), 173.

4. For this relationship, see Hans-Georg Gadamer, "Rhetoric and Hermeneutics," in *Rhetoric and Hermeneutics in Our Time: A Reader*, trans. Joel Weinsheimer (New Haven: Yale University Press, 1997), 45–59. In that same volume, Richard E. Palmer argues that the Reformation made rule manuals for interpretation necessary because Scripture was being interpreted without reference to the church fathers (115).

5. David Buttrick, *A Captive Voice: The Liberation of Preaching* (Louisville: Westminster John Knox, 1994), 8.

would surely admit that he is exaggerating a bit here, but does he have a point? In his foreword to the English translation of Barth's *Homiletics*, Buttrick notes that Barth banished introductions from sermons.[6] Buttrick suggests that this is due to Barth's famous rejection of any "point of contact" between God and humanity. This is true as far as it goes, but what it misses is the profoundly rhetorical nature of Barth's critique of the modern sermon. Barth does not pretend that the sermon is not a human construct. On the contrary, he insists that what he calls the "secular" forms through which God speaks to us can never do justice to God's voice.[7] Precisely for this reason, the rhetorical construction of the sermon has to be very careful and deliberate in order to bend it toward God's will.

Sermons should be natural, honest, and direct, characteristics that, in Barth's view of human nature, do not come naturally. Barth would agree with Kristin Linklater, who argues that the natural voice rarely coincides with the habitual practices of most speakers. Instead, it takes years of hard work to remove the obstacles that have built up over a lifetime. For Barth, however, the goal of a liberated voice will always be utopian and therefore unrealistic unless that goal is put in the context of a disciplined hearing that saves the whole person, vocal folds included. The reason it takes such great effort to speak in one's own voice is that we resist saying only what we hear in the scriptural text. We are free, Barth always insists, only to the extent that we are obedient to the Word. We can preach the Word effectively, in turn, only when we find our voice by immersing ourselves in the biblical text. Otherwise, preaching will sound a false note, and congregations will be either unmoved or moved in the wrong direction.

Barth did not like sermon introductions because he thought the Word of God cannot be captured by a general theme about which the preacher can wax poetic, pretending to be a master of the day's metaphor. The preacher is not putting on a show; rather, the preacher is showing

6. Karl Barth, *Homiletics*, trans. Geoffrey W. Bromiley and Donald E. Daniels, foreword by David G. Buttrick (Louisville: Westminster John Knox, 1991). For Barth's criticisms of introductions, see 52–53, 82, 121, 123. For the best analysis of Barth's use of rhetoric in this book, see James F. Kay, "Reorientation: Homiletics as Theologically Authorized Rhetoric," *Princeton Seminary Bulletin* 24 (2003): 16–35. Kay notes that Barth liked the term *announcement (Ankündigung)* more than *proclamation (Verkündigung)* because the former is less likely to be interpreted in psychological terms as a summons to an existential or heartfelt decision. Kay notes that Barth rejected introductions for both theological and psychological reasons, and he criticizes Barth for not doing a better job of demonstrating how those two levels of criticism cohere.

7. Karl Barth, *Church Dogmatics* 1/1, trans. G. W. Bromiley (Edinburgh: T & T Clark, 1936–1977), 168, 175.

the congregation what it might mean to be a hearer of the Word. The preacher must be open to being contradicted by the Word, which is quite a rhetorical feat! Rhetoric is hardly excused by Barth from sermon preparation: "The sermon demands an orderly language which is appropriate from the standpoint of content as well as expression. Form and content, then, are not to be separated in preaching. The right form is part of the right content."[8] Hardly a better definition of the task of classical rhetoric can be found in all of twentieth-century theology. Of course, this statement has to be put in dialectical tension with the section on form from the *Dogmatics*.[9] We can never be satisfied with the human shape of proclamation, because the content of the Word always exceeds our words. What this means in practice is that there cannot be a general rule that governs the preparation of the sermon. Sermons, for Barth, are a radically occasional genre. They are utterly of the moment. "Having a specific hearer to address, a sermon must be very personal."[10] By "personal" Barth does not mean the sermon should be full of stories about the preacher. Instead, it should be prophetic in addressing the particular situation of the congregation.

The occasional and prophetic nature of the sermon is thus of one piece with Barth's theology of the Word. The sermon is as particular a form of address as is the incarnate Word by which it is addressed. The Word is a particular person, not a general principle. This person, whose history is God's own, speaks a personal word—as should we. "If God speaks to man, He really speaks the language of this concrete human word of man" (1/2:532). Although Barth does use general concepts in describing Jesus Christ—most notably the idea of reconciliation and the theme of the judge judged in our place—he is ordinarily very suspicious of such generalizations. For Barth, danger lurks in the shadows of abstraction, while salvation flourishes only in the clarity of the particular. This is not a rejection of rhetoric. Instead, it is an elaboration of the very heart of rhetorical norms. Like any form of public speech,

8. Ibid., 120. Barth shows more sympathy for the discipline of rhetoric than most of his followers, who dismiss it out of hand. See, for example, Dietrich Ritschl, *The Theology of Proclamation* (Richmond: John Knox, 1960). Barth was not hesitant to connect preaching and rhetoric in the *Church Dogmatics:* "One usually judges the truth of human speech by the nature of its theme on the one side and by the situation and concern of the speaker on the other. Naturally this may and must apply to Church proclamation too" (1/1:92).

9. The Word's "form is not a suitable medium for God's self-presentation. It does not correspond to the matter but contradicts it. It does not unveil but veils it" (*Church Dogmatics* 1/1:166). This statement needs careful interpretation. The Word is disproportionate to all of our words due to an economy of excess. Nevertheless, our words can be a suitable medium for revelation, due to God's trinitarian nature and thus God's decision to speak creation into being in order to share the divine sound.

10. Ibid., 89.

the sermon should accommodate the needs of the audience by using all appropriate means to convey the subject matter. In the case of the sermon, the congregation needs to hear the Word of God, not the anecdotes and stories of the preacher, and the means by which to do that is to exegete Scripture.

The Devocalization of God?

The criticism of Barth's relationship to rhetoric takes yet another form when it is alleged that for all of his talk about the Word of God, Barth was hesitant to let God speak.[11] Barth is known for his fundamental and pronounced distinction between the Word of God and the words of mere humans. Confusing the two, he thought, was the root of all modern heresies. He came of age right before World War I and wrote at a time when too many Christians were claiming that God was on their side, without bothering to ask if God did not say more than what they already took for granted. The church that spoke a human word had ended up affirming the various ideologies of the age without being able to speak a word of protest. To his critics, Barth was not interested in what his contemporaries had to say. To Barth, he had heard enough from his contemporaries to know that they needed to hear something other than what everyone was saying all around them.

The charge that Barth, in effect, devocalizes the Word often comes from evangelical theologians who worry about his handling of the authority of Scripture. The most sophisticated version of this charge can be found in Nicholas Wolterstorff's *Divine Discourse*. Wolterstorff knows Barth's argument that the Word of God takes a threefold form in revelation, Scripture, and proclamation. Wolterstorff suspects, however, that Barth really reduces God's speech to revelation. "When we arrive at the end of the maze, we find just one mode of divine discourse—not three!"[12] It is true that Barth understands Jesus Christ as the form of God's original speech. This necessarily makes the other two forms of the Word—Scripture and proclamation—secondary and derivative. Witness to revelation is not revelation, for Barth. If it were, then God's voice would be frozen in print and subject to our manipulation and

11. In an important essay on voice, acting, and theology, Kevin J. Vanhoozer makes this charge against Barth. "The Voice and the Actor: A Dramatic Proposal about the Ministry and Minstrelsy of Theology," in *Evangelical Futures: A Conversation on Theological Method*, ed. John G. Stackhouse (Grand Rapids: Baker, 2000), 70.

12. Nicholas Wolterstorff, *Divine Discourse: Philosophical Reflections on the Claim That God Speaks* (Cambridge: Cambridge University Press, 1995), 63.

abuse. God's voice is truly a voice; that is, it is free, and its freedom is not an abstraction. The freedom of God's voice, however, does not make it unpredictable, because God's voice can be identified as the voice of Jesus Christ. For Barth, the question is how God can be God and yet be given to us in revelation. For Wolterstorff, the question is how we can hear God today in the human words of the Bible. He worries that Barth's separation of revelation from Scripture renders God mute. For Barth, Wolterstorff argues, "witnessing is human speech, nothing more."[13] Wolterstorff can even say of Barth that "God speaks by way of a human being only if God *is* that human being—Jesus Christ. This is fundamental in Barth!"[14] Although the complexity of Barth's position can cause confusion about his theology of sound, I hope to show that Wolterstorff's understanding of Barth is fundamentally wrong.

True, Barth can sound as if he is denying the possibility that we can hear God speak today. For example, he says that the biblical witnesses speak "in the name of the true God, because they have heard His voice as we cannot hear it, as we can hear it only through their voices" (1/2: 506). The *only* in that sentence is a bit troubling. It is the case that we can recognize the Word of God because we have heard it in the biblical witnesses, yet it is also true that we can hear that Word in other voices and at other times. Barth can be read as arguing that God is silent today except where we can find the record of God's speech in the past. In other words, because the biblical witnesses believed what they heard, we can be saved by hearing what they believed, but we cannot hear what they heard. The more generous reading is that Barth properly insists on the biblical shape of all revelatory sound. The biblical witnesses had a unique relationship to God that allows us to listen to what they heard. We too can hear God today, but we listen to God along with the biblical witnesses, because it is only in learning to listen to their voices that we can be sure we can recognize the divine voice.

The entire thrust of Barth's theology is an attempt to think about how we can hear God in a way that maintains God's freedom to speak when, where, and how God's wants to speak. Barth's insistence on the extrinsic relationship of the Word to Scripture must be put in the context of his desire to protect the freedom of God from human attempts at manipulation and objectification. Just because God can speak through everything, God is not bound to speak through any one thing. God thus did not have to choose to speak through the Bible. It is the Son, not the Bible, who is eternal. However, God *has* chosen to reveal the divine self to the biblical witnesses. When the Bible is truly heard, its sound points

13. Ibid., 68.
14. Ibid., 70.

us to its divine source, but we cannot thereby claim to have a firm grasp of God's nature. Indeed, it is the soundfulness of revelation that checks the metaphysical temptation to treat God as a knowable object.

Revelation is always an event, and so the event of God's speaking through the Bible is an unpredictable occasion, totally dependent on God's grace. An *event* is Barth's term for an occasion that is singular and unrepeatable. God's voice is an event because it cannot become a property of any object in the world; it cannot be recorded by any human instrument. The Bible is not a tape. If it were, merely reading it would reveal God's Word. Reading is not enough, however. Without the Holy Spirit, the Bible is a dead letter, undeliverable and unsigned.

Ironically, it is Barth's urgency in defending God's freedom to speak that leads him to a complex and not fully satisfying doctrine of Scripture. Barth's nuanced position is that God can cause the Bible to be God's Word, but the Bible does not intrinsically represent God's voice. When we read the Bible, Barth says, we "recollect, in and with the Church, that the Word of God has been heard" (1/2:530), but we ourselves do not hear God's voice. The Bible records how other people once heard God, but it is not a recording of God's voice. God appropriates Scripture through a free decision to make it communicate God's will, but such appropriation leaves the Bible only extrinsically related to God's voice. God could speak through anyone or anything; why God chose the words of the Bible must remain a mystery. There is no natural or organic connection between God's nature and the holiness of Scripture. The Bible is necessary for us, but God is not bound by our needs. *Deus dixit* and *Paulus dixit* are two separate things.

The problem with Barth's position on Scripture can be attributed to his resistance to being tagged with the label of neo-orthodoxy. He worked hard to distinguish his position from the rising tide of fundamentalism that was threatening to submerge the church in pseudo-scientific jargon about literal truth. One of the consequences of that effort was a negligent handling of the doctrine of inspiration. Barth sometimes writes as if the Bible were written without any inspiration from God at all, leaving the impression that God appropriates these words as God's Word only after they have already been written. He is too quick in dismissing the doctrine of inspiration as implying "a freezing, as it were, of the relation between Scripture and revelation" (1/1:124). In a most unfortunate image, Barth declares that Scripture is "taken and used by God Himself, like the water in the pool of Bethesda" (1/1:11 and 1/2:530). Of course, God made the pool of Bethesda, just as God providentially provides us with the Bible, which is why God can use anything God wants to convey the divine message. However, to say that Scripture is like the pool of

Bethesda is to suggest that there is no more plausibility in the Bible's speaking for God than in a puddle of water's doing so.

Significantly, all of Barth's comments about the extrinsic relationship between God and the Bible must be understood as referring to the Bible apart from the Spirit. When the Spirit is included in the relationship between God and the Bible, a completely different understanding of the doctrine of Scripture emerges. In a theological move that is startling in its brilliance, Barth defines the Holy Spirit as the ground of our hearing. "The Lord of speech is also the Lord of our hearing" (1/1:182). This is revolutionary because traditionally, since the day of Pentecost, the Spirit has been understood as the source of enthusiastic speech. For Barth, the Word must be not only preached in the Spirit but also heard in the Spirit. Hearing is not a question of anthropology.[15] Hearing is not an art that we can perfect through the proper method, because "hearing God's Word is faith, and faith is the work of the Holy Spirit" (1/1:185). If the Son is best understood as the Word of God, then the Spirit is how the Father and the Son listen to each other—and how we hear them as well. It is the Spirit who makes the Bible sound like God.

This is Barth's position: When we hear in the Spirit, Scripture *becomes* the Word of God, but outside of this event, it is not possible to say that Scripture *is* the Word of God. The relationship between Scripture and grace is thus unpredictable and uncontrollable. The wisdom of the Bible is Christ crucified (1 Cor. 1:18–31), and this makes sense only when we hear Christ speak in the Scriptures; reading the Bible otherwise will never convince us of the wisdom of a God who died on the cross. We hear Christ speak in the Bible, in turn, only when we hear the Bible preached in the power of the Spirit. What is important to note is that the preacher cannot use just any book for the sermon's text. Contrary to what Barth sometimes says, then, the sound of the biblical words has a status that is completely different from the sounds of a flute concerto or a socialist tract. God's relationship to the Bible is not, in the end, arbitrary or capricious. God does not adopt these words to speak on

15. But Barth does limit God's Word anthropologically. He assumes that "God's Word is not spoken to animals, plants, and stones but to men" (1/1:201). Since he argues that we do not need to hear God speak in order for God to be a speaker, this restriction seems artificial and unjustified. Also problematic is Barth's rejection of an anthropological locus for divine revelation. He does this because he does not want to turn the event of revelation into a human experience (which would subject it to human control). He also does not want to place some people on a higher spiritual plane than others by suggesting that they have "an organ, a capability" for God's grace that others lack (1/1:209). We all have ears for the Word, although God speaks to us in different ways. Nonetheless, his whole discussion of revelation suggests that our hearing is, indeed, the anthropological locus for divine speech.

God's behalf any more than God adopted Jesus to be God's Son. God chose to be known as the speaker of these words when God chose to be known as the Word. Although, as Barth says, the Bible is the product of "a unique hearing" (1/1:115), this does not mean that we cannot listen along with the witnesses to God's speech. These words are a unique witness to revelation because they are the words that God determined to speak to us at one time and for all time. Only thus can it be said that God still speaks through the Bible today.

Still, Barth resists giving an account of precisely how it is that God speaks to us through the Bible today. In the next chapter I will provide a more thoroughgoing performative solution to this problem than Barth allows. Wolterstorff, by contrast, is looking for a theoretical solution. He wants to know the conditions that make hearing God's voice today credible, and he uses speech act theory to clarify those conditions.[16] In fact, in the last few years a remarkable group of theologians has opened a way of examining the question of God's voice by turning to speech act theory.[17] This group includes not only Wolterstorff, one of the most prominent contemporary philosophers of religion, but also Kevin J. Vanhoozer, one of the most thoughtful and creative evangelical theologians. It also includes established scholars like Anthony C. Thiselton and promising theologians like Michael S. Horton and Richard S. Briggs.[18] Speech act theory has been applied to homiletics by David J. Lose.[19] Their perspective is exciting, because speech act theory provides a sophisticated set of tools that takes seriously a phenomenon—God

16. For critical reflections on Wolterstorff's use of speech act theory, see I. Howard Marshall, "To Find Out What God Is Saying: Reflections on the Authorizing of Scripture," in *Disciplining Hermeneutics: Interpretation in Christian Perspective* (Grand Rapids: Eerdmans, 1997), 49–55, and Stanley J. Grenz, "The Spirit and the Word: The World-Creating Function of the Text," *Theology Today* 57 (October 2000): 357–74.

17. First articulated by the British philosopher J. L. Austin in the 1950s, speech act theory became popular in America—at a time when the social sciences were gaining in prestige—precisely because it seemed like a way of analyzing language with the most technically advanced tools, in the hope that such analysis would solve traditional and seemingly intractable philosophical problems. But what kind of act is speech act theory? If every kind of speech can be categorized as a form of action, then how can there be a theory of speech in the first place? Speech act theory is itself a kind of action, a performance, so to speak, which needs to be understood in terms of its institutional and rhetorical context.

18. Thiselton was probably the first theologian to utilize the technical vocabulary of speech act theory. See Anthony Thiselton, "The Parables as Language-Event: Some Comments on Fuch's Hermeneutics in the Light of Linguistic Philosophy," *Scottish Journal of Theology* 23 (1970): 437–68. Also see Michael S. Horton, *Covenant and Eschatology: The Divine Drama* (Louisville: Westminster John Knox, 2002), and Richard S. Briggs, *Words in Action: Speech Act Theory and Biblical Interpretation* (Edinburgh: T & T Clark, 2002).

19. David J. Lose, *Confessing Jesus Christ: Preaching in a Postmodern World* (Grand Rapids: Eerdmans, 2003), 102–10.

as speaker—long associated with naive and simpleminded religious groups.

A basic theological problem, however, haunts all of their efforts. It is helpful to sort out the kinds of speech that humans produce, but none of those categories can illuminate the utterly unique speech of God. If God truly speaks, and if God's speech is immediately effective, then God's speech is of a kind unlike any other. The authority of God's voice lies in the fact that we recognize it without needing to draw upon any of our prior experience. We cannot compare God's voice with the other sounds we hear around us. It is just the opposite; everything sounds different once we have heard God speak to us.

Barth said it best: "The question: What is God's Word? is utterly hopeless if it is the question as to the category in which God's Word is to be put or the syllogism by which it might be proved" (1/1:159). God's Word is *sui generis*. "All our delimitations can only seek to be signals or alarms to draw attention to the fact that God's Word is and remains God's, not bound and not to be attached to this thesis or that antithesis" (1/1:164). The Word is spoken according to no known human mechanism or design. "We cannot utter even a wretched syllable about the how of God's Word unless the Word of God is spoken to us as God's Word" (1/1:164). To put the Word into a human category is to treat it as one of the realities of this world, which it most decidedly is not. The Word not only says something absolutely new to us—God is with us—but it also places us "in an absolutely new situation which cannot be seen or understood in advance, which cannot be compared with any other" (1/1:161). This rules out the very presuppositions of applying speech act theory to revelation. "The man who has heard God speak and might still ask about the related act is simply showing that he has not really heard God speak" (1/1:143). God's Word creates what it says, which is not a model for how we speak. Nor can our speech be a model for how God speaks. All human speaking is, in the end, a muted echo of God's own speech, so that theology cannot begin with distinctions about human speech and then apply them to God. The only theory that can even begin to do justice to God's speech is a dramatic and rhetorical one—a theory capable of suggesting the ways in which God's speech is the very stuff of creation and redemption.

The God of Sound

Ambiguities in Barth's understanding of the scriptural voice of God should not distract us from the overwhelming role that sound plays in his theology. His work is so dominated by a constellation of voice terms that it is surprising that no major studies have been done on the role of voice, sound, and orality in Barth. As with all of his work, his interest in sound is fundamentally theological. The very reason God became human was so that "His Word [could become] hearable" (1/2:167). Barth can also state that "God has spoken, speaks now and will again speak" (1/2:800). Theology is thus all about listening: "Modern dogmatics is finally unaware of the fact that in relation to God man has constantly to let something be said to him, has constantly to listen to something which he constantly does not know and which in no sense can he say to himself. Modernist dogmatics hears man answer when no one has called him" (1/1:61). Indeed, Barth anticipates performance theories of interpretation when he argues that, for Scripture, "the writing is obviously not primary, but secondary. It is itself the deposit of what was once proclamation by human lips" (1/1:102). It is the sound of Scripture that saves us, not its appearance on the printed page.

This does not mean that Barth is insensitive to the significance of the printed word. In an improvement on Luther's nearly singular focus on orality, Barth affirms the written form of Scripture in his discussion of the way the canon functions to preserve the Bible's autonomy and independence over and against the church.[20] Precisely because it is written, the Bible can be preached. "Because this book is there as the Canon, it must be preached, as in that age it was preached, with a volume and intensity that surprises us today" (1/1:109). The Bible was written down so that when Christians speak up they will all sound basically alike.

If the Bible were not a written text, the church would be tempted to mistake its own voice for the voice of God. Without the printed voice of God, the church would be left to its own chatter. Indeed, self-dialogue is how Barth understands the form of temptation that is particular to the church. When we talk to ourselves before we learn to listen to an external Word, we are parodying God's own eternal conversation, where God is the One—the only One—who can hold a private counsel.

So how do we think about the sound of God? Barth's approach to this question is as original as it is systematic. In the very first volume of the *Dogmatics*, which will be the focus of the remainder of this section, Barth anticipates much, if not all, of the theory of orality that Walter Ong developed over twenty years later. The whole point of the *Dogmatics* is to distinguish true from false talk about God, but Barth begins this volume with the astonishing claim that "there is no genuinely profane speech" (1/1:47). Because God is the One who speaks the world into being, all sound has its origin in God, and all talk is talk about God. Nothing we

20. See *Church Dogmatics* 1/2:473ff.

say can be anything other than an echo of God's Word. This does not mean that all church talk is proclamation, Barth warns. "If the social work of the Church as such were to try to be proclamation, it could only become propaganda, and not very worthy propaganda at that" (1/1:50). Proclamation, in a way, is the highest form of human speech, because it tries to say what God wants to say to us. Yet calling it the highest form of human speech suggests that proclamation is on a continuum with other forms of speech, which would be untrue. Proclamation is utterly different from every other speech act. That is the puzzle that the *Dogmatics* sets out to address.

One piece of the puzzle is the apostle Paul's language of the herald. "Proclamation is human speech in and by which God Himself speaks like a king through the mouth of his herald, and which is meant to be heard and accepted as speech in and by which God Himself speaks" (1/1:52). This is clear enough; the problem is that Barth understands the Word of God to be totally other than the words we speak, so that an account still has to be given of how God speaks through the herald. Ultimately Barth will ground the possibility of proclamation in the Chalcedonian formulation of the incarnation. Human flesh can be filled with the sound of God because God speaks through the incarnated Son. Later in this chapter I will show how Barth in turn, and more radically, grounds the incarnation in the dialogue between the Father and the Son, a dialogue that is sustained and disseminated by the Spirit.

We can be heralds of God's Word, but God speaks volumes more than we can ever say. In a famous passage in the first volume of the *Church Dogmatics*, Barth says that "God may speak to us through Russian communism, a flute concerto, a blossoming shrub, or a dead dog. We do well to listen to Him if He really does" (1/1:55). Given Barth's early association with socialistic politics and his abiding love for Mozart (I'm not sure what to make of the dead dog), this is not a random list. In fact, Barth's theology can be difficult to read precisely because it is like listening to a symphony with various movements that are repeated as they are developed. Nevertheless, Barth does not take this remark very far; it has the feel of a throwaway line. Unless we want to start a new church or declare ourselves to be prophets of the new age, we would do well, Barth advises, to listen for God in the place where heralds have been commissioned to speak on God's behalf. Even in the church, preaching is no guarantee of making God's voice audible. The effective sermon is a miracle in a sense that is analogous to the incarnation. The sermon consists of human words that nonetheless reveal the divine; the sermon remains human throughout this transformation. (Hearing God in a dead dog does not make the dead dog the Word of God.) If this were not a miracle, then preachers could claim to do the work of dispensing God's grace, which would turn proclamation into magic and not revelation.

God speaks because that is who God is; we speak in order to know who created us. Barth can be as earthy as Luther on this issue. "We have no reason not to take the concept of God's Word primarily in its literal sense. God's Word means that God speaks" (1/1:132). He rejects Paul Tillich's interpretation of speech as one of many symbols of the divine. He also insists that he is not divinizing a human characteristic. He admits that God's speech is spiritual, but he pointedly asserts that the character of this spirituality is distinct but not totally different from a material, corporeal, or physical event. It is primarily spiritual, he says, yet it comes to us always in a natural and physical form. It is also rational, by which he means that it is a form of communication and not an irrational manifestation of the holy in the sense that Rudolf Otto was then making popular. God's speech does not primarily leave us in awe and fascination; instead, it makes life-changing demands on us as it asks our obedience. God always speaks a concrete word, and it is a word that is nothing other than the divine self. "What God speaks is never known or true anywhere in abstraction from God Himself" (1/1: 137). Divine speech is a matter of truth. It also has a personal quality. "The personal character of God's Word is not, then, to be played off against its verbal or spiritual character" (1/1:138). On the contrary, God's revelation is personal precisely because it is verbal. With these comments, Barth anticipates Kristin Linklater's argument that the voice is the fullest expression of personal identity.

Barth understands that his analysis opens him to the charge of anthropomorphism. After all, God does not have vocal cords! Barth turns the table on this charge, however, by arguing, "The doubtful thing is not whether God is person, but whether we are" (1/1:138). In Jesus Christ we know what a human voice sounds like. God defines sound; we do not. God is "Lord of the wording of His Word" (1/1:139). God defines sound because God does not have to listen before speaking, or better put, listening and speaking are coincidental in God, since God is triune. True, Barth takes the freedom of God to its logical conclusion by insisting that "God did not need to speak to us" (1/1:140). God did not have to speak to us, but God could speak to us because God is eternally the Word. In chapter 9 I will return to the implications of the fact that the Word and not silence is eternal. Barth prepares the way for my remarks when he bluntly states that "death is dumb" (1/1:141). The resurrection means not only that death is dead but also that silence is not finally silent. Silence does not have the last word.

Unfortunately, because Barth tends to limit the act of hearing God's voice to the past, he tends to portray the modern human condition as involving a pervasive divine silence that drives humanity to either invent its own gods or seek God's Word in the church. He thinks that God withholds the divine voice from the modern world even though he argues, as he must, that if God speaks at one point in time, then God always speaks. "The time of the direct, original speech of God Himself in His revelation, the time of Jesus Christ (which was also and already that of Abraham according to John 8:56), the time of that which the prophets and apostles heard so that they could bear witness to it—that is one time" (1/1:145). The time of God's speech is, in fact, a time of contemporaneity. But Barth goes on to say that the time of the church is another time. "These are different times distinguished not only by the difference in periods and contents, not only by the remoteness of centuries and the disparity in the men of different centuries and millennia, but distinguished by the different attitude of God to men" (1/1:145). Those who heard God speak directly were in a unique position. All proclamation today is derivative because it is a repetition of their witness.

This conclusion by Barth not only contradicts his earlier statement that God can speak through anything at any time, it also contradicts his own understanding of eternity. It makes more sense to say that when we hear God speak, our identification of God's voice should be evaluated by the church in reference to how Christians recognize that voice in Scripture and proclamation. Barth will have none of that. He thinks that God speaks, but he also thinks he knows that in the present age God is silent. I do not know how Barth, or anyone else, could possibly know that.

What Barth wants to keep in focus is the necessity of Spirit-filled proclamation if we hope to hear God today. Even concerning proclamation, however, Barth's confidence that we can hear God when the Spirit moves us through a sermon is tempered by warnings that we should not be overly zealous in expressing this confidence in words. When talking about God's voice, the Christian should adopt a very careful tone.

Barth is known for his sometimes brash and polemical style, but like all great writers, he usually kept his rhetoric under strict control, even when he wanted to sound out of control. One of his warnings sounds as if it were directed at himself. It probably was: "I am thinking rather of a certain assurance of voice, speech and attitude with which, it seems, we think we can work on the new or older field, a certain confidence with which we think we can take those great concepts on our lips and analyze them and interrelate them constructively or in other ways, a certain sprightliness with which we speak about the things denoted by them as though we were speaking about them because we know how to speak about them with comparatively so little freedom from restriction" (1/1:162–63).

Theology is all about tone, in a way, yet "one cannot discuss tone in general" (1/1:163). Whether a certain tone is appropriate for the occasion is determined by the needs of the moment. Barth gives a typically Barthian spin on the performance theory of preaching: we do not perform what we know; instead we only know what we can perform. "The man who is really determined by God's Word will perform this act. There is no real knowledge of the Word without performance of this act" (1/1: 219). There are no rhetorical rules that tell us how to respond to a particular audience with the right tone. In this, as in all things, we have to trust in the Holy Spirit.

God Speaks! Creation according to Augustine, Luther, and Barth

If speech is more than a figurative way of talking about how God acts, then there are a lot of questions that need answering. How does God make sounds? Moreover, what does it mean to say that God speaks from eternity, if nobody is around to hear the divine voice? This question is puzzling, along the lines of the riddle: if a tree falls in the forest without anyone around, does it make a sound? It is no wonder that the question of the sound of God strikes many people today, even the very devout, as far-fetched and impious. Nevertheless, the implications involved in the unfolding of this question are enormous. If God spoke the world into being, to whom was God speaking? Could it be that God talks to the divine self? But in that case, why would God need to talk at all? Could John Donne be right that silence precedes the Word? In a sermon preached on the conversion of St. Paul, he said, "But how many millions of generations was the Word in heaven, and never spoke? The Word, Christ Himself, has been as long as God has been, but the uttering of this Word has been but since the creation."[21] What then was the Son before the Son was the Word? And how could the Son have been the Word from eternity if God did not say anything until the time of creation? These are surely the hardest questions that a theo-acoustics must try to answer, yet there are few contemporary theologians who even try to ask them.

Augustine, Luther, and Barth did not shy away from these questions. Before beginning with Augustine, however, it would be helpful to briefly

---

21. John Donne, *The Sermons of John Donne*, ed. Evelyn M. Simpson and George R. Potter (Berkeley: University of California Press, 1962), 6:216. For a brilliant explication of God's triadic speech, see Oliver Davies, *A Theology of Compassion: Metaphysics of Difference and the Renewal of Tradition* (Grand Rapids: Eerdmans, 2001), 262–66.

note the Platonic context in which Augustine worked by showing how two prior theologians, Philo and Origen, dealt with the same set of issues. Philo, who is traditionally read as trying to translate Hebraic thought into Greek, set the tone for the hermeneutics of God's speech in all subsequent theology that was influenced by Platonism. In his *Life of Moses* (De vita Mosis), Philo marvels at the passage in Exodus 20: 18, which states, in the Septuagint version, that the people saw God's voice.[22] Philo is further convinced of the visual nature of God's voice by the story of the flaming bush. In *On the Decalogue* (De Decalogo), he writes, "Then from the midst of the fire that streamed from heaven there sounded forth to their utter amazement a voice, for the flame became articulate speech in the language familiar to the audience, and so clearly and distinctly were the words formed by it that they seemed to see rather than hear them."[23] He goes on to gloss this miracle by a rather rationalistic comment. Why is God's voice visible? "Because whatever God says is not words but deeds, which are judged by the eyes rather than the ears."[24]

Origen inherited Philo's ambition to make faith look more Greek by devocalizing God's speech. In his *Contra Celsum*, Origen talks about a "generic divine sense which only the man who is blessed finds on this earth."[25] One form of this sense is a capacity to hear sounds that have no objective existence in the air. The prophets, he argues, had this sense, which explains their ability to hear God's voice. "They heard what they say they heard" (44–45), but what they heard was not something the ordinary person could have heard, because it did not sound like sound. God has a voice, but it "is such that it is heard only by those whom the speaker wishes to hear it" (121). It is heard only by those who have a "superior hearing" (122), those whose souls have not been hardened to the point of deafness. This is an example of the elitist understanding of a special spiritual organ (an inner ear) that only some people possess that Barth tried hard to avoid.

It is important to note the audience for which Origen was writing. Origen was doing apologetics—defending the faith from a rigorous (though frequently ignorant) philosophical attack—and he was responding to a culture that was still under the influence of the Greek privileging of sight over sound. In correcting Roman misconceptions about Christianity, Origen is forced to go out of his way—certainly beyond the boundaries

22. *Philo*, trans. F. H. Colson (Cambridge: Harvard University Press, 1935), 6:555.

23. Ibid., 7:29.

24. Ibid., 7:31.

25. Origen, *Contra Celsum*, trans. Henry Chadwick (Cambridge: University of Cambridge Press, 1953), 44.

of the biblical ethos—in speculating about a spiritual sense that transcends physical perception. His chief aim is to show that Christians do not really believe that "the utterance of God which is mentioned in scripture is . . . vibrated air" (121). If Romans think Christians are under the impression that God needs air to speak, they surely underestimate Christian intelligence. At the very least, they underestimate Origen's own ability to interpret Scripture allegorically in order to accommodate pagan complaints about its backward features.

Origen is right, of course, that God does not need air to speak, but Origen goes too far in arguing that God therefore does not have a soundful voice. Clearly, the sound of God is a metaphysical category. How God speaks may be beyond our intellectual comprehension, but according to biblical revelation, God's speech is not beyond our auditory perception.

Augustine confronts the question of God's speech in his reflections on Genesis, and he wrote about Genesis repeatedly throughout his career. I will focus on his *De Genesi ad litteram* (The Literal Meaning of Genesis), which he began in 401.[26] There are many complexities in Augustine's understanding of creation that go beyond the issue of God's voice. It is helpful to keep in mind that Augustine thought the days of creation were necessary categories to help us understand the orderly arrangement of the world, but in point of fact all things were created by God simultaneously. He is thus not so literal in his interpretation as the title of his work suggests. Actually, by a literal reading he means the intention of the author, and in this case the author is God. So what does God want to tell us about God's own self with the words of Genesis?

Augustine wastes no time in getting to the heart of the issue of God's voice. He asks how it is possible that God said, "Let there be light." Speaking, for Augustine, is a temporal activity. Indeed, in book 11 of his *Confessions* the pronunciation of the syllables of words is the paradigmatic experience of temporality. God is unchangeable, and thus God's speech cannot be subjected to time. Does this mean that God does not speak? Augustine entertains the idea that God spoke the world into being by means of a creature. But how could God create the world through speech and yet speak through a part of that creation at the same time? Moreover, what material would carry God's voice if no matter had yet been made? And what language would God have spoken, if the fall had not yet brought about the variety of tongues? Augustine thus concludes that these words ("Let there be light") were not "spoken by the sound of a voice; for a voice, whatever it is, is always corporeal" (28). Not only

26. St. Augustine, *The Literal Meaning of Genesis*, vol. 1, trans. John Hammond Taylor (New York: Newman, 1982).

does sound require both matter and time for its movement, but it also requires someone to hear it. "Shall we say, then, that there was such a sense of hearing in that formless and shapeless creation, whatever it was, to which God thus uttered a sound when He said, Let there be light? Let such absurdities have no place in our thoughts" (28; also see 186–87). God clearly does not speak unless someone is listening.

So why does Genesis insist on portraying God as a speaker? Augustine solves this riddle by proposing that we think of creation as happening in stages, even though in God it happened all at once. In the first stage of creation, God decided to create the world, the pattern of which is in the eternal Word. Augustine thus understands the Word more along the lines of an image than a sound. Indeed, he imagines God's decision along the lines of light because it does not take place in time. It is a kind of eternal illumination in God. "God in His eternity says all through His Word not by the sound of a voice, nor by a thinking process that measures out its speech, but by the light of Divine Wisdom, coeternal with Himself and born of Himself" (23). That God made all things through the Word, as the Gospel of John clearly states, does not mean that the Word was the instrument through which God spoke. Instead, it means that the idea (or what Augustine calls the exemplary cause) of creation exists eternally in the Word. As Augustine explains, "When we hear, And God said, 'Let there be . . .' we are given to understand that the reason of a thing created was in God" (55). The oral dimension of creation is thus to be translated into a Platonic theory of the Forms. Light precedes sound for Augustine.

In the second stage of creation, God infuses this eternal pattern into the minds of the angels. The light in "Let there be light" (Gen. 1:3) is thus not the visible light of this world but the inner illumination of the angels. They are given a sneak preview, so to speak, of what is yet to come. This happens in one flashing moment of enlightenment (keeping with the theme that true knowledge is immediate and thus not temporal). Even this stage of creation, then, is not the product of a divine conversation. "God therefore did not say, 'Let this or that creature be made' as often as the sacred text repeats And God said. He begot one Word in whom He said all before the several works were made" (54). The Word God speaks is who God is and thus is more like the light that radiates continuously from the sun than a sequence of sounds. It is one word that illuminates, not a series of words.[27]

27. There are two other stages of creation that are not important for my purposes. The third stage is the actual work of creation, while the fourth stage is God's pleasure in the goodness of creation.

Another way to understand Augustine's position on the divine voice is to examine his theory of divine causality. From this perspective, it is clear that there is for Augustine a kind of double creation: God first creates all things simultaneously and then actualizes each substance to become what it was meant to be. The first kind of causality is exemplary. This is the pattern of creation that is eternally present in the Word. These causes are like Plato's Forms, and they take no effort or time on God's part to imagine. They are to be distinguished from what Augustine calls causal or seminal reasons that God implants in all living creatures to cause them to develop and grow according to God's plan. Augustine develops this elaborate two-stage creation in part to explain the two different accounts of creation in Genesis. He also uses it to explain biblical references to God's voice. When God says, "Let there be light," God is calling a spiritual creature (angel or human) toward God *(conversa ad Creatorem)* and thus forming that creature through an inward illumination that makes it possible for the creature to know eternal truth. The communication of the divine plan to the angels, then, is at the same time the formation of the angels as free creatures capable of knowing the mind of God. The light plays the same role for us. It is the light that calls us out of nature to be creatures who can respond to God's will. The light comes from the Word, but not in the form of a voice.

Given how Augustine denies God a voice in the creation of the world, it may come as a surprise that he argues that God literally spoke to Adam and Eve in the garden.[28] Augustine lays the groundwork for this argument by making an important distinction: God speaks either through God's own substance or through a creature. In creating and sustaining the world, God speaks through God's own substance, which for Augustine means that God illuminates from within. Humans are separated from the angels, however, by needing a more external form of illumination. "But when God speaks to those who are unable to grasp His utterance, He speaks only through a creature" (68). God can thus speak to us in a dream or a state of ecstasy, presumably employing an angel for this purpose. Only if Adam were in perfect harmony with God, intuitively grasping God's utterance as the angels do, would there have been no reason for God to speak to Adam through another creature. Augustine even speculates that God appeared to Adam and Eve in human form, "using a creature appropriate for such an action" (167). What Augustine means when he argues that God speaks to us directly only through a creature is hard to discern. Clearly, God communicates as God through an inner word that needs no vocalization. When God wants to be heard by those who

28. St. Augustine, *The Literal Meaning of Genesis,* vo.l. 2, trans. John Hammond Taylor (New York: Newman, 1982), 59.

are deaf to such illumination, God speaks through an angelic agent. God causes the agent to speak on God's behalf. Just as humans can use novel words to enhance language, God can use miraculous events to accentuate the divine speech.[29] Is such mediated speech the same thing as saying that God speaks to us with the divine voice?

In his own commentary on Genesis, Luther quotes an obfuscating passage from *De Genesi ad litteram*, where Augustine tries to explain that "God said" means "it was determined from eternity." Luther's retort is characteristically quick and blunt: "The simple and true meaning must be adhered to."[30] He goes on to say that we should restrict our thinking to the literal meaning of the text; to stray beyond that leads to darkness and mischief. He pointedly refrains from asking what the light was that illuminated the unformed mass of heaven and earth. Luther could hold so tightly to the divine voice because he followed one of Augustine's own principles: "The Divine Word and Son of God does not live a formless life."[31] For Luther, "God said" means Jesus Christ was there from the very beginning, saying the same Word then as he said throughout the Bible and still says today. God does speak to us through someone, but it is no creature; it is the eternal Son.

Luther is thus led to defend the anthropomorphites who speak about God as if God has bodily parts. As I have previously shown, Luther cannot imagine God not having the whole apparatus of speech. If Augustine risks silencing God, and thus making silence speak louder than the Word, then Luther corrects Augustine with a more consistently christological account of creation. As a result, he reverses Augustine's prioritization of light and sound. In fact, Luther does not worry about who heard the Word before the world was created. "No one heard it spoken except God Himself, that is, God the Father, God the Son, and God the Holy Spirit" (19). Using the trinitarian formula in this statement is important because it is communication that constitutes God's threefoldness. God can speak to God's self because God is not a solitary figure. If God were one and only one person, living all alone, so to speak, then God talking to God's self would be as crazy as anybody else caught doing the same thing. If God is really differentiated, however, then it would be hard to imagine what else God would be doing from all eternity.

Luther too had his hesitations about the divine voice. "He does not speak grammatical words; He speaks true and existent realities. Accord-

29. See Brian Stock, *Augustine as Reader* (Cambridge: Harvard University Press, 1996), 9.

30. Martin Luther, *Luther's Works*, vol. 1, *Lectures on Genesis, Chapters 1–5*, ed. Jaroslav Pelikan (St. Louis: Concordia, 1958), 18.

31. Augustine, *Literal Meaning of Genesis*, 1:24.

ingly, that which among us has the sound of a word is a reality with God."[32] This might seem to stretch the analogy between God's voice and our own to a breaking point, if it were not for the fact that Luther takes God's voice literally. Words are true and meaningful only in God and not in us. "Thus sun, moon, heaven, earth, Peter, Paul, I, you, etc.—we are all words of God, in fact only one single syllable or letter by comparison with the entire creation" (21–22). For Augustine, God says only one Word, but for Luther, the divine discourse orchestrates a universe of visible sound. We speak "only according to the rules of language; that is, we assign names to objects which have already been created" (22). We follow rules, while God's speech rules.

Luther does refer to the traditional distinction between the created and uncreated Word. The uncreated Word abides in God. It is a divine thought, an inner command, an eternal utterance, and a distinct person. It can be all of these things because what God says is who God is, which makes the analogy of divine to human speech tenuous indeed. Nevertheless, Luther embraces the idea that the Word is best understood as true sound. It was this Word that Adam heard in the garden when God told Adam what not to eat. This brief sermon—which was, according to Luther, the original sermon, demonstrating that creator and preacher are interchangeably attributed to God—"would have brought to its conclusion the whole study of wisdom" (105) because no other words would ever have been needed. If it had not been for the fall, "we would have had no need for paper, ink, pens, and that endless multitude of books which we require today" (105). It is no accident, Luther claims, that the serpent attacked Adam and Eve with spoken words. The fall was not brought about by an inflammation of desire. "For the chief temptation was to listen to another word and to depart from the one which God had previously spoken" (147). It is our lack of attention, our inability to focus, our reluctance to listen that leads us astray. Luther was convinced that what he called "Satanic oratory" (155) was at work in Adam's day as it was in his own.

Not only was the fall caused by words; it also changed the nature of sound. When Adam and Eve turned their back on the original sermon, they lost confidence in God. It is as if they no longer knew where sounds were coming from when they lost the source of all sounds in God. Sounds without a known origin are menacing. Luther makes the fascinating suggestion that when the Bible says Adam and Eve heard God "walking in the garden at the time of the evening breeze" (Gen. 3: 8), what they really heard was the wind that preceded God's appearance. The wind now struck them as a terrible noise and thus a premonition of

32. Luther's Works, 1:21.

the punishment that awaited them. "They were so fearful that even in the bright light of day they were afraid of the rustling of a leaf" (170). The distortion of sound is the beginning of fear and self-doubt. Eve listens to the serpent as if she were talking "with a puppy that has been raised in the home" (171). It is our ears that are the source of our promiscuity. From now on, God's voice—"Where are you?"—will strike humans as a call to judgment. God's voice has not changed, but how we hear it has. Luther imagines God saying, "It was not my voice that frightened you; but your conscience convicted you of sin" (176). Luther thus works his theology of law and grace into the framework of God's voice. The history of sound is one long anticipation of the sweet words of Jesus.

That history is Luther's as well. Luther battled depression through-out his life, and in his darkest moods he heard the voices of creatures accusing and condemning him. He is led to think about these episodes in his lectures on Genesis when he reflects on Cain, who heard the voice of his slain brother crying out from his spilled blood. Cain is an example of someone who is seized by a spirit of sadness that changes their soundscape. "Even when they speak with people whom they know and in turn hear them, the very sound of their speech seems different, their looks appear changed, and everything becomes black and horrible wherever they turn their eyes" (287). At the far end of sound, where we are so distant from God that we no longer hear in the noise around us even an echo of God's voice, sound takes on a nightmare quality that can drive us to despair.

Fortunately, preaching is the sound that sets all sounds straight. In his sermons on the Gospel of John, Luther portrays preaching as an incarnational act that gives birth to the Word in the words of the sermon: God "condescends to enter the mouth of every Christian who professes the faith." Preaching thus "must be viewed and believed as though God's own voice were resounding from heaven."[33] We hear in God's voice—even in spite of our sin—grace, mercy, and goodness. Reason cannot bring a person to faith, simply because faith is a matter of hearing, not think-ing, something new. Luther goes so far as to say, "Whoever wants to be a Christian must be intent on silencing the voice of reason."[34] We can recognize only one voice at a time, and the singular voice of Jesus is easily lost in a crowd.

In his sermons on the opening chapters of John, Luther brings his systematic theology of sound to a climax. He makes it clear that God

---

33. Martin Luther, *Luther's Works*, vol. 24, *Sermons on the Gospel of St. John, Chapters 14–16*, ed. Jaroslav Pelikan (St. Louis: Concordia, 1961), 66–67.

34. Martin Luther, *Luther's Works*, vol. 23, *Sermons on the Gospel of St. John, Chapters 6–8*, ed. Jaroslav Pelikan (St. Louis: Concordia, 1959), 99.

has "from all eternity a Word, a speech, a thought or a conversation with Himself," and that "there is no analogy between the word of mortal man and the Word of the eternal and almighty God."[35] For Luther, John borrowed the ideas of his prologue from none other than Moses, so that Genesis and the Gospel of John interpret each other.

When God spoke to Moses on Mount Sinai through trumpet blasts and thunder, the people were afraid. Rather than selecting one or two to come up to the mountain, God descended to the people so that they could hear better. This story anticipates the Gospel narrative. "Therefore Christ was to speak so plainly and gently to us that we might believe His words and testimony and cling to them." The two Testaments do not speak with two different voices. When God called Moses to lead the Israelites out of Egypt, "Moses had to listen to this sound and believe in it." And when God told Moses, "Strike the water!" with the rod, it was not the staff that divided the sea. It was the Word of God that spoke, and "the deed followed immediately." Luther even imagines Christ assuring the Israelites that he will take them to the other shore, so that the sound of the parting waters "was not meaningless but . . . was the voice and Word of God Almighty."[36]

The foundation of the mutual implication of Genesis and John's Gospel is a simple parallel: If salvation comes from hearing Jesus, then the whole world can come from nothing less. The comforting words of Jesus are not limited to what he spoke during the time of the incarnation. Before all time, God is "pregnant with a Word or a conversation" which is incomprehensible to us (10). The prophets and the psalmist understood this (Luther refers to Ps. 33:6), but nobody put it better than John. Luther is aware that his position can be misinterpreted. He keeps the Arian heresy constantly in mind, because he does not want to portray Jesus as something like the first of all creation to speak. Jesus is not one of us, but since we too speak, we can become more like him.

Throughout these sermons, Luther repeatedly insists that "reason is blind; man must hold his ears to Christ's mouth and listen to His Word" (467). He can also say that reason must be blinded, perhaps an allusion to Mark 9:47, where Jesus says that if your eye causes you to stumble, you should tear it out. Luther is more interested in the eye itself than what the eye might see. He thinks that "the sense of sight or the eye is the most acute member of the human body" (292). Luther also likes the passage in John that describes the Spirit as a blowing wind (John 3:8). Sight is the source of most of our temptations, but we cannot see the

35. Martin Luther, *Luther's Works*, vol. 22, *Sermons on the Gospel of St. John, Chapters 1–4*, ed. Jaroslav Pelikan (St. Louis: Concordia, 1957), 9.
36. Ibid., 309 (first two quotes), 311, 313.

wind; we feel or hear it instead. The wind of the Spirit carries the sound of God. "It begins at the ear and ends at the ear" (293). Most important, we do not know whence the wind of the Spirit comes, which means that we cannot control it or predict its path. Luther makes fun of philosophers because they "cannot even understand the sense of hearing. No philosopher or sage has ever been able to say how it happens that the ear can catch the report of a gun discharged two miles away and how this sound travels as fast as any arrow from a crossbow" (295–96). If these simple sounds are a mystery, then how much more so is the voice of God. God can speak through anything. "Holy Scripture presents the Word to us everywhere" (304).

Luther uses the water of baptism as an example of how we can feel God's speech. Yet what can the water accomplish without the Word? Everything comes back to the sound of a particular voice. "When the Word is heard, then we feel its sound before our ears" (304). The image is synesthetic. It is the ear that most intimately comes into contact with God, by touching God's voice.

Barth follows Luther, rather than Augustine, on the significance of God's voice. Barth, in fact, can be understood as systematizing Luther's insights into a trinitarian account of sound. God's speech is not, for Barth, a metaphorical way of talking about, say, how God makes God's divinity manifest through nature. By calling the divine speech an action, Barth means it is a word spoken at a specific place and time. It is also a word spoken by a specific person. That is, it is a word spoken by the Word who is Jesus Christ. The Word is decidedly not like the phenomenon of light. Barth says as much when he argues that the Word "is not universally, i.e., always and everywhere present" (1/1:158). The only general concept that really fits the Word is the concept of sound, precisely because sound is never generally perceived.

Much of Barth's doctrine of creation is an explicit rejection of Augustine's. For example, he does not hesitate to reverse Augustine's prioritization of light and sound: "Thus even the separation of the cosmos from chaos by light depends on the Word of God" (3/1:118). He also rejects Augustine's notion that if God were to be a speaker, he would need someone to listen: "Proclaiming His own glory as the Creator of light, God gives most eloquent proof of His concern for the creature. As yet there is no eye nor ear nor heart to perceive this gratefully" (3/1:119). Barth calls the counsel that takes place during creation a "divine soliloquy" (3/1:182). This counsel is also more than a soliloquy, given the repetition of the phrase "Let us." It is more like a divine conversation, and this conversation imagines the creation of humanity: "A genuine counterpart in God Himself leading to a unanimous decision is the secret prototype which is the basis of an obvious copy, a secret image and an obvious reflection in the coexistence of God and man, and also of the existence of man himself" (3/1:183). Barth dismisses the idea that the "Let us" reflects a divine counsel between God and the angels. How could God need help in deciding to be the creator? What advice could the angels have given God? No, the counsel is within God, which demonstrates that God is sound before light, and thus Word from all eternity.

Before creation, nothing returned God's voice. That is to say, nothing spoke back to God outside of the three Persons of the Trinity. That out of which God called the world into being is often called *nothing*, but this can suggest that there really is something to nothingness. This nothingness is usually understood visually, as a kind of darkness, but it might be better to call the nothing that preceded creation *silence*. However, this has the parallel problem of appearing to grant silence an ontological status. Silence became a reality only when God addressed the world into being. Before that, the divine sound was all there was.

A Note on the Preexistence of Jesus Christ

That God speaks creation into being through the Word raises the thorny question of the preexistence of Jesus Christ—not whether, but how. That is, what was the form of Jesus Christ before the incarnation? Karl-Josef Kuschel has argued that Barth moved from an abstract account of the "wholly other" God to a strong affirmation of the preexistence of Christ for primarily political reasons.[37] The more Barth rejected natural theology in order to combat religious idealism in all of its forms, the more he located all of God's activity in the person of Jesus Christ. There is something to Kuschel's analysis, but Barth's political motivation, at least after the second edition of his Romans commentary, was subordinated to a theological logic. For Barth, grace is not a general phenomenon that can be attributed to different kinds of experience. Jesus Christ is not a theophany, revealing a universal truth that can be found outside of Christ. Election means that God chose from all eternity to be determined by the identity of Jesus Christ. More technically put, Jesus Christ is both the subject and the object of election, the One who elects and the One who is elected.

This does not mean that human nature as such has been imbued with something of the divine nature. Barth accepts Luther's premise that we are saved in spite of our sin, and thus he rejects any notion of the divinization of humanity. To clarify this matter, as Bruce McCor-

37. Karl-Josef Kuschel, *Born before All Time? The Dispute over Christ's Origin*, trans. John Bowden (New York: Crossroad, 1992).

mack has documented, Barth recovered the Reformed doctrine of an anhypostatic Christology.[38] What this technical term means is, among other things, that God became incarnate in human nature but not in a particular human person. This rules out every kind of adoptionism: there was no human person in whom God decided to become incarnate. There is only one person who is the Son of God; there is no separate human "hypostasis." There is a hypostatic union of two natures in Jesus Christ, divine and human, but it is the divine that becomes human, not the other way around. The result of this action is a unique unity that exists in no other form. If a human being were chosen by God to become the Son of God, then God's decision would transform all of human nature by making it receptive to the divine. For Barth, the antithesis between God and humanity is overcome not by an alteration in humanity but by the attribution of our sin, guilt, and alienation to Jesus Christ. Barth thus denies (or at least radically modifies) the reciprocity of the two natures that are united. Human attributes can be ascribed to the Logos, who is the Second Person of the Trinity, but the divine does not become a property of the human.

Much has been made in recent years about Barth's revival of the anhypostatic doctrine.[39] For my purposes, this doctrine helpfully emphasizes the extent to which the Son is not merely an aspect or example of a general phenomenon called *divinity* that was at some point united with humanity. Instead, the Son is already Jesus Christ even before the incarnation. Indeed Barth cautions, "It has to be kept in mind that the whole conception of the *logos asarkos*, the 'second person' of the Trinity as such, is an abstraction" (3/1:54). This does not mean that Barth thinks the Son was always enfleshed, so that the eternal Word was eternally blood and bone. He goes to great lengths in *Church Dogmatics* 1/2 to deny that Jesus Christ is a demigod. He notes that the Bible uses the term *flesh* to denote human nature after the fall. Nevertheless, he can make the remarkable claim that "the Word is not only the eternal Word of God but 'flesh' as well, i.e., all that we are and exactly like us even in our opposition to Him" (1/2:151). The point is that the eternal Son is not "a formless Christ who might well be a Christ-principle or

38. Bruce L. McCormack, "Revelation and History in Transfoundationalist Perspective: Karl Barth's Theological Epistemology in Conversation with a Schleiermacherian Tradition," *Journal of Religion* 78 (1998): 18–37; and McCormack, *Karl Barth's Realistic Dialectical Theology: Its Genesis and Development, 1909–1936* (Oxford: Clarendon, 1995), 361–67.

39. One common objection to the anhypostatic doctrine is that it denies the human personality of the incarnate Logos. For Barth, there is only one personality of the Logos, and that is the Son of God. He rejected nineteenth-century Christologies that link our salvation to a Romantic reading of Jesus' personality. The divine is hidden in Jesus. We are not saved by Jesus' personality, heroic or otherwise, but rather by God.

something of that kind" (3/1:54). If we could purify *flesh* of all its fallen connotations—indeed, if we could use *flesh* to designate what we truly are in terms of what Jesus always has been—then it would be appropriate to say that the Son has always been the flesh that we will one day become.

Barth has sometimes been criticized for reducing the three Persons of the Trinity to mere modes of one divine being. He does use modal terminology, calling the Son the second mode of existence of the inner divine reality. Such language should not distract from the radical nature of his thought. The incarnation is not an alien activity on God's part. Indeed, anything God does can be said to be what God is. God is not a being who first exists and then subsequently decides to do one thing or another. That would make God not only temporal but also undependable. If the Son was always the Son, then the Son was begotten (not created) by the Father in anticipation of the role the Son would play in the creation of the world. Barth says as much: "In respect of His Son who was to become man and the Bearer of human sin, God loved man and man's whole world from all eternity, even before it was created, and in and in spite of its absolute lowliness and non-godliness, indeed its anti-godliness. He created it because He loved it in His Son who because of its transgressions stood before Him eternally as the Rejected and Crucified" (3/1:50–51). To speculate about who the Son was before the incarnation—*asarkos*—is beside the point. There was never a time when the identity of the Son was undetermined by the Father. If we know God only through the incarnate Son, and that knowledge is real knowledge, then the incarnate Son is really who God is.

Bruce McCormack is right when, in a controversial essay, he argues that for Barth "the second person of the Trinity has a name and His name is Jesus Christ."[40] God is thus from eternity determined to be for us. As McCormack puts it, "God is already in pre-temporal eternity—*by way of anticipation*—that which he would become in time" (100). More specifically, the Second Person of the Trinity exists in "a form which is constituted by the anticipation of union with the humanity of Christ" (104). Everything, of course, depends on what is meant by the idea of anticipation. However it is understood, McCormack argues that Barth should have taken his emphasis on the preexistence of Jesus Christ to the logical conclusion of understanding the Trinity as a function of the doctrine of election. That is, God's decision to elect Jesus Christ (and, by implication, us too) is the ground of God's self-differentiation as three

40. Bruce McCormack, "Grace and Being: The Role of God's Gracious Election in Karl Barth's Theological Ontology," in *The Cambridge Companion to Karl Barth*, ed. John Webster (Cambridge: Cambridge University Press, 2000), 100.

Persons. McCormack's argument that election precedes (or constitutes) the Trinity is daring and speculative, and its implications have yet to be fully worked out.

At the very least, we can say that election and Trinity need to be thought more closely together than is usually the case. A more prudent position than McCormack's would see the two as so closely tied together that neither can be the foundation of the other. The reason election is Trinity and vice versa is that the relationship among the divine Persons is an act of communication that is projected beyond the boundaries of the Trinity itself. This point can be made from the perspective of the Third Person of the Trinity. Barth follows church tradition by arguing that the Holy Spirit constitutes the bond between Father and Son. He calls the Spirit "the innermost secret of God" (3/1:56), which can sound as if he is portraying the Spirit as the silent bond of love that the Father shares with the Son. When two people share a sacred bond, we call that bond love, but there is warrant in Barth's theology to suggest that the particular form of the bond shared by the Father and the Son is best called speech or sound. The Trinity is bound by sound, which creates a divine space that is both a unity and a diversity. In that sound (the divine conversation) God already envisions what humans will be. Indeed, since sound takes time, it is the interval between the words exchanged by the Father and the Son that opens up the space for creation. That is, something other, and thus something temporal, is already implied by the divine decision to be as an act of communication.

The Spirit thus can be conceived as not only the bond that unites the Father and Son but also a kind of musical interval between them that makes creation possible. "We may say in a word that it is in God the Holy Spirit that the creature as such pre-exists" (3/1:56). The term *interval* denotes space more than sound. As interval, the Spirit opens up the space for what will eventually be us. That space is harmonious, not divisive. For that reason, the trinitarian interval is best understood as the resonance of the loving conversation between the Father and the Son—the way their speech reverberates in creative ways beyond their shared intimacy. Sound, after all, is movement—the movement of molecules of air, vibrating at different frequencies. Of course, God does not need air to speak, because God is Spirit, but the Spirit is best understood not as empty space but the divine breath. The air carries sound for us, but for God sound is carried by the Spirit.

The divine communication is thus the metaphysical condition for human speech. Says Barth: "It is by the communication and impartation of that in which God exists as God that it comes about that man can exist as man" (3/1:57). That is a complicated statement, but I take it to mean something like this: God is God as One who distributes the divine self among the three Persons of the Trinity. This distribution is best understood as a kind of communication between Father and Son. The Spirit is how that communication happens, and that same Spirit makes it possible for us to share God's love with each other as well. Because the Father loved the Son, a love that we can best understand as a kind of speech, the Father through the Son spoke the world into existence and, furthermore, created a creature who echoes the divine sound. The Spirit is God's airless breath, but in us the Spirit works through the air to enable the Word to be carried from mouth to ear.

How Barth holds together Trinity and election as an eternal unity can be seen in his doctrine of creation. For Barth, there is an ultimate harmony between Creator and creature that is grounded in the relationship of Father and Son. "As God in Himself is neither deaf nor dumb but speaks and hears His Word from all eternity, so outside His eternity He does not wish to be without hearing or echo, that is, without the ears and voices of the creature" (3/1:50). Creation, then, is in some sense entailed in the Trinity itself: "If it is true that the world and man are created in Jesus Christ, i.e., for His sake and for Him, in actualization of the compassion in which from all eternity God turned to the creature in the person of His Son bearing and representing it, then creation does not precede reconciliation but follows it" (3/1:76). Of course, this is the height of theological speculation, because, as Barth acknowledges, nobody can know what took place at the creation of the world. Nevertheless, Christians do know what took place in Jesus Christ, and that gives us a clue to the origin of the world as well as its destiny.

Barth, who is famous for insisting that God did not need the creation, and thus that the creation was a free decision of the divine will, can even go so far as to suggest that creation is entailed in the differentiation of the Trinity. "If by the Son or the Word of God we understand concretely Jesus, the Christ, and therefore very God and very man, as He existed in the counsel of God from all eternity and before creation, we can see how far it was not only appropriate and worthy but necessary that God should be the Creator. If this was God's eternal counsel in the freedom of His love, the counsel actualized in the manger of Bethlehem, the cross of Calvary and the tomb of Joseph of Arimathea, it was not merely possible but essential for God to be the Creator" (3/1:51). From the very beginning of time, God the Father was speaking to another, and that speech entailed something more than mere possibility but something less than strict necessity for God to create something other than God's self. That God was already sound, in other words, is the basis upon which it is possible that God could hear an echo.

A theology of sound also suggests it is no accident that we humans take the form we do, because in the Son, God already anticipated us.

God did not become incarnate in Jesus in order to be like us; we were created to be speakers and listeners, that is, to be like Jesus Christ. In a careful theological exegesis of Genesis, Francis Watson has come to the conclusion that the "image of God," which has been given so many different interpretations over the centuries, cannot be separated from the concept of a visual likeness. This would explain the ban on creating images of God; humans already are that image, and thus they should not try to make God into some other likeness. What Watson is offering is a consistently christological anthropology. "If Jesus is like God, then, in so far as they are like Jesus, all humans are like God."[41] Without this christological principle, the image of God quickly degenerates into speculative talk about human rationality or the superiority of humans over animals or, even worse, mysterious spiritual capacities that are allegedly inherent in human nature. My only contribution to Watson's analysis is to suggest that the image of God is more auditory than visual. We are echoes seeking a return to our source.

In sum, my position commits me to arguing that the Son from the beginning possessed some kind of spiritual-material body, a body that is not identical with but nonetheless hints at the glorified body of Jesus after the resurrection. The complexity of this thought suggests that theology must steer between two errors. First, theologians should not, for reasons that are less obvious than one might suppose, portray the Son as fully human from the very beginning. Second, theologians should not portray the eternal Son as completely unrelated to the humanity that God creates in time. The problem with portraying the Son as fully human from eternity is not only that it conveys a crudely anthropomorphic portrait of God (by suggesting that God is like us, which gets the relationship the wrong way around) but also that it leads to a premature divinization of human nature (by suggesting that in our present, earthly form we are already godlike). The problem with a purely spiritual understanding of the Son is even more grave. If the Son was not always the spoken Word of God—the One through whom God was already speaking when God spoke the world into being—then there is no basis upon which we can say that we were created for the Son and for the purpose of eternal fellowship with the Trinity. The idea that God speaks means not only that Jesus Christ was the voice of God in the incarnation but that the very same Jesus Christ has always been God's voice.

The idea that the preexistence of Jesus Christ is the prototype for all subsequent creation is necessary for understanding the whole spectrum of Christian faith. If God were not speaking a creative Word from the

41. Francis Watson, *Text and Truth: Redefining Biblical Theology* (Edinburgh: T & T Clark, 1997), 291.

beginning, then the idea that God speaks the world into being is mere anthropocentric metaphor, and the theology of the Word collapses into a miasma of colorful but misguided language. Moreover, if God did not speak through some kind of formed body, then what kind of body did Jesus have upon his resurrection, and what kind of body will we have in the afterlife? It is the destiny of all living creatures to be blessed with a glorified body that is sufficiently similar to our earthly existence as to enable us to remember and remain in continuity with the past and sufficiently different from our earthly existence as to enable us to enjoy God forever. The heavenly end of all life is possible only on the basis of the beginning of all life in the relationship between the Father and the Son. Also, if the Word of God is not physical, effecting change in the world, then how can the Word transubstantiate the elements of the Eucharist? And finally, if eternity were truly silent until the creation of the world, then what hope is there for singing in heaven? To this final question—the sound of heaven—I will return in chapter 9.

eight

Reading, Hearing, Acting

Toward a Christian Acoustemology

Reading Alone

Elizabeth Achtemeier has put the matter best by putting it simply: "The Christian church is the community that expects to hear God speaking through its Scriptures."[1] This fundamental claim needs unpacking because for many Christians the Bible is primarily a text to be read rather than a script to be performed out loud. Thus hermeneutics, the art of interpretation, dominates discussions of the Bible, rather than rhetoric, which is the art of public speaking. Thinking about the Bible as a written document leads to all kinds of epistemological problems and puzzles. If the Bible does not speak to us, then we have to figure out how to make it talk. But if the Bible is silent, then how can we be sure that we are not spinning its words to make it say what we want to hear? Thinking about the Bible as an oral document leads to a different set of questions that are acoustemological rather than epistemological. Just how radical is the change from a silent to a vocal understanding of Scripture?

---

1. Elizabeth Achtemeier, "The Canon as the Voice of the Living God," in *Reclaiming the Bible for the Church*, ed. Carle E. Braaten and Robert W. Jenson (Grand Rapids: Eerdmans, 1995), 119.

To answer that question, we need to begin with a scene from Augustine's *Confessions*. When Augustine moved to Milan in 384, he began attending church in order to hear the sermons of the local bishop. Augustine was an ambitious professor of rhetoric, and Ambrose was a celebrated bishop known for his eloquence, so it made sense for Augustine to want to hear the famous preacher. Augustine also sought the bishop's company—Augustine's mother, Monica, was especially enamored of him—for intellectual exchange, but Ambrose was always busy.

When Ambrose was not attending to the needs of his congregation, he was reading: "When he read, his eyes scanned the page and his heart explored the meaning, but his voice was silent and his tongue was still."[2] Ambrose evidently made a practice of reading silently, even though he was frequently surrounded by other people when he read, people who would have liked to have heard what he was reading. "Perhaps," Augustine speculated, "he was afraid that, if he read aloud, some obscure passage in the author he was reading might raise a question in the mind of an attentive listener, and he would then have to explain the meaning or even discuss some of the more difficult points."[3] Or perhaps, Augustine continued, he wanted to save his voice, which was easily made hoarse.

As Alberto Manguel has pointed out, this is the first recorded description in Western history of someone who made a habitual practice of silent reading.[4] Scholars debate that claim, but there is no debate that in the ancient world, reading out loud had been the norm since the beginning of written language. How else would Philip have known that the Ethiopian eunuch was reading Isaiah before joining him in his chariot (Acts 8:26–31)? Letters were invented as signals of sound, enabling people to speak to others even in their absence. The reader lends her voice to the silent marks on the page, resuscitating the dead images with the breath of life. As Manguel notes, "the primordial languages of the Bible—Aramaic and Hebrew—do not differentiate between the act of reading and the act of speaking: they name both with the same word."[5] For the ancients—due in part to the low percentage of literacy, as well

2. Augustine, *Confessions*, trans. R. S. Pine-Coffin (New York: Penguin, 1961), 114.
3. Ibid.
4. There are certainly scenes in ancient Western literature that precede the *Confessions* that depict someone reading silently, but Manguel argues that these are rare exceptions, not the norm. A passage in the Bible from 1 Samuel 1:13 suggests that it was even uncommon for Jews to say their prayers silently: "Hannah was praying silently; only her lips moved, but her voice was not heard; therefore Eli thought she was drunk."
5. Alberto Manguel, *A History of Reading* (New York: Viking, 1996), 45. Also see Bernard M. W. Knox, "Silent Reading in Antiquity," *Greek, Roman and Byzantine Studies* 9 (1968): 421–35.

as the lack of punctuation in ancient texts, which meant that for basic comprehension it was necessary to read them out loud—reading was a social, not a private, activity. Consequently, libraries used to be very noisy places.

By contrast, today we have to make a conscious decision to read out loud; our sluggish tongues resist the effort. A phone call seems like an impossible labor given the speed of an e-mail (although instant messaging shares something of the intimacy and temporal progression of spoken conversation). Martin Luther began the Protestant Reformation when he proposed ninety-five theses for public debate, but his insistence that the Word is a matter for preaching was eventually undermined by the printing press, which established an exclusive intimacy between the reader and the text. Reading became a process that no longer required acoustical space. Instead of taking place in a room full of people, it occupied the interior space of the reader's crowded thoughts. Reading became a monologue rather than a dialogue, with the consequence that it was disconnected from the social regulation that comes from organized group activities.

One of Luther's goals in enabling more people than ever before to have a direct relationship to the Bible was to erode the authority of Rome. What he could not have anticipated was a shift in the balance of power from the community to the individual. When reading becomes silent, sound—which is the social dimension of meaning—just gets in the way.

Reading as Hearing

Reading is not a bloodless affair. We love books, as Wayne Booth has argued, because we love people, and we read so much because we find the people who write books to be very good company.[6] When we read a good book, we establish a relationship with the author. A relationship with a person whom we know only on the printed page is possible through the recognition of a scripted voice. This makes reading not only a personal but also an ethical act. When somebody is trying to tell us something, we feel compelled to respond. His or her voice enters us in an intimate way even as it obligates us to focus our attention externally. This is not true of mechanically produced sounds, even though the proliferation of talking toys in our society demonstrates how much we trust technology to meet basic human needs. Children grow bored

6. Wayne Booth, *The Company We Keep: An Ethics of Fiction* (Berkeley: University of California Press, 1988).

with such toys quickly, even when these toys have been programmed to listen and talk back.

Perhaps literary theorists resist the idea of reading as a matter of hearing because they associate it with an immature and unreflective relationship to books. We read to children, and then teach them to read out loud, but we expect them to advance to the more sophisticated mode of silent reading.[7] If they have to pronounce words with their lips, then they are not really reading. They are doing something more like talking to themselves. Speed readers are so quick because they treat words as signs that can be scanned in spatial groupings. They do not slow down to dwell on sound, which is transmitted more slowly than light. Verbalization gets in the way. Yet surely speed reading is more of a trick than a skill. Applying lessons in hyper-efficiency is not the goal of reading. The more we love a book, the more slowly we will read it, absorbing its words by saying them in our own voice.

There are many debates about the relationship between the "real" and the implied author, but the fact remains that good books are written in distinctive and recognizable voices. Voice here is more than a metaphor. The term *literary voice* is more than just another way of talking about style. Words come alive on the page because we connect them to a person who is saying them. It does not matter if we do not know a lot about that person; what matters is that the voice of the text has power precisely because it is a personal communication. Scripted voices are revelatory because they are invitational, and they are invitational only because they are distinctive and personal.

The revelatory nature of the human voice explains why, for most readers of most texts, authorship matters.[8] Just look at the anger that

7. On the other hand, children understand the voices of texts instinctively, perhaps because they have not yet been taught that reading is for the eyes only. The transition from hearing parents and teachers read a story out loud to reading by oneself is so gradual that reading can long remain a vocal affair. Francis Spufford, in a lovely reflection on childhood reading, describes the phenomenon well: "The silence that fell on the noises of people and traffic and dogs allowed an inner door to open to the book's data, its script of sound. There was a brief stage of transition in between, when I'd hear the text's soundtrack poking through the fabric of the house's real murmur, like the moment of passage on the edge of sleep where your legs jerk as your mind switches over from instructing solid limbs to governing the phantom body that runs and dances in dreams. Then, flat on my front with my chin on my hands or curled in a chair like a prawn, I'd be gone." Francis Spufford, *The Child That Books Built* (New York: Metropolitan, 2002), 1–2. Books open up a world in part because our parents opened them to us with their own voices, teaching us to trust the voices we hear on the printed page.

8. Although Roland Barthes announced "the death of the author" as a consequence of the death of God, some theologians and Bible scholars have followed literary critics in arguing that authorship does not matter. This allows them to downplay the importance

is aroused when amateur literary sleuths claim that Shakespeare did not write his plays. It is not as if they are saying that the plays are no good. Nonetheless, by suggesting that someone else wrote them, they are calling into question the ways we read and perform them today. If Christopher Marlowe really did fake his own murder, flee to Italy, and send manuscripts back to England that were eventually published under the name of a wealthy but obscure former stagehand named William Shakespeare, then the plays would still be great, but we would have a different interpretation of their Italian settings and their obsession with disguises and altered identities. We would hear a different voice in the plays, and that would change how we interpret them.

Authorship matters because it helps shape the way that we hear texts. It can also change the way we hear sounds. After the bombing of Iraq began in the second Gulf War, a video was broadcast of Saddam Hussein defending the resolve of the Iraqi military. Analysts pored over the video not only to ascertain when it was made but also to figure out if it was indeed Saddam's voice on the tape. If it was not, then the tape would have a totally different meaning. The audio content of the tape would not change, but how we listen to it would. It would, in fact, sound different.

So how do we recognize a voice in a text? Clearly, a scripted voice can remain the same even through a variety of genres and literary styles. Arguably, great authors are great precisely because they can maintain a unique voice while producing many different kinds of literature. John Updike's voice, for example, is consistently recognizable whether he is

---

of historical criticism, but it also forces them to devocalize Scripture. Stephen E. Fowl, for example, in an exceptional book that admirably defends the theological ground of all biblical interpretation, goes out of his way to dismiss the significance of textual voice. "I can advance no argument by claiming that my interpretation conforms to the 'voice' of scripture and my opponent's does not allow the 'voice' of scripture to be heard." *Engaging Scripture* (Oxford: Blackwell, 1998), 26. What matters for Fowl is not bad interpretations of the Bible but bad practices of Christian faith. Thus Fowl can state that "the authority of scripture is not a property of the biblical texts any more than a meaning or an ideology is a property of those texts" (203). The practices of the church speak louder, for Fowl, than the words of the Bible.

A. K. M. Adam offers a rigorous hermeneutical development of this position. The literary critic Stanley Fish once asked, "Is there a text in this class?" The question to be asked of Adam is, "Is there a Bible in the pulpit?" Adam's answer is, essentially, no. The Bible is not behind the pulpit. Instead it is in the mind of the congregation. The church not only closed the canon of Scripture, it also keeps rewriting Scripture by interpreting it anew. The Bible is silent, for Adam, unless the church gives it a voice. See A. K. M. Adam, "Docetism, Käsemann, and Christology," *Scottish Journal of Theology* 49 (1996): 391–410; "Matthew's Readers, Power, and Scripture," *SBL Seminar Papers* (1994): 435–49; and *Making Sense of New Testament Theology: "Modern" Problems and Prospects* (Macon, Ga.: Mercer University Press, 1995).

writing poetry, short stories, allegorical tales, autobiographical essays, book reviews, or epic novels.[9] We can recognize his voice on the page even if we have never heard him speak in person. People who read him extensively can know his voice intimately without knowing him personally. Nevertheless, reading Updike is not like recognizing the voice of a loved one in a letter. We draw on memory and experience to fill in the gaps between the words in a love letter, which can help to avoid misunderstanding. Our relationship to a literary voice is no less imaginative, but we are usually forced to draw from our memory of other texts to help us to interpret any individual text. It helps to read a lot of an author in order to have a full sense of the author's voice. The fact that we must use our imagination in reading a book does not make textual voices any less auditory. What voices give us is the presence of an other, even when we must imagine him or her in our own head.

Reading the Bible for the voice of God is not all that different from reading a novel for the voice of its author. Christians believe they have a personal relationship with God that is both derived from and supportive of their practice of attending to God's voice in the Bible. Not all Christians, of course, read the Bible in order to listen for God's voice. Among evangelicals and fundamentalists, the doctrine of infallible inspiration can be used to silence the sound of the Bible when it pictures God as having inscribed words on the printed page like the carved tablets Moses received on Mt. Sinai. This makes the Bible something to be looked at and revered as a sacred object rather than something to be performed and heard. As a result, the doctrine of infallible inspiration can turn the Bible into a dry and lifeless text of abstract propositions. This does not mean the doctrine of divine inspiration is without truth or value. Properly construed, it can highlight the ways in which God uses human writers as resonators of the divine voice.

A resonator, however, is not the same thing as a ventriloquist's dummy. God speaks through the biblical writers, but they modify God's sound as it moves them. The apostle Paul, for example, has a voice that is undeniably his own, as do the other authors of biblical books, whether we can identify those authors historically or not. But Christians do not read the Bible to have a relationship with Paul. We read it to have a relationship with God. It is God's voice we want to hear, even as we listen to Paul. How does that happen?

9. For an analysis of Updike's voice as it relates to theology, see Stephen H. Webb, "Writing as a Reader of Karl Barth: What Kind of Religious Writer Is John Updike Not?" in *John Updike and Religion: The Sense of the Sacred and the Motions of Grace*, ed. Jim Yerkes (Grand Rapids: Eerdmans, 1999), 145–61.

There are two ways that God speaks through Paul even today. One way is to argue that God authorizes (to borrow a term that Wolterstorff develops in his book *Divine Discourse*) the words of Paul to be God's own voice to us. We hear something that God wants to say to us in Paul's scripted voice because Paul is not speaking for himself. God chooses to speak to us through the voices of the biblical writers, just as Augustine was converted by the child saying, "Take and read." The idea of authorization, however, does not take us far enough in understanding what difference it makes to claim that God is the author of the Bible. It suggests that it is Paul's voice we hear in the text, even if we subsequently decide that God wants us to hear Paul's message as God's own.

How can it be said that we hear God speak the words of the Bible in God's own voice? And how can we make sure that this voice is not of our own creation? These are two related but separate questions. The problems entailed in the second should not make us have exaggerated worries about the first. At the outset it should be said that we imagine printed voices according to what we know about the person we meet in the text. If we know that person only by what he or she has written, then we look for clues to how they sound in the text itself. A scripted voice is only as distinctive as the text is coherent. This does not mean that the text must speak in the same voice at all times in order for the reader to hear the author's voice. On the contrary, complex literary texts can speak in many voices, all of which can be heard in the voice of the author. Even when a novel is written from the perspective of an omniscient narrator, characters will be given voices of their own, without thereby detracting from the narrative voice. Some literary critics argue that great novels are invariably multivocal—peopled with characters who carry out a dialogue among themselves—but the ways these characters speak and understand the world will still be stamped by the distinctive voice of the author.

The voice we hear in a text, then, is both our own and not our own. Just as there is a visual imagination, there is an auditory imagination. We can recall images in our mind that are colored by our own perspective but nonetheless reflect actual perceptions of things in the world. Just so, we can hear voices in our head that speak to us in someone else's voice. A useful analogy can be made to the inner voice we use when we think. The precise nature of this inner voice is elusive; it comes from within but is not produced by our body like the natural voice. We hear it, but it does not travel through the air. We cannot trace it to a source, since we are the source we would be trying to track. This is paradoxical. Hearing our inner voice implies that we can step outside of ourselves in order to listen to ourselves, but if we did this, to whom would we be listening? The important point is that the inner voice is not the same thing as talking to ourselves. It is more immediate and less self-conscious than that. It is the closest experience we have to being present to ourselves. It is also the closest experience we have to getting inside someone else's voice. It shows just how close speaking and hearing are to being the same thing, since the speaker must listen to her own voice and the hearer must let the other person's words resonate from within.

It is interesting that Barth portrays preaching as a kind of silent yet vocal reading to oneself. "The sermon will be like the involuntary lip movement of one who is reading with great care, attention, and surprise, more following the letters than reading in the usual sense, all eyes, totally claimed, aware that 'I have not written the text.'"[10] To read is to perform, no matter how still we sit.[11]

The Joy of Public Reading

Words have "mouth-pleasure," as the poet Donald Hall puts it.[12] This is especially true of an oral text like the Bible, which was written to

10. Karl Barth, *Homiletics*, trans. Geoffrey W. Bromiley and Donald E. Daniels (Louisville: Westminster John Knox, 1991), 76.

11. Alla Bozarth-Campbell, in a much neglected but very valuable contribution to the orality of interpretation, treats the written text as a mere cipher of potentiality that becomes real only when actualized by the voice. Her theological language is explicit: "The poem as potentially speaking subject remains voiceless until it is taken into a body and allowed to resonate from within. The gesture of the human body can release the word from its own interior." Alla Bozarth-Campbell, *The Word's Body: An Incarnational Aesthetic of Interpretation* (Tuscaloosa: University of Alabama Press, 1979), 14. Throughout this book she uses the Christian idea of incarnation as the hermeneutical key for interpretation, but she tends to reverse the meaning of this theological doctrine. In her view, the word is not complete until it is heard and understood, and understanding is always demonstrated when one uses the word in new ways, so that the word is without life until it is given voice by the hearer. Although she tries to follow a trinitarian line of inquiry by showing how the creative word must be enfleshed in writing before it takes shape in the audience's response, her position is more Hegelian than orthodox in arguing that only at the end of this process does the word come into its fullest meaning. Nonetheless, she demonstrates how every theory of language is ultimately nothing more than commentary on Christology. *Logos* is inseparable from *theos*.

12. Quoted by Catherine Madsen in her brilliant essay on orality and the liturgy, "The Common Word: Recovering Liturgical Speech," *Crosscurrents* (summer 2002): 242. Sven Birkerts's meditation on reading in *The Gutenberg Elegies: The Fate of Reading in an Electronic Age* (New York: Fawcett, 1995), offers some useful observations for Christian worship. He is especially nuanced in his understanding of how reading works to transport us from one world to another that is no less real. "Reading is not on a continuum with the other bodily or cognitive acts. It instigates a shift, a change of state—a change analogous to, but not as totally affecting as, the change from wakefulness to sleep" (80). The church teaches us how to read by immersing us in the world of the Bible. That is why reading

be spoken. It is full of the mnemonic patterns that enable listeners to remember what they have heard. Rhythm aids recall, as do formulaic sayings and other rhetorical devices. Indeed, everything used in worship—not just the Bible but also the ancient creeds—was written for the ear more than the eye.[13] Christianity was passed down from generation to generation through oral modes of education. As William A. Graham has observed, "the actual contents of the scriptural book (or, more correctly for the early Christian centuries, of the scriptural books) were transmitted largely through liturgical reading, catechetical instruction, and quotation and exegesis in sermons."[14] Vestiges of these practices survive in evangelical churches like the one I grew up in, where in the early 1970s we would compete to see who could memorize the most Bible verses. Unfortunately, such rote memorization often stood in the way of hearing the Bible afresh. We breathlessly rushed through the words, hoping not to miss any, because the point was to give every word the same literal weight. The only drama was who would win the prize for getting the most words right.

These memorization games were a perversion of the oral culture that once sustained the centrality of the Bible in the home as well as the church. The stress on memorizing every word was a reaction against the liberal insistence that the Bible can be understood only when its words are put in the broadest historical context. Both sides of this division fundamentally misunderstand the relationship between orality and meaning. As Donald Juel has eloquently pointed out: "The whole

---

the Bible together and out loud in church is so important. Birkerts also, unfashionably, emphasizes the role of the author in creating the world of the novel. The author's presence saturates every page, creating "a world held fully in the suspension of a single sensibility" (81). Interestingly, Birkerts is no fan of books on tape. Being read to, for him, is a passive activity that stifles the imagination. He likens it to watching television; the result is that it reduces the pleasure of reading to "a companionable blur, a string of easy cadences to the ear" (142). Of course, most people who listen to books on tape do so in the car, commuting to work, and that shapes the listening experience. What Birkerts laments is the impossibility of what he calls a "deep reading" in a situation where one is listening to a tape while dodging traffic. He defines deep reading as an inward, private, and meditative activity. Being read to is, for Birkerts, a violation of the reader's right to imagine the book on her own terms. In the church, by contrast, readers have no rights. When we hear someone read Scripture to us, the whole service is designed to enable what we can call a "deep listening." Deep listening is communal, public, and active. It demands that we listen in order to liberate us to speak.

13. Thomas Farrel argues that the Nicene Creed of 325 was designed to be remembered by catechumens who were formed by a primarily oral culture. "Early Christian Creeds and Controversies in the Light of the Orality-Literary Hypothesis," *Oral Tradition* 2 (1987): 132–45.

14. William A. Graham, *Beyond the Written Word: Oral Aspects of Scripture in the History of Religion* (Cambridge: Cambridge University Press, 1987), 120.

interpretive enterprise suggests that public reading is unimportant to understanding the scriptures. The Bible is a mute companion whose access to the imagination is dramatically limited to the sense of sight. The Bible is strangely silent among its most devoted students."[15] It is not quite correct simply to say that a reader must interpret the text before performing it. Instead, oral performance—which is a kind of reoralization of the text—is interpretation. The inflection of one's voice determines the meaning of words written on a page.

Consequently, the public recitation of Scripture should be one of the highlights of the worship service. In the early church, public reading would have been a special event even in urban areas where rates of literacy were relatively high. As Ronald E. Osborn notes, "the office of reader [lector] carried distinction, signified at Rome by the action of the bishop in ceremonially handing over the sacred scrolls to the person being appointed for that responsibility in the liturgy."[16] The reading of Scripture before the sermon should be a miniature sermon in itself, and the fact that laity are invited to read the Scripture in most traditions shows that all believers are called to preach the gospel. "Hear then the Word of God" is rightly said before the reading of Scripture in church. Separating the reading from the preaching properly suggests the priority of Scripture, but it can also improperly suggest the isolation of the Word from proclamation. The Reformers, in fact, were skeptical about having a separate place in the service for Scripture reading. In a way, the whole worship of God is nothing more than the oral performance of the Bible.

Reading the Bible out loud is a profoundly theological act. After all, it is no accident that the Christian tradition considered the Word to be first and foremost a person. In oral societies, words have so much personal power that they are treated as entities with their own agency. As Walter Ong observes, "In a society where the only known word is the pure, evanescent spoken word, it is easier to think of objects as words than it is to think of words as objects."[17] Reading out loud gives us a glimpse of the social conditions that made the identification of God with the Word so plausible. Reading the Bible out loud is also practically useful. It helps to answer some of the most pressing questions that arise from the written text. What did Jesus sound like when he stilled the storm,

15. Donald Juel, "The Strange Silence of the Bible," *Interpretation* 51 (January 1997): 6.

16. Ronald E. Osborn, *Folly of God: The Rise of Christian Preaching* (St. Louis: Chalice, 1999), 401.

17. Walter J. Ong, *The Barbarian Within and Other Fugitive Essays and Studies* (New York: Macmillan, 1962), 51.

rebuked Peter, or chatted with Martha and Mary? Does it matter that the only leper who showed gratitude for being cured praised God with a loud voice (Luke 17:15)? When Pilate asked if he were the Messiah, how did Jesus say, "You say so"? How do we know, unless we try saying these words out loud ourselves? Of course, vocalizing the words of Scripture is no guarantee that they will be fully and truly understood. Such vocalization is not even a necessary condition for divine revelation, since God can work through any medium. Nevertheless, the Word of God is never more at home, so to speak, than in the sound of the human voice.

Reading the Bible out loud is an act of interpretation that involves many of the same skills that actors bring to a script. Luther was so attentive to the oral aspects of the Gospels that he could give stage directions for their public reading. "Emphasis and a raising of the voice must be observed at the words 'it is written of me' and at the words 'I have desired.'"[18] Books on homiletics, however, are often hesitant to make the connection between church and the stage. David Buttrick, for example, argues that too much acting on the part of the preacher will "fill in the gaps of biblical narrative and smooth over abrupt, surprising turns of narrative, so that the mystery of God-with-us may gradually be edged out of the narrative and be replaced by psychologies of faith."[19] There is some truth to such warnings. Acting is hard to do well, although that does not mean that some elements of acting cannot be of service to the church. As Richard F. Ward points out in one of the best books on what preachers can learn from actors, such warnings tend to perpetuate outdated stereotypes about acting and unwarranted suspicions about the theater.[20] It is as if acting were too frivolous to be mixed with the somber rituals of the church. Perhaps if more attention were given to the dramatic qualities of the Sunday reading of Scripture, there would be less interest in performing actual dramas during worship, something that has become popular in many "seeker" churches.

The lack of attention to the art of public reading is surely the reason why the Sunday morning Scripture reading is usually less than satisfy-

18. Martin Luther, *Luther's Works*, vol. 29, *Lectures on Titus, Philemon, and Hebrews*, ed. Jaroslav Pelikan (St. Louis: Concordia, 1968), 221.

19. David Buttrick, *Homiletic: Moves and Structures* (Minneapolis: Fortress, 1987), 334. No theologian has thought more carefully about the rhetorical construction of the sermon than David Buttrick. He analyzes the full range of speaking skills involved in preaching, from pacing, cadence, and tone to the use of "sound clusters" that are the natural poetry of human speech.

20. Richard F. Ward, *Speaking of the Holy: The Art of Communication in Preaching* (St. Louis: Chalice, 2001), 24–25. Also see Clayton J. Schmit, *Too Deep for Words: A Theology of Liturgical Expression* (Louisville: Westminster John Knox, 2002), chap. 3.

ing. The public reading of Scripture is not exactly like acting, but it is not completely different from it either. It is distinguished from acting by its overtly ritualized setting, but that does not mean that it lacks dramatic elements. It is close to readers' theater, a dramatic genre that is now largely out of fashion.[21] Like any performance, practice is required. People need time to do more than practice pronouncing words they do not know. Choices have to be made about what the text should sound like, which makes it all the more upsetting when ministers ask someone to read the morning Scripture when they walk through the door, giving them no time to practice. Ministers need to address the reading of Scripture as a theological task that entails a literal embodying of the Word. Readers should not be discouraged by the idea that reading is a kind of performance. Rather, they should be honored that they too can proclaim the gospel with joy and gladness.

The best readers of Scripture opt for a style that is what we might call "high conversational." Good readers try not to deflect attention from the Bible with too much variation in cadence and pitch. They use their regular voices, yet they heighten the sense of purpose in their tone. They speak plainly but seriously, as if the Word of God were written especially for each listener, and each listener will know what to do with it when the reading is done. The reader is delivering a message that is not her own, so she is not free to present it however she wishes. Regardless of how well she understands it, she wants her words to convey some of its urgency and weight. And she can hope that her listeners are already sufficiently familiar with the text that she need not pause over its more technical difficulties.

Some public readers use a false voice in order to compensate for their nervousness. Reading Scripture on Sunday mornings is serious work, but it should also be, paradoxically, a release from the usual pressures that even the most confident performer experiences when standing before a large crowd. No matter how anxious we are, the voice we use in reading Scripture is the gift God has given us at that moment, and thus we can suffer no embarrassment or humiliation. This does not mean that the reader should perform this task in a thoughtless manner. The obligation the reader has to the text and the congregation is to use her natural voice, because no other vocal act is as natural as this one. Our voices are a gift from God, so what better way to employ them than in reading God's gift of inspired words? Most of the time we use

21. See Gordon C. Bennett, *Readers Theatre Comes to Church* (Richmond: John Knox, 1972). Also see Clayton J. Schmit, *Public Reading of Scripture: A Handbook* (Nashville: Abingdon, 2002), and Audrey J. Williamson, *The Living Word: A Study of the Public Reading of the Bible* (Kansas City, Mo.: Beacon Hill, 1987).

our voice in a rushed and strained manner. Our voice reflects all of the tension we carry in our body, and we inevitably pitch our voice from a particular part of our body rather than letting it flow freely from the body as a whole. When we read Scripture, God authorizes our voice as the sound of God's will. We cannot accomplish God's will by ourselves, but we can be the mouthpiece of God's plan. Every time we read the Word, God works through us, but we do not know what God will do with a particular reading. The Holy Spirit blows where it will, even as it is carried aloft by the sound waves of our breath. Every time we read the Bible in church, then, we can be confident that God has ordained his Word for a public reenactment and that God's Word will accomplish whatever God wills.

Public reading does not demand a sacrifice of our body, as if we should be ashamed to give mouth to what more properly should be an inward and silent illumination. The Word is meant to be proclaimed, and thus it must be heard before it can become an object of contemplation. Ministers probably avoid drawing an analogy between reading and drama because they fear that readers might adopt a melodramatic tone. The opposite mistake of using an ascetic monotone is just as disheartening. Readers sometimes think they need to use a monotone voice in order to imbue the occasion with ceremonial seriousness. Certainly a reading that draws attention to itself and thus distracts from the message of the text would be inappropriate. But this does not mean that the reader should not use the full range of her voice to enact the text. The reader of Scripture animates the text by performing it in the context of that particular congregation on that particular day.

The public reading of poetry is making a comeback in America, and as a result people are growing more accustomed to an animated reading style. Poetry jams are beginning to have an impact on the way poetry is written, even though most poetry continues to be written to be read in a quiet nook rather than heard aloud in a busy bar. Interestingly, poets are rarely the best readers of their own work, because reading a poem aloud requires a different skill from writing a poem. Literary style is not equivalent to what Helen Vendler has called "intonational style."[22] Poets often affect a mannerism in their public readings that is absent from their writing. When poets try to play the role of the sacred priest, the keeper of the mysteries, they can be tempted to use an affected voice and subsequently lapse into a singsong chanting. Rather than letting their work speak for itself, they become guilty of what a theater critic would call overacting. Poets, in other words, make for bad preachers.

22. Quoted in Judith Shulevitz, "Sing Muse . . . or Maybe Not," *New York Times Book Review,* December 1, 2002, 31.

The Bible includes long sections of poetry, and even in its more prosaic portions, its unfamiliar syntax as well as its inherent richness can sound a lot like poetry. The reading of Scripture in church is thus not dissimilar to a poetry jam. All sound requires agency and action—physical movement that produces vibration. The reader of Scripture need not strive to be a hollow tube through which God speaks. On the contrary, when we read words that have been designated by God as God's Word to us, we can speak those words with our whole body, knowing that God too spoke in a body like ours. Our bodies have been redeemed because the breath that God blew into Adam and Eve is the same breath that Jesus exhaled and the same breath that the Spirit continues to blow today.

Kristin Linklater speaks of the moment of nothing that occurs after we release our breath and before we draw another. This moment of the breath cycle is a pause in which we are alone with ourselves facing the myriad possibilities that are the consequence of our freedom. It is a moment of emptiness in which we wait to be filled, and thus it is a moment of faith.

The Church as Community Theater

Although many seminaries still teach the rudimentary skills required for successful public speaking, communication programs in colleges and universities often treat this kind of instruction as old-fashioned and irrelevant.[23] Perhaps communication studies departments do not offer speech courses because public speaking is held in such low regard. Furthermore, with all the latest developments in information technologies, who could blame most students for thinking that they will probably never give many public speeches anyway? The category of *performance* is preferred over *speech* because it is so much broader. A performance

23. For an overview of this development, see Charles L. Bartow, "In Service to the Servants of the Word: Teaching Speech at Princeton Seminary," *Princeton Seminary Bulletin* 13 (1992): 274–86. With America's surging role in the world after World War II, Americans became obsessed with mastering the art of public speaking. Speech departments expanded as universities recognized the need for all students to be proficient in the art of public speaking. Learning to speak well, however, was not enough. Americans also wanted to apply their mechanical genius to figuring out how persuasion works. To gain legitimacy for their discipline, speech professors increasingly neglected the traditional study of rhetoric for the more exciting promise of the burgeoning behavioral sciences. They hoped that they could understand the power of communication by analyzing its component parts and measuring the impact of the available media. Thus the study of speech would be of crucial use to America's new post-war role as the world's voice of democracy. By the eighties, communication studies further evolved into the analysis of any kind of performance, thus completing a trajectory from the practical to the theoretical.

can be defined as any meaningful pattern of human activity, regardless of the form of address. Anything and everything can be considered a performance, from watching TV to mowing the lawn.

The study of homiletics is not impervious to this academic trend of broadening the idea of communication.[24] Preachers do a lot more than preach, and thus they need to be acquainted with the latest theories about what makes for effective communication. Nevertheless, even at the risk of appearing to be hopelessly old-fashioned, Christianity has an irreversible commitment to the dignity of the human voice. The performance that sustains Christian worship is the proclamation of the Word in the sermon as well as the sacraments.

Western culture has long lived off the interest that has accrued to the heritage of Christianity's theology of the Word without reinvesting in this endowment. It is no coincidence that with the decline of Christianity's influence on the West, we are seeing a decline in the power of the spoken word as well. The doctrine of the Trinity is the only intellectual bulwark in the West against the apotheosis of the eye. Three institutions in particular depend on the intimacy of sound for their continued viability: live theater, classroom education, and the church. Putting theater and the church in the same sentence might seem surprising, but the sanctuary is an auditorium, just as the stage is a sacred refuge for actors. Not all religions or all arts are audiocentric, but this religion and this art are. Audiences have to want to hear what someone from their own community has to say for theaters and churches to flourish. You cannot just change the channel when you hear someone speaking in a play or at church. Minimally, the human voice demands our politeness, so that we feel obligated to try to pay attention. When audiences find such listening to be a burdensome chore, stage and pulpit will find themselves in the same sinking boat. This is ironic, given the long history of competition and mutual incrimination between the theater and the church.[25] Only institutions that are so close together could be

24. The literature on preaching and performance is vast and growing. An early work that pointed in this direction is Nicholas Lash, *Theology on the Way to Emmaus* (London: SCM, 1986), chap. 3. He draws on the example of performing King Lear. I have also found the following works helpful: Rowan Williams, "The Literal Sense of Scripture," *Modern Theology* 7 (January 1991): 121–33; Michael Cartwright, "The Practice and Performance of Scripture: Grounding Christian Ethics in a Communal Hermeneutic," *The Annual of the Society of Christian Ethics*, 1988, 31–55; David Scott, "Speaking to Form: Trinitarian-Performative Scripture Reading," *Anglican Theological Review* 77 (1995): 137–59; and Stephen C. Barton, "New Testament Interpretation as Performance," *Scottish Journal of Theology* 52 (1999): 179–208.

25. For the best overview of the relationship between church and theater, see Hans Urs von Balthasar, *Theo-Drama: Theological Dramatic Theory*, vol. 1, *Prolegomena*, trans. Graham Harrison (San Francisco: Ignatius, 1988). For excellent commentary, see Aidan

so acrimonious, however, and though these institutions seem to want to have little to do with each other today, they have never been more intimately linked.

Film, to put it bluntly, is to be blamed for many of the problems faced by both the theater and the church.[26] Perhaps the secret of the power the cinema has over us can be found in the impetus of the visual to lay bare all of reality to inspection. As I argued in chapter 2, the eye can see a large number of things simultaneously, while we hear units of sound sequentially. True, movies are technically nothing more than a sequence of still photography, but they play on the biological quirk of the human retina to hold an image for a fraction of a second after it has disappeared. The rapid shuffling of images literally overwhelms the eye. As a result, the movies, unlike a series of photographs, leave little space for reflection. Indeed, as movies developed, they became increasingly accomplished in controlling every aspect of the audience's response. Audience responses are not just anticipated but designed and refined by test groups and marketing experts. Rather than liberating the audience with an external word that must be internalized by the hearer in a dialogue with oneself, movies mesmerize the viewers with a carefully calculated orchestration of elements that are meant to control one's every reaction.

This is especially true of cinematic sound, which fills the auditorium to the point where silence is rarely heard—except when silence is used to signal the significance of an upcoming sound. By the 1970s, as Gianluca Sergi has shown, young people brought to the movies aural expectations based on rock concerts and sophisticated hi-fi systems. Hollywood responded with multichannel technology that surrounds the viewer and adds a sonic dimensionality to the space of the theater. As Sergi states, "the contemporary Hollywood aural experience elevates the spectator to a state which we may define as that of a super-listener, a being (not to be found in nature) able to hear sounds that in reality would not be

---

Nichols, *No Bloodless Myth: A Guide through Balthasar's Dramatics* (Washington: Catholic University of America Press, 2000).

26. For an excellent theological critique of film, see Gerard Loughlin, "Looking: The Ethics of Seeing in Church and Cinema," chap. 12 in *Faithfulness and Fortitude: In Conversation with the Theological Ethics of Stanley Hauerwas*, ed. Mark Thiessen Nation and Samuel Wells (Edinburgh: T & T Clark, 2000). For a cultural analysis of the sacred dimension of film, see William Dean, *The American Spiritual Culture and the Invention of Jazz, Football, and the Movies* (New York: Continuum, 2002), 178. Neal Gabler, *Life: The Movie* (New York: Knopf, 1998), argues that the movies function as an American theology (238–39). For a surprising and fascinating history of how the church responded to the emergence of film, see Terry Lindvall, *The Silents of God: Selected Issues and Documents in Silent American Film and Religion, 1908–1925* (Lanham, Md.: Scarecrow, 2001).

audible or would sound substantially duller."[27] Cinema sound systems are powerful enough to move the air and vibrate the seats, pounding the listener with sound waves. The soundtracks of films, then, sound nothing like what we hear in everyday life, except to the extent that our everyday lives imitate the movies. The result is that the cinematic sound of someone getting punched in the face sounds real to us in a way that real violence does not.

Film is the ultimate rationalization of sound, immersing the viewer in a sonic sea but also subordinating sound to a visual source. No sound in a movie is incidental. When the source of a sound is hidden, the sound can be menacing and mysterious. Every cinematic sound has a reason, just as every scene must be scored. Movies rely on the way sound draws us out of ourselves to keep the plot moving along. The images on the screen would be lifeless otherwise. When films are inexpertly dubbed or the synchronization of sound and image is off, we immediately protest and refuse to watch. We want the sound of movies to be louder than life, moving through us like light. If it is true that we live in a society that is increasingly administered, that is, if our senses are the object of a seamless web of persuasion and control, then films represent the apex of the loss of sensory freedom.

Not all the blame for declining attendance at churches and theaters can be attributed to movies, of course. If film makes listening easy by distracting the ear with a parade of sights, the proliferation of magazines and newspapers has had a similar effect. Indeed, the Sunday newspaper has probably had just as devastating an impact on churchgoing as film has had on live theater. Church, after all, is a time for people to feel connected to their local community, sharing news in the form of joys and concerns as well as the good news of the gospel. To appreciate public speaking, people have to be involved in their immediate surroundings. Newspapers, by blurring the line between the local and the national, weaken the importance of local ties. It turns out that all the news that is fit to print is endless. A certain economy of scale drives the construction of a national—and increasingly global—conversation about people whom nobody really knows. Newspapers and magazines must have a broad circulation in order to be profitable—locally or family-owned newspapers are becoming increasingly rare—so they must persuade their readers to relocate their desire for gossip from the local to the national. The result is an atomized reading public, more curious about the intimate lives of stars who live on the other side of the country than

27. Gianluca Sergi, "The Sonic Playground: Hollywood Cinema and Its Listeners," in *Hollywood Spectatorship: Changing Perspectives of Cinema Audiences* (London: British Film Institute, 2001), 125.

about the people who live in their own neighborhood. If people were most interested in the affairs that really have an impact on them, then the media giants would be cut down to a more human size.

Much the same can be said about theater. Community theater actors rarely make their living exclusively from their art; they have to work other jobs in order to support their passion for the stage. Community theater actors tend to live in the same town where they act, and so they are rightly perceived to be "more like us" than the actors we see on film and television. When they speak to us on the stage, we hear voices that echo our local sounds. They offer less of an illusion than the stars who speak from the magical world of fame that is far removed from our everyday concerns.

Neither the theater nor the church can survive in a world where the local does not matter. Before the rise of print culture, people were more connected to religion through both their local church and their larger, frequently transnational church body. Print encourages more abstract connections, which has led not only to Hollywood but also to forms of nationalism and patriotism that could never have materialized in more oral societies. This is true from the very beginning of the printing press, which was first used not to attack Rome but to popularize the crusade against the Turks. Even the publication of the Bible contributed to social fragmentation. As Elizabeth Eisenstein notes, "in the form of the Lutheran Bible or the King James' Version, the sacred book of Western civilization became more insular as it grew more popular. It is no accident that nationalism and mass literacy have developed together."[28] And not just nationalism, but the universal ambitions of the Enlightenment were also inconceivable without printing. The "men of letters" who mastered print were able to distinguish between true and false religion on the basis of literacy and not sound, just as they were able to supplant the particularity of public speech by constructing the much broader audience of all those who want to listen to the voice of reason by reading the right books and newspapers. In print, abstract entities like the "nation-state" or the "community of scholars" can come alive because our loyalties are carried further by sight than by sound.

If print expands our sense of space, sound limits it. Both theater and the church are viable social institutions only to the extent that they honor the limits of sound. It is often said that the church is the people, not the place, but it also needs to be said that the church is not just the physical presence of people. The church is the space made by the people's voices. The church is an acoustical space, configured by

---

28. Elizabeth L. Eisenstein, *The Printing Revolution in Early Modern Europe* (Cambridge: Cambridge University Press, 1983), 162.

the resonance of sound. Honoring sound is one way of describing the historic task of architecture. For most of Western history, the size of buildings and the layout of cities were determined by the physics of sound. This might seem like an odd claim, especially since most theorists of sound connect it to time and not space. After all, sound vanishes quickly, leaving no trace in space. Nevertheless, the role of rhetoric in the ancient world literally shaped the construction of space. Because speaking and hearing, more than reading and writing, were at the heart of education and culture, proximity was a necessary feature of social life. The Roman forum was crowded because people had to be close to the speaker. Likewise, the Israelites were united because they could assemble together to listen to the word of God. "Then Moses said to Aaron, 'Say to the whole congregation of the Israelites, "Draw near to the LORD, for he has heard your complaining"'" (Exod. 16:9). Before the electrical amplification of sound, leadership was frequently determined by the strength of one's voice.

When Protestantism enhanced the role of sound in worship by displacing the altar with the pulpit, the space of worship had to change as well. Churches became more like auditoriums, an architectural process that has been documented by Jeanne Halgren.[29] A similar transformation took place in movie theaters. Movie theaters were once called picture palaces because they were so roomy. The orchestral music that accompanied silent movies needed a large hall to allow for long-lasting reverberations. With the coming of the talkies, theaters had to be redesigned to enhance the fragile features of the human voice. Technology has alleviated the need for intimate spaces to a degree. Yet the sound of the movies—and many sermons as well—now comes through an electronic system that only ironically can be called "speakers." Technology can record the human voice, but we still have a deep desire to hear performers in person. We go to movies where the sound is recorded and engineered, but would we go to church if the music and the sermon were all on tape? Why not stay home and watch church on TV?

Why not indeed? Except for the qualitative difference in hearing sound "live" as opposed to hearing it recorded, the church would have little to offer in competition with the Kingdom of Entertainment that is America. The Protestant churches thus share a common destiny with the theater. With so many programs on TV and video, live drama is finding it harder and harder to compete for the consumer's dollar. One option for the theater community is to stage grand spectacles that are even more glitzy and glamorous than anything on TV. To attract a public

29. Jeanne Halgren, *When Church Became Theatre* (New York: Oxford University Press, 2002).

that sees everything in terms of the movies, these musicals are often based on a particular film, as if theater can compete with the cinema only by referring to it.

Megachurches are in many ways the ecclesial complement to Broadway productions. After centuries of protesting against the drama of the Catholic Mass, these Protestant churches have learned to mount their worship services with all of the resources of theatrical productions. Their very size makes the congregants more spectators than participants, seeing rather than hearing. True, we have a hunger for God that cannot be filled with words alone. We want to be overwhelmed with the divine, transported and amazed rather than instructed and encouraged. But this is the job of the Eucharist, not film clips and rock bands. The Eucharist stages the central drama of our lives and points to our hope in the eventual saturation of all things with the divine presence. The Eucharist is the Word made visible, and it should be all the show we need on Sunday mornings.

Most of the megachurches in America are evangelical and independent, free of hierarchical structures that bind them to a particular denomination. They can absorb the popular culture and speak its language by combining a strong sense of belonging with the lure of technological sophistication. In a way, this has always been the methodology of the evangelical churches. As historian Richard Hofstadter notes, "the 'star' system prevailed in religion before it reached the theater."[30] If the church looks like a dim reflection of the world of entertainment today, it is only because the bright lights of the movies can better fulfill its visual functions.

Consumerism has always been a more visual than auditory affair. As historian William Leach has extensively documented, the transformation of Americans into consumers in the twentieth century was largely a matter of "eye appeal." When Ezra Pound visited New York, he thought electricity had made "the seeing of visions superfluous. Here is our poetry, for we have pulled down the stars to do our will."[31] The visual world of advertisement portrays a disembodied utopia of abundance that serves no material purpose other than being an outlet for private fantasy and distraction.[32]

30. Richard Hofstadter, *Anti-intellectualism in American Life* (New York: Knopf, 1963), 86.
31. Ezra Pound, quoted in William Leach, *Land of Desire: Merchants, Power, and the Rise of a New American Culture* (New York: Vintage, 1993), 344.
32. Collecting (collecting anything), rather than gift giving (which keeps goods in circulation), is thus the paradigmatic economic activity of the modern market. See Jackson Lears, *Fables of Abundance: A Cultural History of Advertising in America* (New York: BasicBooks, 1994), esp. chap. 4.

Neither the church nor live theater can compete with the movies, but neither can the church compete with the stage in terms of its professionalism. Most churches must be content to be more like community theater and less like Broadway. Community theaters draw local crowds, not tourists. They work best in smaller towns or cities where audiences can get to know the actors, because audiences are less likely to be judgmental toward a performer when she or he is one of them. People support community theaters because they are doing more than just seeking an evening's entertainment. The audience is striving to create a community for the arts, where amateurs can hone their talents without having to depart for the big lights of New York or Los Angeles. Audiences are willing to overlook flaws in productions as long as the communicative intent of the production is honest and sincere. They suspend their sophisticated skepticism in order to participate in a process where they have an integral role.

Churches and community theaters are two of the only institutions in our culture that are not inundated with irony. People have to believe in what they are doing if these institutions are to survive. They cannot pay for much of the labor that sustains them, and thus they provide an occasion for giving, which demonstrates the power of sharing in a marketplace driven by profit. And just as many theaters have fallen on hard times, with the massive proliferation of entertainment options, so too many churches have lost their vigor and excitement. The best community theaters, however, retain the urgency of their mission by joyfully maintaining that the show must go on. Small churches, stoically trying to stay afloat in the religious marketplace, could do much worse than to follow their example.

nine

The Lasting Word

Silence, Music, and the Synesthetic Destiny of Sound

The Sound of Silence

In his phenomenology of sound, Don Ihde develops the neglected category of an auditory horizon.[1] We usually think of horizons as spatial, but there is also a horizon of sound. The spatial horizon is that which we do not see directly. If we make the horizon the center of our visual field, it ceases to be the horizon and another horizon takes its place. Horizons cannot be objectified without introducing another horizon into the picture. This is another way of saying that all of our experience is framed while the frame itself is never experienced. We cannot see everything at any one moment; instead, our seeing is made possible by the way it is limited.

The visual horizon can be a good metaphor for the way knowledge works in general. A framework is always presupposed in implicit or indirect ways by what we perceive and understand. That is, without already knowing something, we cannot know anything.

Hearing is no different; there are noises on the fringe of our awareness that we must block out in order to hear what we want to hear.

1. Don Ihde, *Listening and Voice: A Phenomenology of Sound* (Athens: Ohio University Press, 1976).

221

Just as the visual horizon is a spatial category, the auditory horizon is temporal, because sound is more connected to time than space. Sounds emerge out of a congestion of noises that could be anywhere and trail off into a void that is nowhere. To make sense of a sound, we have to remember it even as we are listening to it, because it moves through time so quickly.

Ihde argues that the border of sound is silence, but this would be like saying that the border of vision is darkness. Just as the act of seeing is surrounded by a horizon of sights that we do not directly see, the act of hearing is surrounded by a horizon of noise, which is the category of sounds we block out. We have to have heard something in order to listen to anything in particular. Silence, then, is not the opposite of sound; if it were, we could hear it simply by stuffing our ears. Consequently, escaping sound is an elusive goal. If we try to hear silence, we will always hear something making noise instead. Silence, in other words, cannot be the object of an intentional activity. The only way to draw silence near is to let go of all intentional activity, but even then there is a good case to be made that silence is never experienced in its pure state. After all, meditation teachers often instruct students to focus on their breathing in order to distract the ear from its vulnerability to unwanted sounds.

Silence is not the natural state of matter in motion, which is why freeing nature from sound takes years of training and involves sophisticated techniques. In that regard, there is a peculiar intimacy between the worlds of meditation and science. In fact, things can be silent only when we examine them as static objects, using our eyes at the expense of our ears. Perhaps this is why the construction of mental images is often a crucial learning tool in meditation. Meditation, like scientific analysis, is a highly intellectual activity. Indeed, all abstract thinking is made possible by the prior process of deafening ourselves to the sounds of the world. Even in our scientific age, however, things still have a way of speaking to us. The atonal and monotonal voice of science, expressed in the language of numbers, laws, and statistics, gives a voice to the sonic meaning of nature, even if that voice is flat and indistinguishable. Moreover, meditation rarely aims at silence as an end in itself, preferring instead to free the mind for fresh perceptions of sound.

Meditation can be linked not only to scientific abstraction but also to the romantic goal of reenchanting nature by excavating the silence that lies beneath a harsh urban soundscape. Romantics, in fact, have long contended that silence is the auditory depth that makes sound possible, and it is this belief that guides the practice of meditation. Christians cannot grant sound this metaphysical status. For the romantics, sound is divine when it is natural, but for Christians, it is natural only when it is a response to the divine.

In fact, all arguments about sound come down to religion, because there is no neutral theory of sound that does not imply or articulate a metaphysics or a theology. Take this statement by R. Murray Schafer: "All the sounds we hear are imperfect. For a sound to be totally free of onset distortion, it would have to have been initiated before our lifetime. If it were also continued after our death, so that we knew no interruption of it, then we could comprehend it as being perfect. But a sound initiated before our birth, continued unabated and unchanging throughout our lifetime and extended beyond our death would be perceived by us as—silence."[2] This is a Buddhist or Hindu understanding of sound, with its emphasis on an eternity that is ultimately without a personal voice. Christians, of course, believe in a triune God who, even before we were created with ears, was speaking a creative Word. That Word is the sound that precedes, uplifts, and attracts us. By not being silent, it is a sound that creates our hearing and invites our own saying in return.

Silence is constructed, not natural. Music is used to create the proper mood for meditation, just as laboratories are constructed to keep noise to a minimum level. Christians construct silence through music and prayer, but they do not treat silence as an end in itself. The church is not a meditation room, and Christians do not believe that silence has the last word. As the apostle Paul wrote, "there are doubtless many different kinds of sounds in the world, and nothing is without sound" (1 Cor. 14:10). For Christians, silence is part of the discipline of waiting patiently for the kingdom of God. Silence is pregnant with expectation, as in moments during the worship service when the congregation observes a silence in preparation for the reading of Scripture or the proclamation of the gospel. Moments of silence give meaning to our anticipation of communion with God. Silence, musically bestowed, drums out the noise that prohibits human speech from carrying the Word.

From a Christian perspective, if God is silence, then all is lost.[3] Our voices would have no echo, and our prayers would be in vain. This still leaves open the question of what kind of sound we should imagine God to be. Of course, God transcends all earthly objects, including the vibration

---

2. R. Murray Schafer, *The Tuning of the World* (New York: Knopf, 1977), 262.

3. It is interesting that the priestly realm of the Jerusalem temple was clothed in silence, perhaps as a way of distinguishing the Hebraic cult from the magical incantations of its pagan neighbors. The inner circle was largely silent, but the outer circles were full of prayer and song. Israel Knohl, "Between Voice and Silence: The Relationship between Prayer and Temple Cult," *Journal of Biblical Literature* 115, no. 1 (1996): 17–30. Carol Newsom has speculated that this silence was influenced by 1 Kings 19:12, which describes God's revelation to Elijah as, in some translations, "a small still voice." See Carol Newsom, *Songs of Sabbath Sacrifice: A Critical Edition* (Atlanta: Scholars Press, 1985), 303.

of air that carries sound. Apophatically speaking, God is neither silence nor sound. Or, conversely, God is both silence and sound, a singing silence or silent song. Silence and sound are both in the service of the Word. The eternity of the Word, though, privileges sound over silence and suggests that it is the destiny of all things to sound like the first sound through which the world was created. As Simone Weil has stated, "the whole creation is nothing but [the Word of God's] vibration. When human music in its greatest purity pierces our soul, this is what we hear through it. When we have learned to hear the silence, this is what we grasp more distinctly through it."[4] The sound that we can imagine God to be is thus none other than the sound of the Son, who spoke to the apostles and speaks to us still.

From Noise to Music

Just as silence has been romanticized in the modern period, so has noise, and with no more plausibility. Noise has played a role in modern life that is frequently neglected by social historians. Noise is particularly effective at wreaking havoc on our sense of ethical obligations. Psychologists have demonstrated that people are less likely to stop to help a stranger who has dropped books on a sidewalk if a loud lawn mower is running nearby. Other studies have shown that people socialize more with their neighbors when their streets are quieter. The levels of noise in urban environments require us to spend increasing amounts of energy blocking out what we do not want to hear.

Noise is a problem for artists as well as city planners. Much of modern art, as Jonathan Crary has persuasively shown, is a reaction to the dismal fate of perception, especially auditory attention, in the modern world. Attention has been disrupted, fragmented, and reconstructed by communication technologies in order to advance mass consumption.[5] The same can be said for modern music. The avant-garde of the twentieth century tried to capture the brutal reality of noise without configuring it into conventional harmonies of meaning. "Of all the emphatic sounds of modernism, noise is the most common and the most productively counterproductive."[6] Twentieth-century music thus became mired in dissonance and atonality.

4. Simone Weil, *Waiting for God*, trans. Emma Craufurd (San Francisco: Harper & Row, 1973), 124.

5. Jonathan Crary, *Suspensions of Perception: Attention, Spectacle, and Modern Culture* (Cambridge: MIT Press, 1999).

6. Douglas Kahn, *Noise, Water, Meat: A History of Sound in the Arts* (Cambridge: MIT Press, 1999), 20.

At its best, the musical appropriation of noise can serve to protest the false idealization of sound and to proclaim the liberation of the auditory from social control. For Theodor Adorno, the noisy revolution of music was made necessary by the horror of Auschwitz.[7] The familiar and the conventional are forever tainted by the sounds of fascism's triumphant march through the first half of the twentieth century. Tonality is irrational, Adorno thought, precisely because it pretends to reflect an orderly cosmos that no longer exists. Every harmony can only sound manipulative in the aftermath of the Nazi orchestration of society. As a result, purity of sound must give way to unpitched noise.

While the traditional function of music was to transform sound into something that speaks to the rhythms of being human, the abrasive cacophony of atonal modern music denies the simple pleasures of listening. The iconoclasm of atonality pays no attention to the natural limits of the ear. In its own way, the radically new language of atonality was as utopian and idealistic as the traditional music it tried to replace. Its attempt to change the way people hear was bound to fail, primarily because it was destined to be defined by the sounds it tried to interrupt. Adorno's own "negative dialectics" suggests that any protest against the status quo will merely amplify what is being rejected. Popular culture uses noise to imprison us within a thought-numbing assault of sound, but enhancing that noise will only strengthen the imprisonment. The aesthetics of dissonance is a pact with the devil, since ugly noise is ultimately destructive, no matter how much it is solemnized by a sophisticated musical score.

No American tried harder to hear music in every sound, no matter how dissonant, than Charles Ives (1874–1954). Perhaps only an American growing up at the end of the nineteenth century could have had the optimism, innocence, and confidence to turn his back on European tradition in order to capture the chaotic noise of a burgeoning democracy. Unorthodox, experimental, and extravagant, Ives used dissonance and atonality long before most European composers. He wanted to teach people how to listen anew, as if he were creating sounds from scratch. When he was a boy, he heard one of his father's choir members sing off key, and his father's advice never left him: "Don't pay too much attention to the sounds—for if you do, you may miss the music." He mixed two styles in his works. One is nostalgic and mournful, conveyed through allusions to folk tunes, barn dances, jigs, waltzes, and other sounds that he remembered from his youth. The other is brash and boisterous,

---

7. For an analysis of Adorno's impact on modern German music, see Alex Ross, "Ghost Sonata," *New Yorker*, March 24, 2003, 64–71.

purposely mixing keys and tones to create a music that is gloriously out of tune.

Many of his works were not performed until decades after they were written, and Ives was thought to be a crank and an eccentric until his genius was recognized near the end of his life. His idiosyncrasies reached a feverish pitch with the utopian dream he called the Universal Symphony. It was so colossal in scale that he left it as a gift to future generations by inviting others to help finish it.[8] He wrote it to be played by several orchestras in valleys and with choruses on mountaintops, speaking to each other of the depths and heights of human experience. He did not expect that the resulting "conversation" would ever match the language of conventional harmony. It is as if he imagined heaven to be full of the untutored voices of those who sing off key, and yet by the sheer exuberance of the effort, everyone would learn to sing their part no matter how out of tune.

Voices Carry

Ives heard in the sounds of his youth a truth that he could express only in fragmented form. Similarly, Christians believe that composers can make music out of noise because they have heard something healing in the origin of sound. A moving musical rendition of this theological conviction can be heard in Gavin Bryars's *Jesus' Blood Never Failed Me*, one of the most remarkable pieces of music of the twentieth century. In 1971 Bryars stumbled upon a bit of audiotape of an old man singing a short verse: "Jesus' blood never failed me yet, Jesus' blood never failed me yet, Jesus' blood never failed me yet. There's one thing I know for he loves me so." Bryars never knew the tramp (as he is called in the liner notes), who died before Bryars decided to pay a musical tribute to his heartfelt tune. The result is a string quartet composition that accompanies the tramp's song—which is continually repeated throughout the piece—with a gentle reverence and empathy, as if Bryars is afraid to drown out the tramp's gentle but broken voice.

First we hear the tramp's voice alone, then low strings and full strings, reminding us that even the loneliest voice is never without an echo. Theologically construed, the strings sound like the angelic hosts that Jesus could have called upon to save himself from his anguished death on the cross. Finally, almost miraculously, we hear Tom Waits's gravelly voice. At first Waits sings softly, just below the tramp's range, and then

8. Two composers have taken Ives up on the offer: Johnny Reinhard and Larry Austin.

Waits's voice becomes stronger, as if he has surreptitiously stepped beside the homeless man in order to accompany him home. Then there is a remarkable musical transformation. Waits's voice gently rises, as if he is now carrying the tramp on his own musical shoulders. What is nearly impossible to do in life—that is, to aid someone without appearing condescending or patronizing—is accomplished here with a grace that can be only musically expressed. Waits subsumes without replacing the tramp's tune, carrying it to new heights without leaving the tramp behind. Waits is the Son carrying the tramp with his voice, showing us how Christ can take our tuneless songs and make them sublime, or Waits is the Father harmonizing with the cries of the tramp/Son at the moment of greatest sorrow.

The Vocal Heart of All Sound

Bryars's composition, like all great music, gives us a sonic foretaste of heaven. The strings and the voices work together for this end, but it is the unexpected soaring of Waits's voice—the way it carries the rest of the music, as well as the tramp himself—that makes this orchestral piece so theologically singular. This music thus reaffirms the Bible's central preoccupation with voice. The prophets, for example, sometimes attacked instrumental music due to its association with pagan revelry (Isa. 5:11–12), an attack that was continued by some of the church fathers, including John Chrysostom. Instruments can dehumanize music by drawing attention away from the moral timber of the human voice. Perhaps for this reason, the use of instruments in religious worship was a relatively late development in Israel. King David organized elaborate musical ceremonies around the placement of the ark of the covenant in Jerusalem (1 Chron. 15:16–25), and harps and lyres were used in the Jerusalem temple (trumpets and flutes were added by the time of the second temple). After the destruction of the second temple, however, the rabbis prohibited the religious use of musical instruments, which put cantorial music at the center of Jewish worship. This decision was anticipated by the hostility of the Pharisees toward the temple orchestra. The apostle Paul's attitude toward music was shaped by the Pharisees. Paul uses musical instruments as metaphors, but he favors simple hymns and songs (Col. 3:16) rather than "a noisy gong or a clanging cymbal" (1 Cor. 13:1). The result is that throughout much of its history Christianity shared with Judaism a belief in the superiority of vocal over instrumental music. A general aesthetic principle seems to be at stake in the biblical approach to music: the singing voice reveals the spiritual depth of human nature and thus points to a divine source for all sound,

while instrumental music tends to dissolve individual identity by drawing attention to itself rather than a transcendent source.

Music and human speech have been associated since time immemo-
rial. Some scholars argue that the origin of music lies in the natural
prosodic variations in the human voice. It is even possible that music
was born in the cooing tones mothers use with their babies. The history
of Western music in the modern period, however, is in the direction of
separating music from its verbal associations. Modern instrumental
music tries to distance itself from the human voice much as modern
art has tried to distance itself from the human form. So-called absolute
music purifies music of any external reference. Absolute music tells no
story and delivers no message and thus is a language in only the most
analogical sense, stripped of the connotations of the human voice. When
this happens, instrumental music veers dangerously close to becoming
idolatrous, because it makes sound an end in itself. Yet instrumental
music is always the product of people and objects in motion—vibrating, sliding, blowing, and banging. The instruments are masks of sound
that point beyond themselves to the humans who play them, a point
that is demonstrated by the fact that seeing music performed, where
one can watch the musicians at work, is more satisfying than hearing
a disembodied recording. Recordings, in fact, can become too perfect,
removing the all-too-human sounds that make a concert so immediate
and powerful. So while vocal music is a more direct celebration of the
human body as the source of sound, even instrumental music, which
enhances human bodies with pieces of wood, metal, and strings, demonstrates how the human voice, in the end, must be the measure of all
earthly sound.

The argument that all sound has its telos in the human voice sounds
implausible to many people today, due to the role of television in our
society. It is impossible to calculate the effect of television on our perceptions of the human voice. Not only does the TV disembody voices, but it
also drones on and on, making the human voice the background noise
we wrap around ourselves like a security blanket. The more rushed our
days become, the more it seems we need a constant chatter of voices to
keep us company, distracting us from the loneliness our speeding lives
are designed to cover up. Television does have its own pedagogy, but
what it teaches us is how not to listen, or how to listen with only one
ear. No wonder the sermon on Sunday mornings is becoming a lost form
of communication. We want to listen to someone speaking only while
we are also doing something else, making every minute count as we
multitask our way through the day. Voices no longer denote presence,
because attending to someone's presence is a demanding obligation
that is ultimately moral in character. Voices on the television promise

a parade of frictionless and contentless conversation that requires no labor because they offer absolutely nothing to think about. The talk on TV is so constant that it results in a reduction of the human voice to pure sound—a buzzing that keeps us from asking any questions or making any reply.

The human voice is at the heart of all sound this side of heaven only because Jesus Christ speaks to us with a voice that is both human and divine. No one should say, Luther warns us, "True, Christ preaches sweetly and excellently, but who knows what the Father says up in heaven?"[9] In heaven, no other word will be addressed to us by God than the Word of Jesus Christ. If so, then the old-fashioned images of heaven depicting a choir singing praises to God's glory forever and ever are not as sentimental as one might think. In the consummation of creation, even nature will be given a voice to praise God. As Isaiah writes, "the mountains and the hills before you shall burst into song, and all the trees of the field shall clap their hands" (55:12). The sounds of heaven will not be the earsplitting cacophony of a roaring Babeldom but the uplifting harmonies of a community that speaks "as those who are taught" (Isa. 50:4). If noise lies at one extreme of sound, then choral music lies at the other. And if all sound echoes the Word spoken by God in Jesus Christ, then the choral music of heaven will accompany the solo of Jesus' voice, and all noise will be joyful.

Wordless Music

Much wordless music in our society, like the comforting sounds projected from an unwatched television, sets a mood but delivers little intellectual content. Even songs with words can be essentially wordless. Everyone has experienced the way certain melodies stick to the neural circuits of our brains. The words to the song—whether it is "YMCA" or "The Lion Sleeps Tonight"—do not matter, even though they worm their way through our day. Just reading the names of these songs might be enough to pass them from one person to another, like a parasite seeking a new victim!

Praise songs used in contemporary worship services can work like this. Praise songs demonstrate not only the power of repetition but also the lingering effect of linking sound to motion, which involves the whole body in the act of remembering a tune. In many evangelical churches, most of the music comes before the sermon, and appropriately so.

9. Martin Luther, *Luther's Works*, vol. 24, *Sermons on the Gospel of St. John, Chapters 14–16*, ed. Jaroslav Pelikan (St. Louis: Concordia, 1961), 165.

Even wordless music should move us toward hearing the Word. Praise songs are a popular way of creating a worshipful mood, but the way they subordinate the message of the song to its emotional effect can be troublesome. Praise songs have their place, but they need to be placed in the context of the spoken word. As Eryximachus told Socrates upon dismissing the after-dinner flautist in Plato's *Symposium*, "Let us rather spend our time in conversation."

In a brilliantly provocative essay on music, J. Bottum suggests that the power of music in our culture has led people to equate morality with a set of feelings rather than a system of ideas.[10] At one point in Western history, as Bottum acknowledges, music was an expression of a coherent understanding of human nature. That connection has been severed because there simply is no coherent account of human nature to which music can correspond, unless one reduces human nature to a model of stimulus and response. Historically, music not only reflected but also directed notions about human nature, but now musical styles change so swiftly that they reflect little more than the capitalist demand for new products to titillate consumer desire.

The best evidence that much contemporary music makes only minimal intellectual demands on us is that it presents nothing against which we can feel the urge to rebel. Even when a composition includes lyrics, much contemporary music aspires to a certain wordlessness, so that the words become subsumed into sound. Aficionados can spend countless hours poring over the printed lyrics of a popular song, trying to decipher its message, but most of the time the meaning remains immanent to the music. Country music is dismissed as a regressive genre precisely because it tries to keep words—and a story line—at the heart of the song.

Allan Bloom was more right than wrong in *The Closing of the American Mind* to accept Nietzsche's definition of music as antirational and then to lament music's triumph in American culture.[11] To equate music with emotion is not to denigrate its evocative power. On the contrary, sound has an emotional capacity that sight does not, which accounts for music's immense hold on us. However, the emotions when unmediated by thought can lead directly to impulsive actions, which explains why every store in America uses music to get customers in the proper mood to buy.

We live in a period that is awash in music, and the lovers of music are surely more sophisticated about their tastes than ever before, but that

10. J. Bottum, "The Soundtracking of America," *Atlantic Monthly*, March 2000, 56–70.

11. Allan Bloom, *The Closing of the American Mind* (New York: Touchstone, 1988).

is not a good measure of music's cultural value. Musical sophistication slides into decadence when it becomes the basis for creating fan clubs or when it provides a gnostic experience for the elite connoisseur. Indeed, the pervasiveness of music results in an increasingly fragmented world, where music caters to individual taste. The newest technology in sound emission, HyperSonic Sound, represents the culmination of technological attempts to control and direct sound, beginning with speaking trumpets and acoustical tubes. This device, invented by Woody Norris, can target individuals hundreds of feet away by placing sound right in their ears, without disturbing anybody standing nearby.[12] In the future each of us will live in our own world of sound, while the world itself will remain ominously silent.

Eschatology and Synesthesia

If movies represent the most intense perceptual experience of modernity, then that might help explain the eclipse of heaven in the contemporary imagination.[13] We no longer dream of being ecstatically transported into another world of liberation and fulfillment, because we can experience a disembodied bliss here and now while stuffing ourselves with candy and popcorn. Theologians also, however, must bear much of the blame for heaven's decline. Theologians easily fall prey to the false pride of distancing themselves from the sentimentalism of popular piety. For many liberal theologians, heaven is too good to be true. Meanwhile, popular culture does not want God to get in the way of its fantasies about the afterlife. Both sides in the battle between theology and popular culture miss the extent to which God and heaven are interchangeable. Properly construed, heaven is just another name for God—the way God will one day call all things to their proper place. Thinking about God and longing for heaven should be one and the same thing.

Traditionally, heaven has been understood in terms of sight—that is, when theologians have bothered to offer a perceptual scheme of what heaven might be like.[14] Eschatological rhetoric is full of visual images;

12. Marshall Sella, "The Sound of Things to Come," *New York Times Magazine*, March 23, 2003, 34–39.

13. For my own reflections on heaven, see my review of Alice Sebald's *The Lovely Bones*, in *Christian Century*, October 9–22, 2002, 20–22, and of Jerry L. Walls's fine book *Heaven: The Logic of Eternal Joy*, in *Christian Century*, December 4–17, 2002, 41–43. Also see Webb, *Good Eating* (Grand Rapids: Brazos, 2001), chap. 7, "Will All Good Dogs Go to Heaven?"

14. The book of Revelation is fascinating with regard to its oscillation—and one could even say its synthesis—of visual and auditory descriptions of the end times. This book is

we long to see the glory of God and to see God face to face, for example. From this perspective, hearing is the sense of faith, while seeing, which is more direct, is the reward of heaven. This argument is unsatisfactory in several respects. First, it demotes hearing to a lesser status as the perception that does not truly connect us to God, a connection that can be made only by sight. Yet we are saved by hearing, so we must really hear God when we hear the gospel preached. Second, it trades on a discontinuity between this life and the next. Heaven should not be portrayed as a shift from one sense to another but as the fulfillment of all of our senses. Third, it is captured by Enlightenment notions of evidence. Heaven is not the place where we will have visual proof (the beatific vision) of what we have to believe by faith on earth. Seeing is not confirmation of what hearing cannot really know. Faith will be consummated in heaven, not replaced. If earthly faith were to be replaced by heavenly knowledge, then we would have to say that Christians do not really know what they believe.

There is much to recommend the idea, then, that heaven is a synesthesia of the ear quite unlike the cinematic condensation of all senses to the eye. If heaven is defined in terms of the fulfillment of time, that is, as eternity, then sound, not sight, will be its predominant characteristic. This does not mean that the other senses will be excluded from the final restoration of all things. On the contrary, the senses will be consummated in an ecstatic unity that cannot be experienced in earthly bodies. Because all of our senses will be engaged by God's glory, our senses will no longer be fragmented and disconnected. And because God is infinite, our perception of God will also be an infinite process wherein our senses will not know exhaustion or limitation. Their merging together will set them free for forms of knowledge that we can only dream of now.

---

the source of many of our most enduring visual metaphors of heaven, but a close reading of the text shows John, the author, describing what can only be called a soundscape full of shouting and singing. Just when you think John is celebrating the eye, the ear reinserts its primacy. The orality of the book is evident from the beginning: "Blessed is the one who reads aloud the words of the prophecy, and blessed are those who hear and who keep what is written in it; for the time is near" (1:3). When John looks, it is to ascertain the source of sound: "Then I turned to see whose voice it was that spoke to me" (1:12). Voices speak like thunder and trumpets, and at one point John hears every creature in heaven and on earth singing praise to the Lamb (5:13). Significantly, nobody is able to look into the scroll with the seven seals, and when the seals are opened, their message is proclaimed aloud. John hears the number of those who are sealed from the twelve tribes, and he hears the "great multitude that no one could count, from every nation, from all tribes and peoples and languages" (7:9) singing, loudly, in one united voice. When the beast from the sea appears, it is "given a mouth uttering haughty and blasphemous words" (13:5). The battle between good and evil is, arguably, conducted through sound.

The eschatological synesthesia of the senses in a heavenly consummation needs to be distinguished from what usually passes by that name.
The body of literature on the phenomenon of synesthesia is vast. Interpretations of it range from hallucination caused by a genetic glitch to
mystical revelation associated with a kind of neurological poetry. At the
very least, it is a curious condition. It means the mixture of the senses,
so that people who have it can hear colors and see music. Sometimes
they can see the color of words. Or, as in the case of the psalmist, taste
them: "How sweet are your words to my taste, sweeter than honey to
my mouth" (Ps. 119:103). Everybody can experience a kind of low-grade
synesthesia, because at about twenty hertz, where the lower frequencies of sound become tactile vibrations, hearing and touch meet. Some
people, however, have their entire spectrum of senses conditioned by
this phenomenon. Some writers on this topic speculate that synesthesia is the natural state of infants, who cannot distinguish among the
senses. In some ways, it is a good metaphor for what happened with the
Reformation. The sermon was not only heard but felt, tasted, touched,
and seen as well. The spoken word flooded the senses.

As a metaphor, synesthesia has long enchanted the literary imagination. Ordinarily we are unnerved when other people experience the
world in ways that are radically different from our own. Romantics
have found in such exceptional cases a clue that points to what they
think is normative for all sense perception. As Kevin Dann writes, "the
popular romantic image of synaesthesia has functioned as a sort of
ersatz mystery, a stand-in for truly transcendental knowledge."[15] Dann,
who has written one of the best books about synesthesia, makes the
sobering point that the fact that it is a hard-to-describe condition does
not make it ineffable and mystical. Nevertheless, for the romantics,
synesthesia promises a means of overcoming the fragmentation of the
senses. Even more, it offers a glimpse into utterly new and transcendent
worlds, validating the key romantic argument that the imagination is
more fundamental than ordinary perception. Some romantics even associate it with an original wholeness of experience that has been lost
in human history—a kind of edenic state to which we can return only
in moments of sensory rapture. If Babel (Gen. 11:1–9) was a "second
fall," then salvation comes from the recovery of an Adamic language
that transcends the grating discord of linguistic diversity. Much modern
occult literature blends this Christian theme with a Hindu quest for a

---

15. Kevin T. Dann, *Bright Colors Falsely Seen: Synaesthesia and the Search for Transcendental Knowledge* (New Haven: Yale University Press, 1998), 181. Also see Greta Berman,
"Synesthesia and the Arts," *Leonardo* 32 (1999): 15–22.

sacred chant that would give voice to the sound of an eternal silence, as in Madame Blavatsky's *The Voice of Silence* (1889).[16]

Such thinking leads to the idea that synesthetes are the saints of the modern world who experience a unity to which ordinary mortals can only aspire through the metaphor of poetry. And that is precisely what the romantics did, proliferating cross-sensory or intersensory metaphors in an attempt to express the sublimity of a perception that transcends the limits of rational thought. Romanticism thus secularized the biblical drama of innocence, fall, and redemption, with synesthesia playing the role of grace. Yet while the romantics used synesthesia to structure their linguistic wordplay, others would neglect the hard work of poetry and turn to a more direct means of altering states of consciousness. Drugs could re-create synesthesia if poetry proved too difficult, and an entire discourse about stages of cognitive evolution could provide the rationalization necessary to make widespread drug-taking acceptable. This is precisely what happened in the 1960s, when interest in synesthesia reached its peak. As part of the counterculture of the sixties, synesthesia could be used to "solve" the problems of rationalism, materialism, and positivism. Synesthesia serves as a micro-revolution for the overworked senses that modernity has turned into specialized and efficient avenues of perception. More recently, synesthesia has become just another part of the occultist worldview of the New Age—an alternative route of entry into the astral world. The supersensible becomes the medium for the supernatural.

Process philosophy is the most sophisticated intellectual movement to have taken synesthesia seriously. The whole aim of process philosophy is to overcome the specialization of the senses. For Charles Hartshorne, one of the founders of this philosophical school, the basic building blocks of experiences are "occasions" in every sense of that word.[17] Sense experiences are fundamentally holistic, organic units of reality that can be analyzed only when we break them into discrete parts. We feel wholes, in other words, before we assign different parts of the world to our various senses. This is in direct contradiction to the Helmholtzian theory that the qualities of the different sensory modes are irreducibly heterogeneous. What sets Hartshorne apart is that he insists on speaking the language of science, not poetry. He uses our intuitive grasp of the intersensory resemblance of brightness and high-pitched sounds to

16. For a sophisticated version of this argument, see Steve Odin, "Blossom Scents Take Up the Ringing: Synaesthesia in Japanese and Western Aesthetics," *Soundings* 69 (fall 1986): 256–81.

17. Charles Hartshorne, *The Philosophy and Psychology of Sensation* (Chicago: University of Chicago Press, 1934).

argue that all sensory experience, at its most concrete level, is not only comparable but ultimately transferable and even identical. God too relates to us through this process schemata, growing and changing by becoming absorbed in a confluence of relationships.

The fact that romantics of all eras have employed synesthesia to advance their own gnostic (only the nonconformist elite can really see the truth) and docetic (one must transcend the limitations of the body to have otherworldly experiences) agendas should not lead us to dismiss its theological relevance. Romanticism has appropriated and distorted every aspect of Christianity, so bad theology should not be allowed to drive out good ideas. Although we enter the realm of imagination when we talk about heaven, it is not a realm that we should cast aside for that reason alone. Heaven will not be less than what we can imagine of it, which should give us confidence to trust in our feeble descriptions of its glories. Christianity has traditionally affirmed the resurrection of the body, although what kind of body we will have has been subjected to great debates.[18] Will heaven literally be the transcendental unity of the senses? Will we understand God in a way that is radically discontinuous with the way we understand God now? Or will God's own unity point to a reconstruction of the senses along the lines of a synesthesia shaped by one specific sense?

We do not know, but what I am calling the synesthesia of the ear has much to recommend it as the most potent way of imagining the beatific "vision" of God's glory. Hearing as the governing sense of heavenly delight dates back to the ancient world. Pythagoras discovered the rational order of music, the mathematical ratios that constitute harmony, and he also understood that the planets and stars appear to move with perfect regularity. The strings on a musical instrument and the movement of the planets are both expressions of one law binding music and math. Pythagoras claimed he could hear the music of the spheres, though none of his disciples could. It is a dream of a perfectly full sound, uniting all of our perceptions and governing all of our actions, so that the rule of our natures would also be the song of our hearts. It is a dream that Christians share. In heaven we will become like music, absorbing time into the complex harmonies that constitute our souls, transforming our hearts into ears. Perhaps that is how we will experience our spiritual bodies, not as stable constellations of orbiting atoms but as swelling waves of rhythmic surfing—matter transfigured into the harmonic proportions of the divine law.

18. For a good analysis of this question in the context of Paul's first letter to the Corinthians, see Dale B. Martin, *The Corinthian Body* (New Haven: Yale University Press, 1995), chap. 5.

The End of All Sound

Throughout this book I have noted how sound is related more to time than to space, but this is only a half-truth. In fact, sound has the power to disfigure and reconfigure space.[19] In visual concepts of knowledge, the knower sees from a single point of view, which means that the individual's perspective must be supplemented by multiple standpoints. Only God knows everything, because God is everywhere. Hearing points to a different relationship between knowing and space. "Where auditory experience is dominant, singular, perspectival space gives way to plural, permeated space. The self defined in terms of hearing rather than sight is a self imaged not as a point, but as a membrane; not as a picture, but as a channel through which voices, noises and musics travel."[20] The auditory self represents the possibility of organizing subjectivity in ways that overcome the isolation and fragmentation of the visual grid. Translated in terms of heaven, we will attend to each other because we will be full of each other, permeated by each other, instead of inspecting each other from a space we claim as our own.

The heavenly fulfillment of sound can perhaps best be understood in contrast to the sinfulness of the objectifying eye. So much of sin is a result of abstract thinking. Lust is most fundamentally a product of the visual regimen; it takes strenuous mental effort to make impersonal sex exciting. We have to endow the object of our desire with all sorts of features, characteristics, and settings in order to ignite and consummate our passion. This is why much pornography is so tawdry. Most people do not have the time, energy, or mental acuity to turn lust into art, no matter how hard they try. This is also why pornography is more associated with men than women. Men are more driven by the visual imperative to submit all of reality to an inspecting gaze.[21] Of course, there is always more to see when we stare at something, which is why the eye can be so insatiable. Since we can never see enough to see it all,

19. The most sophisticated discussion of how music transfigures both time and space and thus prefigures eternity can be found in Jeremy S. Begbie, *Theology, Music, and Time* (Cambridge: Cambridge University Press, 2000).

20. Steven Connor, "The Modern Auditory I," in *Rewriting the Self: Histories from the Renaissance to the Present* (New York: Routledge, 1997), 207. Sound, he notes, is omnipresent and mobile, while vision is intermittent and fixed.

21. The ear too, of course, can be the source of sexual temptation. There is an erotics of the ear that complements the theology of sound, but such eros is easily corrupted. That the intimacy of the human voice can arouse intense physical longing is a repercussion of the absolute creativity of the divine voice. Voices call to us, and that calling is the source of ethical responsibility, but in our mechanized age, voices are easily disconnected from bodies, which results in various pathologies, such as phone sex. For a literary exploration of the ear as a sexual organ, see Nicholson Baker, *Vox: A Novel* (New York: Vintage, 1995).

we have to imagine the rest, but pornography so fixates the eye that it stultifies the imagination. Ironically, then, consumers of pornography set out to lay reality bare but end up trapped in their own heads, victims of an imaginary life that is eclipsed by the false promises of the visual.

Heaven will be the opposite of such abstract thinking. It will be a flooding of the senses with the definiteness of the concrete and particular. We will perceive as we have never perceived before. C. S. Lewis has meditated on this aspect of heaven in his great novel *Perelandra*.[22] He portrays each heavenly sense experience as complete and fulfilling in itself and thus blames sin on the human desire for repetition. Although he does not say so, one can draw the conclusion that we want to repeat our experiences because our perceptions are fragmented. No single experience can give us what we want, because every experience is linked to one basic sense perception. As a result, we are never satisfied. We compare every experience with what could be the case, and thus a calculative mentality takes the place of gratitude for what has been given to us. Heaven will be a place without habits, because every experience will be inherently unrepeatable and incomparable. Lewis's *Perelandra* offers clues to a profound portrait of heaven, and it demonstrates just how important the neglected topic of the senses is for theology. In heaven each experience will be an end in itself, because it will integrate all of our senses into a new and wholly unimaginable unity.

When theology becomes too abstract, it appeals to the mind, rather than the whole person, by supplying ever new images for religious reflection. Indeed, a great deal of contemporary theology tries to meet the needs of an ever pressured "customer" of cultural meaning who no longer has time for religion. The forces of a global market tempt theologians to modify church doctrine in order to make a composite portrait of faith that will appeal to the broadest audience. Other theologians look for niche markets, targeting disaffected spiritual consumers who need to be lured back into religion with appeals to their specific needs and demands. A theology of the sense perceptions can help show the folly of these approaches. All the flavors of the world combined together would not create a good dish, just as the attempt to combine the best from all the world religions does not make for a good faith. All the colors combined together would create just another color, not something new and unique. Touch is so specific that it is hard to imagine heaven as one big group hug.

Now sound is another matter. All the sounds together could be harmonized in a unique way that nonetheless would do justice to the individual component parts. Sound has that kind of depth. A chorus of

22. C. S. Lewis, *Perelandra* (London: Bodley Head, 1943).

voices is more than a single voice in the way that a blending of colors is not more than a single color. For such a blending of voices, however, there must be individual voices, a score to be followed, and someone to direct and orchestrate the music. Christianity, with its doctrine of the Trinity as the origin as well as the destiny of all sound, provides a coherent account of how sound can be both multiple and unified, intimate and public, bonding and expanding.

Evangelical Christians are especially sensitive to the association of sound with eschatology. David D. Hall notes this connection in the life of Samuel Sewall, a Puritan who lived in the late seventeenth century: "Any encounter with thunder, trumpets, or shrill cries in everyday life stirred associations in Sewall's mind with their meaning in Revelation. Abrupt sounds were the sensate medium of God's anger."[23] All sound is meaningful, and even the most natural event speaks the will of divine providence if it is correctly heard.

The association of sound and divinity did not originate with evangelicals. John Donne (1572–1631), the English metaphysical poet and Anglican clergyman, insisted that while God speaks to us in many ways, we seldom discern the divine voice in the noise all around us. "Princes are God's trumpet, and the church is God's organ, but Christ Jesus is his voice."[24] Donne even argues, in a sermon on Paul's conversion, that Saul was struck blind so that he would be better able to hear Jesus' voice. "Man has a natural way to come to God, by the eye. But God has a super-induced and supernatural way, by the ear. For though hearing be natural, yet that faith in God should come by hearing a man preach is supernatural. God shut up the natural way in Saul, seeing; He struck him blind; but he opened the supernatural way."[25] In another sermon, Donne declares, "The scriptures are God's voice, the church is His echo, a redoubling, a repeating of some particular syllables and accents of the same voice."[26] Donne can be said to have been highly sensitive to the acoustemology of the Christian faith.

So was Jonathan Edwards (1703–1758), whom many scholars consider to be America's greatest theologian. Edwards imagined that all of our

23. David D. Hall, *Worlds of Wonder, Days of Judgment: Popular Religious Belief in Early New England* (New York: Knopf, 1989), 225.

24. John Donne, *The Sermons of John Donne*, ed. Evelyn M. Simpson and George R. Potter (Berkeley: University of California Press, 1962), 6:217.

25. Ibid., 6:217. Cognitive neuroscientists have documented Donne's point by showing how the visual areas of the cortex in the blind can become transformed to heighten the sense of sound. For a profound religious reflection on the shift from visual dependence to new levels of auditory perception, see John Hull, *Touching the Rock: An Experience of Blindness* (New York: Vintage, 1992). For further discussion, see Oliver Sacks, "The Mind's Eye," *New Yorker*, July 28, 2003, 48–59.

26. Donne, *Sermons*, 6:223.

sensible capacities will be exquisitely enlarged in heaven. This is especially true, he thought, of sound, which was central to his conception of the afterlife. Just as adults can attend to the harmonic proportions in a complex arrangement of notes better than children, the saints in heaven will hear harmonies of an altogether richer kind than those even the best-trained musicians are able to hear in this life. Although the idea of choirs in heaven is often the object of derision, Edwards takes it literally.

> Singing is amiable, because of the proportion that is perceived in it; singing in divine worship is beautiful and useful, because it expresses and promotes the harmonious exercise of the mind. There will doubtless, in the future world, be that which, as it will be an expression of an immensely greater and more excellent harmony of the mind, so will be a far more lively expression of this harmony; and shall itself by vastly more harmonious, yea, than our air or ears, by any modulation, is capable of. Which expressions, and the harmony thereof, shall be sensible, and shall far more lively strike our perception than sound.[27]

It is questionable whether such heavenly music should be considered to be anything like sound in the earthly sense. The saints "will have ways of expressing the concord of their minds by some other emanations than sounds."[28] Edwards imagines a truly cosmic community collected together by modes of communication that are worlds away from even our most advanced technology. We will be able to "hold a delightful and most intimate conversation at a thousand miles distance."[29] Sound will disseminate without any sluggishness, he suggests, and we will be all ears, our hearing as keen as that of any canine.

All imagination is born out of the desire for eternity, but as much as the imagination transforms our desires, so will heaven transform our imagination. When we imagine heaven, we must rely on descriptions that we know will fall far short of their object, yet when we enter heaven, we will realize that those descriptions were feeble but appropriate ways of stimulating our delight. In heaven, our voices will no longer be carried along by vibrations but instead will travel at the speed of grace, and the divine voice will sound amazingly sweet.

27. Jonathan Edwards, *The Miscellanies*, ed. Thomas A. Schafer (New Haven: Yale University Press, 1994), 303.
    28. Ibid., 331.
    29. Ibid., 369.

Index of Names